For
Alice and Lee Schryver

VICTOR HUGO
A biography

Other books by Samuel Edwards include:

The Naked Maja
Fifty-five Days at Peking
The Divine Mistress

Available from NEL:

Rebel! A Biography of Thomas Paine

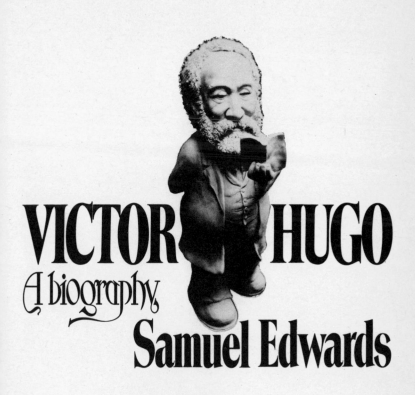

VICTOR HUGO
A biography
Samuel Edwards

NEW ENGLISH LIBRARY
TIMES MIRROR

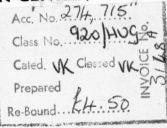
Copyright © by Noel B. Gerson, 1971

First published in the United States of America
by David McKay Company, Inc, New York in 1971

First published in Great Britain by New English Library,
Barnard's Inn, Holborn, London EC1N 2JR in 1975

Printed in Great Britain by Thomson Litho Ltd, East Kilbride, Scotland.
Bound by Hunter & Foulis, Edinburgh.

0 4500 25853

Ego Hugo

—Motto on the "family
crest" designed and
written by Victor Hugo
for himself.

List of Illustrations

following page 148

Many of these illustrations were obtained through the courtesy of the New York Public Library Print Collection.

VICTOR HUGO
A biography

Chapter I

$\mathcal{A}$NDRÉ *GIDE*, one of the more renowned French literary figures of recent times, was not in an entirely playful mood when he asked himself, "Who was the greatest French author of the nineteenth century?"

His reply was as succinct as it was cynical: "Unfortunately, Victor Hugo."

Gide's reaction, which mirrored that of critics throughout the Western world, was inevitable. Hugo, the titan of his age, was not only a superb poet, novelist, dramatist, essayist, and critic who influenced generations of writers following him, but won a degree of hysterical public worship such as no author had ever received. As a man, in both public and private, he was usually if not always insufferable.

Hugo worked on a grand scale, lived on a grand scale, simultaneously observing and defying virtually every convention of his era. Eventually he succeeded in forcing the civilized world to accept him on his own, unique level. He would have been the first to agree with Gide that he stood far above any other French author of his century. After all, the critics of his day agreed with him, a majority of his colleagues followed wherever he chose to lead, and the public—including many thousands who never read the work of anyone else—made him wealthy.

His output was staggering. His disciple and friend, Alexandre Dumas, wrote far more, but Dumas concentrated on the novel, and may or may not have received help from a stable of anonymous assistants. Hugo wrote superb lyric and epic poetry, huge and immortal novels, highly popular plays, and sharp-witted criticisms with equal, dazzling facility.

He proclaimed the virtues of monogamy, yet in later years had scores of mistresses. At the height of his career, he maintained three separate households at the same time: for his wife, his principal mistress, and a woman who might best be described as an auxiliary mistress. He managed to persuade all three to accept the arrangement, but he refused to grant his wife the privilege of maintaining an affair with her own lover. The reason, perhaps, was that he had lost respect for the man not as a rival but as a literary critic. Nevertheless, in his own way, Hugo practiced what he preached. His most celebrated affair lasted for more than a half-century, and although never sanctified or legalized, attained a level of respectability.

It would be gross understatement to say that Hugo exaggerated. He was incapable of reporting anything, trivial or important, in factual terms, and described any and every event in his own grandiose manner.

Therein may lie the clue to this facet of his extraordinary personality. He not only thought in exaggerated terms, but observed others and their actions in his own image.

The events of his life were not only melodramatic, but often tragic. His favorite brother went mad at Victor's wedding, and had to be confined to a sanitarium, where he languished for many years. The eldest of Victor's daughters, his favorite, was drowned in the Seine, and may have committed suicide. He not only outlived his two sons, but his younger daughter became insane after an abortive elopement with a British army officer and spent the next half-century in an asylum.

Hugo was pompous, yet possessed a quiet, sweet humility that was startling. He was a penny-pincher who lived like a monarch, and a profligate when it suited his fancy. A gourmet and a gourmand, he could and did live the life of an ascetic when circumstances he was able to control caused him, on principle, to share the lot of his fellow countrymen during the Prussian siege of Paris in 1870. He worked at his desk as though chained there, but walked several miles every day of his life, and, for two decades, took daily swims in the sea he both loved and feared.

His whole life was a series of paradoxes, beginning in his rags-to-riches-to-rags childhood. He adored his mother, whose correspondence reveals that the judgment of her contemporaries was accurate—she was a shrew who cared little for her children. As a boy he hated his father, who did not see his son until he was almost grown to adulthood, then became his closest comrade and greatly influenced him. He fell in love with his self-imposed image of the girl he married, and too late discovered that she not only was indifferent to him, but had no comprehension of his writing, including the exquisite poems that he dedicated to her.

An aspiring politician whose views ran from orthodox monarchism, through Bonapartism, to liberal republicanism, Hugo yearned for a political career. Although he became a member of both the Chamber of Deputies and the Senate, he failed miserably in his second vocation. His candidacy for the presidency of the Third Republic in 1870 was a huge joke. Nevertheless many considered him the most influential political figure of his day, and he played a major role in the downfall of Napoleon III.

In spite of the many twists and turns in his political philosophy, Hugo was a dedicated patriot. Influenced by Goethe in his youth and something of a Germanophile, he became deeply disillusioned by Germany in his later years. Little interested in the English or in English literature, save the works of Shakespeare, he found refuge on British soil during the two most productive decades of his life.

Aspiring to admission as a member of the French Academy, three times he suffered the humiliation of seeing literary nonentities chosen in his place. And when finally admitted to the Academy, he immediately plunged that body into one of its most bitter feuds.

He imagined himself a man of the people, but so mishandled himself during a political crisis in Paris that he barely escaped lynching by the public. Sought by the authorities at the same time, he escaped from the country disguised as a workman, and years later learned that an official (who probably recognized him), had permitted him to escape (not because the officer admired his politics, but thought his poetry superb).

Even Hugo's final triumphs were paradoxical. He took up residence in a remote workingman's district of Paris because he sought solitude, or so he said. On his eightieth birthday, six hundred thousand Parisians marched past his house in his honor, and he was so overcome that he had to be persuaded to stand on the balcony to receive their salutes. Then moved by the repeated rendition of the national anthem by massed brass bands, he hurried down to the street and joyfully joined in the parade.

He made careful preparations for his final resting place in his will, specifying that he wanted to be buried in a simple pauper's casket in a pauper's graveyard. But France chose to honor him in a manner he would have enjoyed, and would have accepted as his due. A day of national mourning was declared, and his casket was placed in state beneath the Arc de Triomphe. Newspapers reported that two million people filed past the casket, though, like Hugo, they were prone to exaggeration. Residents of other cities came to Paris to pay homage, but the population of Paris was somewhat less than two million at the time.

The supreme paradoxes of Victor Hugo's life are to be found in his literary endeavors. He was a trail-blazer who in the 1820s broke out of the classical mold in which Boileau had mired French literature and soared high above the romanticism of his time, and on into the harsher field of realism. He neither created nor initiated new movements of drama or the novel, and he struck out into "new" poetic territory only by reviving forms that had lain dormant since the sixteenth century. He was no philosophical innovator, either, by his own rare admission. Yet every significant poet, dramatist, and novelist of his age was influenced by his work, and even those who managed to choose a different path, such as Émile Zola, moved forward only after treading in his giant footsteps.

The secret of Hugo's enormous success, which he well knew, was his ability to express the growing trends and make them his own, enabling him to ride the crest of public popularity. The honors accorded him in the many celebrations of his eightieth birthday and at his death five years later were not idle gestures. One phase or another of his writing struck responsive chords among fellow Frenchmen of all classes. He appealed to conservative royalists and radical republicans, to idealists and to liberal but hard-bitten practical politicians such as young Georges Clemenceau, to intellectuals and to average Frenchmen who owned no books other than his.

Victor Hugo was unique in his own time, but if he had lived in any other age he might well have been a failure. He himself liked to believe he was a follower of Voltaire, but his liberty-loving, cynical predecessor would have laughed at most of his work. For all his compassion and his dedication to individual freedom, Hugo was both a rank romantic and a sometimes sloppy sentimentalist.

Hugo was also a virtuoso of the French language, a poet who appreciated the delicate nuances of the French tongue and utilized them as they rarely, if ever, had been previously. As generations of students have discovered, his lyrical work is at its best when read aloud. The author himself noted this. In a letter to his younger daughter, he told her his poems could best be savored when read before an open fire. He added that wine and cheese contributed to the listener's mood, too, and being Victor Hugo, he insisted that the wine be mellow and the cheese ripe.

"Hugo's poetry will live as long as the French tongue is written and spoken, and novelists will be indebted to him for centuries to come. Even his most prejudiced critics realize that he has exerted a permanent influence on literature, that which exists beyond the borders of France as well as within France."

That judgment was accurate. What makes Victor Hugo so maddening to later generations is that he made it himself. The quote is taken verbatim from some informal remarks he made at a dinner party given by younger authors, newsmen, and civic leaders on the eve of his eightieth birthday.

He also came near the mark in his opinions of his personal life. "People approve of me," he wrote his lifelong friend, critic Théophile Gautier, "because I live in a style they want for themselves. But they do not envy me, because they know that my work entitles me to compensations beyond the ordinary." True.

"Women," he declared in an extraordinary letter to Juliette Drouet, his mistress of a half-century, "find me irresistible." Since Juliette was the undisputed leader of the Hugo-worshipping cult, she found nothing strange in the assertion.

But Hugo was dissatisfied with the statement of this

7

fact. Why, he wondered in the next paragraph, should this be so? Was it his appearance? His massive head, white hair, and full beard? Was it his physique, which was more that of a day laborer than of a poet? Or was it, perhaps, his quality of charm, which he could not see in himself, but which he was so repeatedly assured he radiated.

Juliette replied that his appeal was compounded of these and other "virtues," which she enumerated at length. She was not merely feeding her lover's vanity in order to maintain whatever hold over him she possessed. As Hugo well knew, her devotion to him was total. After all, she literally gave up all familiar contact with other members of the human race; she had lived as a courtesan. For years, when they were first together, she "proved" her love for him by obeying almost entirely his request that she isolate herself, seeing and speaking to no one else.

Adversity could not dim Hugo's opinion of himself. After he had spent more than a decade in exile, and had no hope of returning safely to his native land, he informed his son, Charles, "I find it a consolation that I am regarded as more than a writer of verse and story by my fellow countrymen. To them I am a national institution, embodying in my one person all the best that is France."

In Paris, Charles made no secret of his father's view, and the people of France agreed with him so vociferously that Hugo's arch-enemy, Napoleon III, publicly invited the author to return. Hugo refused the invitation, declaring he would not set foot in France until the personal liberties of his compatriots were restored, and thereby made himself even more popular. Whether he was as sincerely devoted to freedom as his self-banishment would make him appear, or whether he struck the attitude because he knew it would win him continuing applause, is still debated among historians.

Nothing would have delighted Victor Hugo more than the knowledge that, almost a century after his death, he still created controversy. His motto, *Ego Hugo*, may have been one of the most precise statements he ever wrote.

Chapter
II

$\mathcal{U}$ICTOR HUGO defies virtually every theory of
the importance of environment in childhood as an influence
on intellectual development. He also mocks the significance
of heredity. No one ever seemed more certainly destined
for existence as a nonentity.

The Hugo family had known no distinctions. They
had lived in Lorraine for a number of generations, and the
name, Germanic in origin, indicated that the first Hugo to
come to the region may have emigrated from the far side
of the Moselle River. Joseph Hugo, the grandfather of
Victor, was a master carpenter whose principal distinction
was that he sired seven daughters by his first wife, and,
after her death, five sons by his second. Carpenter Hugo
also had the right to claim driftwood floating down the
river to Nancy, where he lived. This distinction enabled

him to obtain his raw materials free of charge. His renowned grandson speculated at length, in writing, on the possible acts of heroism Joseph had performed in order to gain this privilege from the city fathers, but the facts are unknown.

Victor Hugo could not be satisfied with a background of commoners, and when his research revealed that a few members of the nobility had been named Hugo, he claimed them as ancestors. One was a Georges Hugo, who had been a captain in the Royal Guards in the sixteenth century and was made a count as reward for his services to the French crown. Another had been a Louis Hugo, a priest, who had ended his career as Bishop of Ptolémaïs. There is no genealogical evidence to indicate that either was actually Victor Hugo's ancestor, however remote.

The author's father, Joseph-Léopold-Sigisbert Hugo, and his four brothers enlisted in the army of the Revolution in 1789. Léopold showed a natural bent for military life. A fifteen-year-old student at the time the Revolution broke out, Léopold left school to enlist, and a year later won his commission in the field. He could read, write, and had studied a smattering of the classics, so he was far in advance of most of his contemporaries.

By 1792 he was promoted to the rank of captain in the Army of the Rhine, where he served under General Alexandre de Beauharnais, the first husband of the Empress Joséphine. Recklessly courageous, Captain Hugo sustained wounds in three engagements, twice had horses shot from under him, and succeeded in calling himself to his superior's attention. In 1793 he won a promotion to the rank of major, and Beauharnais sent him off to Brittany with his battalion to put down a revolt there.

The gallant Major Hugo achieved more than he had intended. His lenient and humane conduct won him the support of many of the ferociously independent Bretons, and the forces of the enemy dwindled. One night the nineteen-year-old officer quartered his men on a farm outside the little town of Petit-Auverné, and there he met Sophie Trébuchet, the niece and ward of the proprietress. A year and a half his senior, Sophie was strikingly attractive, but the Revolution had taken away those who might have been her suitors. She had no dowry, so it is small wonder that she was attracted to the curly-haired, dashing Major Hugo.

Her background was as undistinguished as his. Her father had been a sea captain, and had earned his living for a time in the merciless slave trade with the New World. The only ancestor of any note had been her maternal grandfather, who had held a post as a public prosecutor in Nantes. Intellectually, Sophie was more sophisticated than her suitor. The aunt with whom she had lived after being orphaned was an enthusiastic follower of Voltaire, and the girl had not only read many of his books, but had absorbed much of his philosophy. It was from her that Victor Hugo learned early in his life to cherish personal freedoms, question organized religion, and gaze cynically at the idealists of the world.

But Sophie's dedication to Voltaire was tempered by her own needs, and she presented a demure, lady-like façade. Certainly young Major Hugo, who knew little about girls, had no reason to suspect that she not only held many iconoclastic beliefs, but, beyond this, would turn out to be a man-hating virago. He fell in love with her, maintained a steady correspondence with her after his battalion was ordered back to Paris, and eventually he proposed to her.

Early in November 1797, Sophie's brother escorted her to Paris, and on the fifteenth she and Major Hugo were married. The Church was still banned under the laws of the Revolution, so a civil ceremony was performed. The couple lived in Paris for the next two years, and Léopold Hugo remained very much in love with his wife. There were strains, of course, but the ardent, romantic major resisted his wife's attempts to dominate him and remained the master of his own house. When her stubborn streak irritated him, he managed to overcome his annoyance, and complained only about her secretiveness. No doubt, Sophie was displaying tendencies that would now be called paranoid.

In 1798 the first son was born, and from infancy Abel was as attractive as his handsome parents. He had his father's broad build and his mother's refined, regular features; temperamentally he took after Léopold, who enjoyed life to the full.

The following year Sophie discovered she was pregnant again, which dismayed but did not surprise her. Her principal complaint, which she continued to make for many years, was that Léopold could never get enough of lovemaking, while she, in the words of her third son, Victor, considered herself more refined and civilized.

The family was thrown into its first crisis when the major was ordered to become second-in-command of a regiment in the Army of the Rhine. He insisted that his wife accompany him to Nancy, where he established her in the Hugo family residence while he went into the field with his troops. Sophie hated Lorraine, felt contempt for the families of her husband's brothers, and told him in letter after letter that she wanted to bear her second child at home, in Brittany.

The correspondence of the couple during this time is illuminating. Léopold's letters were filled with endearments, and he told his wife repeatedly that he missed her. Sophie's replies were as cold as they were curt, as formal as they were brief. They were effective, too: she won her battle, and went off to Petit-Auverné.

There her second son, Eugène, was born. He had the unfortunately large nose of the Hugos, but otherwise he was a beautiful baby, and he appeared delicate, which gave his mother a splendid excuse to stay on in Brittany. She soon discovered she wasn't the only member of the family who could be obstinate.

Léopold was exasperated by her remote, impersonal letters, and insisted she join him. He had just been appointed governor of Lunéville, formerly the capital of Lorraine, and wanted his wife at his side when he assumed his new post. However great Sophie's yearning for independence, and regardless of her overwhelming resentment, she was the product of an age in which women obeyed the commands of their husbands, so she went off to Lunéville with her two babies.

Léopold still loved her, but may have wished he had allowed her to stay in Brittany. Political conditions were chaotic, France was becoming restless, and General Napoleon Bonaparte took advantage of the disturbed situation, in 1799, by grasping the helm of France as First Consul. Unlimited opportunities awaited a personable young soldier who nurtured ambitions for advancement. It was difficult for the governor of Lunéville to concentrate on his work when his wife moved into a bedroom of her own, locked the door every night, and refused to have relations with him.

Two years later, in 1801, Léopold's patience was rewarded. He took Sophie with him on a trip to Besançon, the headquarters of his immediate superior, Brigadier Jacques Delalée, where he would report to the district commander, General Victor Lahorie. On that journey, in a small inn high in the mountains, Sophie again conceived.

Léopold had other reasons to feel the journey was successful. General Lahorie, a martinet, an intellectual, and a perpetual conspirator against higher authority, treated him with every courtesy and was very attentive to Sophie. The general asked him to spend the winter at Besançon, and Léopold sent for his children.

The third son was born in the little town on February 26, 1802, in a cramped stone house that consisted of three stories and a garret. Neither parent had reason to suspect the building would become a national monument. On the contrary, both were horrified by the infant's appearance. His head was enormous, his body was tiny, and he himself wrote many years later that his father exclaimed, "He looks like the gargoyles of Notre Dame!" It could not be accidental that the hunchback of Notre Dame became one of Victor Hugo's most famous characters.

General Lahorie was the baby's godfather, and Brigadier Delalée's wife, Marie, was the godmother; they gave the infant their names, and he was christened Victor Marie. The godparents had good cause to believe they were being obligingly polite and nothing more. Little Victor Marie was in such poor health that the attending physician warned both parents that his survival beyond the first month would depend on a miracle. Apparently that miracle took place. The baby survived, but was so ugly his mother could not bear to look at him.

In the period immediately following his third son's birth, Major Hugo became involved, or at least seemed to be a participant, in a conspiracy against the government. According to some historians the real villain was Lahorie, who, for reasons of his own, wanted to make Léopold Hugo a scapegoat, but their conclusions may be based on hindsight. The evidence in favor of their argument is slight. The major, a soldier who cared nothing about politics, must have been innocent of the charges.

Whoever was to blame, Léopold Hugo received transfer orders only six weeks after his third son's birth. He was directed to go to Marseilles to take command of a battalion being sent to Santo Domingo, in the Caribbean, which any true Frenchman regarded as the far end of the earth. The major proclaimed his innocence, and only by protesting vigorously was he able to obtain a stay of the order.

Sophie went off to Paris to intervene on her husband's behalf with Joseph Bonaparte, the older brother of the First Consul, with whom General Lahorie was friendly. As it happened, Lahorie himself had just been transferred to Paris. Léopold remained in Besançon, keeping his three sons there with him.

Students of Victor Hugo's life have spent a century

debating his mother's journey. Did Léopold send Sophie to Paris, knowing that Lahorie was fond of her, and hoping she could influence the General in his behalf? Or was the mission Sophie's idea, which her desperate husband grasped when she presented it to him?

The facts have yet to be discovered, but the outcome of the journey is indisputable. Major Hugo's transfer to Santo Domingo was cancelled. Sophie remained in Paris, leaving her husband in Besançon to cope with their two handsome sons and ugly dwarf of an infant. A wet-nurse and a serving maid looked after the baby.

Léopold was afraid that the youngest of his children was an imbecile, but Victor soon confounded his father with the first signs of genius. At the age of six months he spoke with sufficient clarity to ask for his mother. He continued to call for her during the next year, and when she failed to appear he sank into long, brooding silences. This melancholy became a permanent characteristic and afflicted him for the rest of his life, often appearing without notice and debilitating him after periods of activity beyond the capacity of ordinary men.

Sophie professed to love the children she had abandoned, but was content, for a time, to live with General Lahorie in Paris. They made no secret of the fact that she was his mistress, and although she frequently told friends she missed her children, she made no attempt to gain custody of them.

Léopold had become acquainted with Joseph Bonaparte when both had been living at Lunéville, and now appealed to the brother of the future Emperor for help. In some matters Joseph could be practical, and knowing he had no influence with Sophie, transferred Major Hugo's battalion to the island of Elba. Léopold, accompanied by his sons, arrived at the little city of Portoferraio in January 1803. He could not have been buoyed by Joseph's advice that he forget his wife.

He realized, however, that his marriage had come to an end, and he hired a governess for his children. Her name was Catherine Thomas, and she was very young, very pretty, and highly intelligent. Abel, who was old enough to respond to feminine warmth, became fond of her. So did the major, although several months passed before she became his mistress.

In mid-July 1803, Sophie appeared at Portoferraio, unannounced and unexpected. A major change was taking place in the moral standards of the French. First Consul Bonaparte, who was about to crown himself Napoleon I, had undergone a shattering experience when Joséphine had been unfaithful to him. He made it plain that he expected his officials and their wives to comport themselves with greater dignity. The idea of returning to Major Hugo was more than even Bonaparte could expect of Sophie, but she could attain greater stature if she obtained custody of her children, and she informed her husband she had come for them.

Léopold was in an unfortunate situation. If Sophie took him to court, he knew, she would be awarded the children, unless he could prove her guilty of immoral conduct. And a major compelled to name a general as his wife's lover would ruin his own career. So Sophie won the round, and early in November 1803, she took all three of her sons off to Paris.

Abel, who hated the prospect of being separated from his father and the affectionate Catherine, wept constantly. Eugène's reaction is unknown. Victor, according to autobiographical notes written more than a half-century later, was so elated he chatted with her all the way to the city. He was not yet two years of age.

Sophie rented a large, plain house on the rue de Clichy, in a less than fashionable section of Paris, and there she settled with her sons in genteel poverty. Léopold, generous beyond reasonable expectations, gave her half of his wages every month. If she had hoped General Lahorie would contribute to her support, she soon learned better. The general lived extravagantly, and could not afford to maintain two households, especially as Sophie continued to make him welcome, even though he gave her no funds.

Victor, still resembling a dwarf, displayed such precocity when he reached the age of four that he was sent off with his brothers to a nearby school in the rue du Mont-Blanc. In 1807, when he was five, he could write as well as read. Abel, who was encouraged by General Lahorie and the schoolmaster, was already writing poetry, and Victor—according to no authority other than himself—followed his older brother's example. But no poetry he wrote at that time has survived.

Whether or not he composed at such an early age, he came under the influence of his godfather in a surprisingly beneficial way. Lahorie was a strange, warped man with a personality much like that of his mistress, a suspicious and lifelong opponent of the status quo of any given moment. His relationship with Sophie was far more intellectual than physical, which suited both of them. She loathed sex and he had passed beyond it, being more than a generation older. It was enough for him to be seen around town with a young, attractive woman. And Sophie, daughter of a slaver and niece of a Breton farmer, had found her milieu in the salons of Napoleon's Paris, where her beauty and her association with the General opened all doors. It was an ideal arrangement.

It was helpful to Sophie's sons, too. Lahorie, for all his faults, was a genuine intellectual who enjoyed the company of children. Under his guidance the Hugo boys read the Bible, Greek and Roman classics, and virtually everything of importance in French literature since the dawn of the Renaissance. Although Victor Hugo hated to admit it, he owed the foundations of his education to his mother's lover, whom he secretly considered inferior to her.

While the boy was reading every book within reach, his father began to prosper. Joseph Bonaparte was sent by Napoleon to conquer the Kingdom of Naples, and Major Hugo was a member of that expedition. Repeatedly distinguishing himself in action, Léopold was promoted to the rank of colonel and became governor of the Italian province of Avellino.

As his star rose, that of Lahorie fell. Unable to cure his old habits, he engaged in the dangerous pastime of plotting against the Emperor, and boasted to his mistress that he could outwit Joseph Fouché, the chief of Napoleon's secret police. As no man in France was that wise or clever, Sophie received an indirect warning from Fouché that her own future would be compromised unless she gave up her affair.

Deprived of Lahorie's protection, her funds low,

Sophie took her sons out of school and set off to Italy with them. The journey was the first that the five-year-old Victor remembered, and he forgot none of the details, recalling them with startling clarity many years later. Colonel Léopold Hugo must have been astonished when Sophie descended unannounced on him and Catherine.

But he was so pleased to see his sons that he permitted his wife to stay. There was no possibility of a marital reconciliation, and the situation was complicated by Sophie's attempt to manage Catherine's home. The efforts were not appreciated.

Abel was so delighted to rejoin his father and Catherine that he didn't care what anyone said or did. His mother reacted violently; the boy ignored her jealous rages and spent time each day with Catherine. Victor and Eugène were not consciously aware of the struggle between the two women, and in any event remained loyal to their mother. Certainly Victor had so much to occupy him that domestic disputes could not capture his attention.

He was no longer compelled to attend school, in itself a blessing that only a small boy could appreciate. He had found a new and fascinating interest that he enjoyed as much as books. The soldiers in his father's regiment were real: each day he went off to the barracks, where he watched the men polish their rifles and equipment, and groom their horses. The highlight of the day was the parade before the regimental commander, and Victor loved to stand beside his father as Colonel Hugo took the salute.

Perhaps the greatest of Léopold's surprises was the change that had taken place in his youngest son. Victor's head was still abnormally large, but his body was growing

steadily, and he now had the thick neck,
and deep chest of the Hugo clan. The wi
ment's officers paused to admire him almo
they did Abel, and the colonel was pleased t
could take pride in his youngest son.

It was during this period of Victor's life
first subjected to the open parental tug-of-war th   ..as by
no means commonplace in the households of that century.
Daily Sophie would take her two younger sons aside and
deliver a diatribe intended to convince them that their
father was abominable. Victor loved Maman, so he believed
her.

At the same time, however, he was fascinated by
Papa, that genial giant who took him for rides on his own
horse and taught him to wield a cavalry saber so heavy
Eugène couldn't lift it. Victor was already developing
prodigious physical strength, while the delicate Eugène,
whom Maman sometimes dressed in girl's clothes for her
own amusement, remained weak.

A climax of sorts came one day in the late autumn of
1807 when Colonel Hugo formally entered the name of his
youngest son on the regimental rolls as a cadet officer. That
afternoon Victor, attired in a cadet officer's uniform,
mounted on a pony that was a surprise gift from his father
and Catherine Thomas, took the regiment's salute.

The boy was deliriously happy, the event was the
most significant of his young life, and he made up his mind
to become a soldier, like his father. His mother created a
scene he would never forget, berating him, abusing his
father, and finally tearing his uniform to shreds. The boy's
sense of guilt was so overwhelming he made no protest. Not

til a half-century later could he write, "I felt, that night, that my world had come to an end."

Naples lost its savor for Victor, and he was fortunate, as were his brothers, that the interlude came to an end. Napoleon had promised his brother Joseph the crown of Spain, and Colonel Hugo's regiment was ordered to take part in the march on Madrid. With relief, Sophie returned to Paris after wringing a promise of a larger monthly payment from her husband. Victor appeared to make a rapid adjustment to the change, and returned to his studies, but he frequently read books on battles and military campaigns as well as the classics.

A real military campaign then in progress had an even more profound influence on the lives of the Hugo boys and their mother. Léopold, an officer of great merit, distinguished himself so often that King Joseph promoted him to the exalted rank of major general, made him a close adviser at the court of Madrid, and, as a final honor, granted him a Spanish title, that of Count of Siguenza.

Sophie now had the right to call herself a countess, and her allowance was increased to three thousand gold francs a year. Early in 1809 the sum jumped to four thousand. Loving luxury, she promptly rented a huge apartment, the entire ground floor of what had once been a convent, called the Hermitage of the Feuillantines. Victor and his brothers now lived in a palace of their own, complete with a domed, private chapel and a private, superbly tended interior garden that extended the length of two city blocks.

This was one of the happiest periods in Victor Hugo's life, as he later wrote in *Le Dernier Jour d'un condamné*.

Each morning he, Abel, and Eugène went off to school, and every afternoon they played in the magnificent garden. Abel was the leader, permitting no one to usurp his authority, but the boys were usually engaged in an endless variety of games invented by Victor. He was never at a loss to find a new one, and his imagination appeared limitless. Eugène more handsome and docile than ever, did as the others told him.

Abel had become seriously interested in writing poetry, and the younger boys, not to be outdone, conscientiously followed his example. The industry of the seven-year-old Victor was remarkable, and General Lahorie,, who had now reentered their lives, commended him at length.

The influence of Lahorie at this stage of Victor's life cannot be exaggerated; the boy learned more from him than from the former priest, one La Rivière, whose school he and Eugène attended. General Lahorie was in grave trouble, and Madame Hugo, the Countess of Siguenza, risked her own good name, if not her life, to help him. Napoleon had long regarded the old conspirator as a harmless fool, but Lahorie was conspiring so openly against the Emperor that, early in 1809, Fouché finally issued a warrant for his arrest. Perhaps he was harmless enough himself, but he might influence others, and therefore was dangerous.

So Sophie gave him refuge, and he lived under her roof at the former convent after taking an assumed name, which the Hugo boys had to learn. Outsiders never saw the general, who literally did not set foot outside the property. He exercised by walking daily in the garden while his mistress's sons were at school. With nothing better to occupy him, Lahorie supervised the education of the boys, and was a strict taskmaster. It was he who taught Victor the disciplines that would remain unyielding for all the author's life. It was he who taught Victor to appreciate Tacitus, Ovid, and Homer. And it was he who told the boys stories every night after dinner, thereby inflaming the imagination of Victor, who tried to compete by telling stories of his own.

It was the garden, however, that remained the greatest joy of Victor's life. He made himself a swing beneath a huge chestnut tree, he discovered a dry cistern that was admirable for playing war, and there were flowers of so many varieties that he and his brothers regularly engaged in contests to see who could identify the largest number. There was so much fruit that the boys ate all they could consume, and there were strange herbs, some bitter and some bland, that grew wild in untended areas of the garden.

That fairyland always remained fresh in Victor Hugo's memory. He wrote literally hundreds of poems about it, and it appeared, sometimes in disguised form, in his plays and novels. It represented the ultimate freedom, a heaven on earth where life could be savored to the full, and the man became a carefree boy again whenever he thought of the place.

Idylls come to an end, however, and life in the magic garden was no exception. Late in December 1810, the secret police finally traced General Lahorie, placed him under arrest and carted him off to prison. Madame Hugo tried to use her influence on his behalf, but quickly discovered she had none. The order for her lover's imprisonment had been signed by the Emperor himself, and was irrevocable.

At this juncture, Sophie's brother-in-law came to her with some sage advice. Léopold's younger brother, Louis, himself a former army officer, was now a high-ranking official in the Ministry of Police. Through his efforts Sophie escaped punishment for harboring a refugee. But people were talking about her, Louis told her, and if the Emperor caught wind of their conversations, she might suffer.

She would be wise, he said, to leave the country for a time, and he suggested Madrid as the best place to go. He knew that King Joseph was anxious to give his court an air of permanence, and was trying to persuade his officers to bring their families to Spain.

Sophie not only accepted the advice, but once again prepared for her journey without bothering to notify her husband that she was joining him. That journey also indelibly impressed Victor Hugo. He described it in great detail, years later, in a book of poetry that he dictated, in large part, to his wife, *Victor Hugo raconté par un témoin de sa vie.* Everything the nine-year-old boy saw remained engraved on his mind. Later the scenes he saw, the people he met, and situations he witnessed were used in his plays and novels. The trip was the child's first conscious attempt, as an author, to gather material that he could record on paper.

Sophie and her children left Paris in mid-March 1811, traveling with a large convoy under military protection. The troops were necessary because Spain, although nominally incorporated into Napoleon's realm, was still at war, and guerilla attacks on the French occurred frequently. The Hugo family rode in a large carriage pulled by a team of four horses, the luggage strapped onto the rear, with two armed soldiers riding on the box with the coachman. Because of Léopold's prominence, a full company of troops was assigned to guard the family.

The convoy traveled to Madrid via the little town of Ernani, later to be used in Victor's play, *Hernani*. The boys saw the ruins of Torquemada, and in Burgos, Valladolid, and Toledo there were houses gutted by artillery shells and fire, as well as impoverished Spanish refugees wandering through the streets. The difference between Victor's own situation and that of the supposedly vanquished enemy made a lasting impression on the boy.

Léopold was absent when his family arrived in Madrid, having accompanied King Joseph into the field. When he returned to find Sophie awaiting him, he was furious. He was again delighted to see his sons, however, and immediately enrolled them in the College of Nobles, the school that the sons of Spanish aristocrats traditionally attended.

The year that followed was torture for Victor. He and his brothers were regarded as outsiders by the Spanish boys, who blamed the Hugo children for their country's miseries. Victor and his brothers were snubbed, beaten, and persecuted by their fellows, although they quickly learned to fight back. The College quarters were damp, cold, and gloomy, and the dormitories resembled prison cells; the house and gardens in Paris more closely resembled heaven on earth with each passing day.

On weekends, when the boys rejoined their parents, they found no escape from tensions and unpleasantness. Victor was old enough now to become aware of the sordid domestic situation, which his mother made no attempt to hide from him. Léopold wanted to divorce the woman he called his "demon," but King Joseph still insisted on maintaining appearances. He not only refused to permit the dissolution of the marriage, but commanded General Hugo and his legal wife to dwell under the same roof.

Sophie won a great victory when King Joseph demanded that she be presented at the Spanish court. Catherine Thomas, now banished to a separate dwelling, made such a fuss that the king was forced to placate her, which he did in typical Bonaparte fashion by making her a countess in her own right.

Léopold now learned of his wife's affair with General Lahorie, picking up tidbits of information inadvertently dropped by his sons. He had long suspected the relationship, although unable to prove it, and when he confronted Sophie, she admitted the truth. Not even the desires of his royal Bonaparte master could persuade Léopold to remain under the same roof with his wife. He not only left her, but openly lived with Catherine. Sophie appealed to Joseph for help, but in vain.

During this period of domestic strife, which lasted for an entire year, Sophie frequently confided in her sons and appealed to them for sympathy and loyalty. She was completely successful, as her youngest disclosed twelve years later in a portion of *Victor Hugo raconté*. The boys regarded their mother as the champion of "freedom and poetry," while their father was a harsh giant, a stranger responsible for their "imprisonment" in the College of Nobles.

In March 1812 Joseph Bonaparte finally granted the embattled wife permission to return to Paris. It could not have been too difficult for Sophie to persuade him, as the situation of the French in Spain was deteriorating rapidly, and it would not be long before Joseph and his court beat an ignominious retreat into France.

Sophie returned happily to the Hermitage; the boys resumed their idyllic life. The garden, the house, the private chapel, and their school were the same, and for two more years they lived in their dream world. There was one major change now, however: General Lahorie was conspicuous by his absence.

The general had gone too far in his plotting against the Imperial crown. Had he behaved in prison he would have been released at a convenient time, but he elected to initiate a new conspiracy, drawing in a number of fellow prisoners, and it was inevitable that the plot should be discovered. The Emperor was having troubles of his own in the invasion of Russia and no longer tolerated eccentric conspirators.

In October 1812, Lahorie was executed by a firing squad.

Sophie's decline began the day her lover was put to death. She became less vigorous, increasingly indifferent to the world around her, and even more vindictive in her personal relations, if that was possible. As her husband refused to accommodate her in any way, a startling change took place in her financial situation.

Returning to France with Joseph Bonaparte in the summer of 1813, General Hugo was given command of the garrison at the fortified town of Thionville. There, early in 1814, he decided to take a personal as well as a military stand, and not only stopped sending funds to Sophie, but sent his two younger sons to a school near Saint-Germain-des-Prés, the Pension Cordier, which had a deserved reputation for its disciplines. As was his right under the law, he ordered the boys to have nothing further to do with their mother.

Sophie tried to retaliate by filing suit, and eventually she won a feeble victory. Léopold was ordered to pay her one hundred francs per month, but he was granted a formal separation from her, and the court upheld his right to keep their sons from her.

For two years Victor and Eugène lived and studied at the Cordier, and although the future author hated his father as never before, he studied hard, and the intellectual disciplines were of inestimable benefit to him. He learned, too, to adjust to others, and soon became the undergraduate leader of the school, the other boys referring to him as their "king," a situation that the older Eugène did not relish.

Immersed in his studies and deprived of his mother's company, Victor appeared almost unaware of events taking place outside the walls of the school. Napoleon lost his crown and was banished to Elba, returned from exile to rally his fellow countrymen, and went down to his final defeat in 1815. The conservative governments of the Grand Coalition placed the reactionary Louis XVIII on the throne, and the personal freedoms granted Frenchmen under Napoleon were, in the main, rescinded. Not until later would the significance of contemporary politics become clear to Victor Hugo.

For the present it was sufficient that his father was retired on half-pay and went to live with Catherine at Blois. With no money to spare in the Hugo family, Léopold's younger sons were forced to live on allowances far smaller than those paid to their schoolmates. The Hugo boys enjoyed no frills, ate only staples, and rarely purchased new clothing. Such penury was the first Victor had ever known, and the jolt, coming close on the heels of sumptuous living, was not easy to take. Even more difficult to bear was his inability to rescue his mother, who had moved into a small house, existing there in near-poverty.

In only one way could the frustrated boy release the fury in his soul. He worked from early morning until late at night, developing the compulsive habits that would remain to the end of his days. His fervor for his books paid unexpected dividends in 1816, when the Cordier sent him on to an advanced school that accepted a few of its better pupils. The lycée Louis-le-Grand was devoted to scholarship, and Victor was required to pay no tuition, while his father was charged only a token sum for his room and board.

The fourteen-year-old Victor began to write seriously for the first time. After translating most of Virgil into French, he began to compose poetry of his own. Encouraged by his teachers, the prodigy turned out a quantity of work in his first year at the lycée that was almost beyond belief. In the next two years he actually increased the pace. When he left Louis-le-Grand in 1818 at the age of sixteen, his total composition was breathtaking:

Translations of Virgil

Irtamène, a tragedy in five acts

Le Déluge, a poem of 364 lines

More than a hundred other poems, including elegies, satires, odes, and idylls

A comic opera (subsequently lost)

The boy decided, at the age of fifteen, to enter the annual poetry contest of the distinguished French Academy, and wrote an elegy in Virgilian style, which immediately plunged him into his first literary controversy. The noted judges read his work, and refused to believe that the contestant was only fifteen. Victor appealed to his mother for help, and she went to the Academy herself with his birth certificate. The boy was awarded an Honorable Mention, his first literary recognition.

Victor celebrated by beginning the composition he would enter the following year. He soon changed his mind, however, deciding that the contest was conducted on an infantile level far beneath him. His mother, who believed she had good cause to hate the Bonapartes, was a dedicated Royalist. Most of the poems that the sixteen-year-old boy wrote reflected Sophie's enthusiasms. He would continue to hold these views himself for several years.

In 1818 Victor's formal schooling came to an end, as did Eugène's. The boys were old enough to live where they pleased, and Léopold could no longer prevent them from joining their mother in a small house on the rue des Petits-Augustins. Abel, who had spent two years in the army, went to work as a journalist, and became interested in the book publishing business. Although he continued to write poetry, he soon displayed a knack for making money, and began to contribute to his mother's support.

Abel's assistance made it possible for Victor to enroll as a law student at the University of Paris, but he found his courses dull, and frequently spent his time during lectures composing poetry. He and law were not made for each other, and it took only a year for him to discover this.

Something other than poetry occupied Victor's mind. Unlike most of his friends, he had shown little interest in girls, but he began to make up for lost time. The object of his affections was Adèle Foucher, the daughter of former neighbors, who had been a childhood playmate at the Hermitage. What the brilliant youth saw in Adèle remains a mystery to this day, and can only be explained by his lack of experience. Victor literally knew no better.

Adèle was moon-faced, with curly hair, irregular features, and a figure that, even in her late adolescence, caused no one to stare at her. She had a bland, almost bovine disposition, and was completely lacking in intellectual traits. She made no secret of her shallow thinking, however, and, if nothing else, was honest. As she repeatedly told Victor, she neither understood nor enjoyed poetry. She was flattered by the lyrics he composed in her honor, but freely admitted that they sailed over her head.

The enamored youth refused to accept her candor, and like uncounted other young men in love, insisted she possessed innumerable qualities that were alien to her. He thought her beautiful, too, which was a tribute to the childhood they had shared in Victor's magic garden. Anyone who had been touched by that necromancy could not be less than supremely attractive.

One person who did not share Victor's opinion was Sophie Hugo. Adèle, she declared, was not only homely and stupid, but far beneath the Hugo family socially. She showed no reticence in making her views known to her son, expressing herself with the vehemence of the termagant she had always been. Victor tried to resist, but it was impossible for him to escape the influence of his domineering mother, and he was forced to stop seeing Adèle. For the first time he began to suspect that his parents' marriage might not have been perfect at the outset, and that his mother might be partly to blame for its dissolution.

Poetry remained his great consolation. When he entered a number of poems in a contest held annually by the Academy of Toulouse, recognition of his extraordinary talents was swift. He not only won first prize, with an award of one hundred francs, but took second prize, too, with a purse of fifty francs. Soon thereafter he entered a contest for adults sponsored by the French Academy, and won fifth place out of a field of several hundred. Those who came in ahead of him were men many years his senior, all of whom were professional authors.

Before Victor reached his eighteenth birthday he gave birth to an idea that was destined to set him on the path of his lifelong career. Abel was in the publishing business, and wrote poetry. His younger brothers also wrote. Therefore, the youngest urged, they should pool their collective talents and go into business together. The Hugo brothers would not only storm the literary world, but would earn vast sums of money. Eugène was enthusiastic, as always, and even the relatively hardheaded Abel was swayed by Victor's rhetoric. They would stand together, and together would win fame and fortune.

Chapter III

THE world in which the Hugo brothers were growing to manhood was inordinately complex. The victorious powers that had defeated Napoleon attempted at the Congress of Vienna to restore an era when the rights of kings had been almost divine, and both money and power had been concentrated in a small class of aristocrats. On the surface they had succeeded, but the influence of the French Revolution, followed by that of Bonaparte's Empire, influenced all that came after.

Men who had known true freedom refused to bow their heads. The stranglehold of the Church had been broken in Catholic countries; Protestants and Catholics were equal everywhere; and ghetto walls that had confined the Jews had been torn down. Newspapers and magazines were published everywhere, the public was informed as never before. Only a limited number of political aims were still taboo. Relatively speaking, men enjoyed unprecedented freedom of speech and the right to assemble for peaceful purposes.

Attempts were made to reestablish a repressive code of morality, but the pendulum did not swing back as far as it had once moved. Only in the growing middle class, which became stronger as the Industrial Revolution expanded, were the old-fashioned virtues still extolled, and even in those circles the preceding era had left its stamp.

The European world was shrinking, too. The steamboat would be seen on the waterways of the Continent within a few years, and railroads would connect the cities. Telegraph lines would speed news, and new printing presses would make it possible to print large editions of books at a fraction of their previous cost.

The Hugo brothers were above all concerned with the costs of printing. Abel, the business manager of the trio, estimated that they would be able to earn a profit if they kept down editorial costs. Their magazine, *Le Conservateur littéraire*, would print poetry, fiction, articles, and literary criticism. Abel acted as editor-in-chief as well as business manager, and contributed an occasional poem. Eugène wrote a few pieces, too, and outside submissions of other authors were solicited. But it became evident with the first issue, published in the last months of 1819, that Victor was the mainstay of the writing staff.

During the year that *Le Conservateur* was published bi-monthly, more than seventy-five percent of its editorial content was written by Victor, who churned out articles, narratives, and odes at a dizzy pace. The first version of his novel, *Bug-Jargal*, appeared in the pages of the magazine.

Always wanting more than one string to his bow, even in his earliest days, Victor contributed some of his poems to the Academy of Toulouse contest, where he continued to win every prize offered. Before his eighteenth birthday he won national recognition, and no one was surprised when some of his poems, which had a strong royalist flavor, so impressed the court that he was invited to call on Louis XVIII, who received him at tea and praised him for his efforts.

Even more important, Victor won the admiration of the dean of French literature, François-René de Chateaubriand, who expressed a desire to meet him. Victor called on him, and was so tongue-tied he could not speak, but the great man put him at his ease with a glass of cognac, and the youth poured out his thoughts in such a torrent that Chateaubriand later wrote, "If this young man can discipline his thoughts and his personal fervors, he will become the wonder of France."

Even at that early age, Victor had supreme confidence in himself. When he was shown Chateaubriand's comment, he told Eugène, "He doesn't know I am already disciplined, but otherwise he is quite right. I intend to change all the courses of French literature, and if I cannot improve upon the record of Chateaubriand himself, I shall be nothing whatever."

In 1820 the magazine changed from bi-monthly publication to quarterly, and for the better part of the next two years it continued on that basis. All the Hugo brothers remained active on the staff, with Victor the mainstay. Some issues contained material that he alone wrote.

Abel, who was becoming increasingly prominent in

literary circles, was one of the founders of a royalist literary group, the *Société des bonnes lettres*, which boasted Chateaubriand as its president. Abel's growing importance was evident in his series of lectures on Spanish literature.

Victor was a member of the society, and during the first months of its existence wrote a number of poems that were read at its meetings. But his activities soon dwindled, because of the intense personal pressures that were being exerted on him.

Late in 1821 Sophie Trébuchet Hugo died, leaving her younger sons heartbroken. The nineteen-year-old Victor and his brothers immediately discovered that she had been badly in debt. Although not legally obligated to pay off her debts, her sons pledged themselves to clear her name.

This was easier said than done, and the first sacrifice they had to make was the suspension of their magazine. It had done no better than break even, in spite of the prestige it had garnered, and Abel said he could not afford to keep up its publication.

Victor hoped to obtain assistance from his father while he solidified his position in the literary world. But he had not been in touch with the general since he had left school to live with his mother, and he soon found that Léopold did not approve of the career he had chosen.

"The writing of literature is a laudable ambition," his father wrote from Blois, "provided one has a sponsor. Alas, I am no king, and must make ends meet on my small pension. Were you to elect a career as a lawyer or a physician, I would gladly make sacrifices in order to see you through the university, but to help you to become established in literature would be like the pouring of good wine down an open sewer."

Abel understood the general's position and tried to explain it to his younger brother. But Victor was in no mood to listen. "I shall prove to him," he cried, "that a poet can earn sums far larger than the wages of an Imperial general!"

For a period of almost a year, from the latter part of 1821 through most of 1822, Victor knew genuine suffering such as he had never known before and never again experienced. He lived in a tiny attic room in the rue du Dragon, and was relieved when a cousin from Britanny, Adolphe Trébuchet, moved in with him for several months to help pay the rent. Often the cousins had nothing to eat, and when they acquired funds, they had to spend all of it for food, which they cooked themselves.

Victor owned three shirts, two suits, one of which was presentable, and a single pair of shoes. He wrote incessantly, but only rarely could sell a poem or an article for a few francs. As France was undergoing a financial depression and jobs were scarce, he could find no other work. For months he put aside a special fund so he could buy a blue coat with gold buttons, hoping it would help him create a good impression on the rare occasions when he was invited out to dine.

Victor remembered his own situation in painful detail many years later, when writing *Les Misérables*, and his account of the poverty endured by Marius de Pontmercy was, in fact, a recollection of his own experience:

Life became hard for Marius. It was nothing to eat his clothes, his watch. He ate of that terrible, inexpressible thing that is called the rage of emptiness; that is to say, he

*endured great hardships and great privations. A terrible
thing it is, for it contains days without bread, nights without sleep, evenings without a candle, a hearth without a
fire, weeks without work, a future without hope, a coat out
at the elbows, an old hat which evokes the laughter of young
girls, a door which one finds locked at night because one's
rent is not paid, the insolence of the porter and the cook-
shop seller, the sneers of neighbors, humiliations, dignity
trampled upon, work of whatever nature accepted, disgust,
bitterness, despondency.*

But this year was not completely without hope, and
Victor discovered immediately after his mother's funeral
that he was free to pursue his romance with Adèle Foucher.
He saw her in the street near her house only twenty-four
hours after the funeral, and it is possible, if not probable,
that he went to the neighborhood in the hope of catching
a glimpse of her.

Adèle, who was returning home from an errand,
greeted him with hearty good cheer.

Victor was offended because she not only failed to
offer him condolences on the death of his mother, but had
not appeared at the funeral.

Adèle was shocked, and after telling him she hadn't
known of his mother's death, broke into tears.

Victor wept with her, and their sorrow immediately
reunited them.

Now it was the turn of Adèle's parents to object. Their
daughter was in love with a young man who, however
honorable, had no job, no prospects of work, and was
destitute. They promptly moved to a small country house
they owned at Dreux, more than sixty miles from Paris.

There, they reasoned, their daughter was safe, because her suitor had no money to purchase a seat in a carriage.

Victor, the young romantic, set out for Dreux on foot, and arrived there three days later. Soon after, he wrote to a friend in Paris that he had enjoyed every moment of the long hike, and added, "I look with pity upon all carriages."

His appearance was so disreputable that the local police asked him for identification, but the compleat young poet, much in love, did not carry one scrap of identification and was thrown into the local prison. There he remembered the parents of a former classmate, who not only identified him, but took him into their home, fed him an enormous supper, and gave him clean clothes and a bed.

The following morning he was in the street when Adèle acompanied her father on his morning walk. Although it has been said that Victor Hugo had more gall than any man of his time, his courage faltered, and he merely nodded to the startled father and daughter as he passed them.

Quickly realizing he was accomplishing nothing, Victor returned to the home of his hosts and wrote a letter to M. Foucher. After pretending that the meeting had been "accidental," he went on to say that the mere sight of Adèle had thrilled him, and that he loved her with all his heart, from the depths of his soul.

The letter was delivered by a servant, and that afternoon Victor was permitted to call. He immediately asked for Adèle's hand.

M. Foucher was very wise, and neither agreed nor refused. If the young couple wished to consider themselves informally betrothed, he had no objection. They could see each other at reasonable times and under reasonable circumstances, provided they were chaperoned. But marriage was out of the question until Victor could support a wife in comfort. Her family had no intention of allowing her to live on breadcrusts in an attic for the sake of poetry.

Victor returned to Paris in his own threadbare clothes, on foot, determined to succeed for Adèle's sake.

In the months that followed they corresponded regularly. At least Victor wrote often, and Adèle replied with short, prosaic notes. His correspondence was saved, thanks to Adèle's habit of keeping every scrap of paper she ever received, and was published after his death under the title, *Lettres à la fiancée*. They are memorable principally because Victor Hugo wrote them, and unusual only when he could not express himself adequately in prose and wrote lyric poems for her.

It is not surprising that these poems are the most romantic and sentimental he ever penned. Few, if any, are considered of any merit.

The letters revealed an aspect of Victor's nature that he soon discarded: he was a prude. Not only did it infuriate him when other men dared to glance in Adèle's direction, but he wanted to run them through for their temerity. Fortunately he neither owned nor could afford to buy a sword. He told the girl in letter after 'letter that he believed in a single standard. She should be pure when she came to her husband in marriage, as was the custom, and he, too, should be sexually inexperienced.

Adèle stood far above him, high among the stars, Victor declared, and he would struggle all his days to lift himself as high as her feet. She was divine, he said, and he fell to his knees before her. His soaring verse left the girl unmoved. Victor was so much in love with her—and with his own rhetoric—that he could not see how phlegmatic she was.

One day he wrote her some lyric lines that were abstruse in both concept and execution. Frankly experimental, he was trying out a new verse form in telling her of his love.

Adèle, in her reply, was brutally candid. She had no appreciation of poetry, she said, and could not understand a single phrase of his poems, even though every word was written in French.

Victor was outraged by her self-denigration, and wrote again, this time in prose:

I cannot believe what you have told me. You have a beauty that shines from your face. It is present in your eyes, in your voice and in your heart. Such beauty can proceed only from the soul, and yours is a soul of exceptional beauty.

Poetry is the language of beauty, so it is not possible that you fail to understand me. My words tell you of my love. You understand that love, hence you understand my poetry, since it is written expressly for you. The soul does not lie.

Many years were to pass before it finally dawned on Victor that his betrothed had meant what she had said. By that time they were married and the parents of several children, so it was too late to heed Adèle. He was never in a position to say that she had married him under false pretenses.

Unable to find work of any kind and sustained only by his romance, Victor spent most of his time writing, and in the spring of 1822 Abel came to his rescue. Acting surreptitiously, without his younger brother's knowledge, he obtained copies of all the poems Victor had written over the past year and published them at his own expense under the title, *Odes et poésies diverse*. Victor knew nothing of the arrangement until Abel presented him with the galleys for proofreading.

The edition was small, but all fifteen hundred copies were sold within a short time after publication in June 1822. Victor not only enhanced his reputation, but earned seven hundred fifty francs in royalties, the only money of any consequence that he had ever made. The first copy was presented to Adèle, of course, and the author wrote in the flyleaf, "To my beloved Adèle, the angel who is all I desire of glory or possess of happiness—Victor."

The love poems comprised a small part of the book. Victor had already become a shrewd professional writer, avoiding the personal and preparing his work for the broadest available market. The pendulum of popular taste had swung away from Napoleon's collapsed Empire; royalist views were certain to find an audience. Also, Victor had become friendly with a high-ranking nobleman who had embraced the Church, the Abbé Duc de Rohan, and a number of the poems were devoted to what Victor called "enlightened" Catholicism.

Rohan and the Abbé Lammenais, another priest with strong humanitarian views, had built up a following among young authors of the period, and their idealistic romanticism appealed to Victor, who became their most ardent spokesman. So the book was a curious combination of ideas, espousing a liberal Catholicism and a political conservatism.

At this stage of his life, when Victor was estranged

from his father, his anti-Bonaparte feelings were vehement, and he referred to the Emperor repeatedly as "the Corsican usurper." Shown the book, Louis XVIII was so pleased that he not only summoned the young author to a private audience, where they again drank weak tea, but publicly presented him with a purse of twelve hundred francs. Victor overnight became a person of some consequence, and was assured a hearing whenever more of his work was published.

He was solvent, too, with enough money to support a wife for at least a year or two, so he applied to M. Foucher for permission to marry. Adèle's father kept his word, and plans were made for their wedding.

Late in the summer Victor was taken with a mysterious fever, one of the few serious illnesses he ever suffered, and his relationship with Adèle was such that she was allowed to visit him daily without a chaperone. But the young couple avoided temptation, even though alone in the author's quarters, and both were so pleased by the strength they had showed that they wrote each other several letters of mutual congratulation.

The marriage took place on October 22, 1822, at the Church of Saint-Sulpice, with the Abbé de Rohan performing the ceremony. The bridegroom was escorted to the altar by two friends rather than one. Alfred de Vigny, one of the most popular young poets of the period, had become a close friend; Victor also wanted in this way to acknowledge the influence on his career exerted by his former teacher, Biscarret. Following the ceremony a dinner was held in the hall of the War Council, which M. Foucher rented for the evening, and provided an orchestra for dance music. Victor and Adèle had engaged a suite in a hotel for the night, and planned the next day to make their temporary home with Adèle's parents.

In later years Victor wrote at length about the dramatic incident that took place at the wedding. He and his brother, Eugène, although the closest of friends, long had been rivals. The theme of brotherly competition and hostility appeared many times in Victor's works.

Eugène had also been Adèle's childhood playmate. For many years he had secretly loved her, so Victor believed. Now, as Eugène saw the bride and groom walk up the aisle together and leave the church, he knew he had lost his love forever, and the blow was too great. "A terrible cry of anguish and despair escaped from his throat," according to Victor's account, and he went mad, never to recover his wits.

The story is as macabre as any fiction Victor Hugo ever wrote, and he told it so often that he probably came to believe it. The facts, however, do not jibe with his account, although Eugène may have been in love with Adèle. It is possible to interpret some of his poems in the light of his alleged affections.

Actually, Eugène's grip on reality had been slipping over a period of time, and others, including his brothers, merely assumed that he was becoming rather eccentric. He made several loud comments during the wedding ceremony, and friends were forced to quiet him, but the bride and groom appeared unaware of his interruptions.

Wine flowed at the wedding dinner, and Eugène, who had too much to drink, behaved even more strangely. When Abel tried to calm him he became violent, and the eldest of the Hugo brothers had to ask Biscarret to help him calm the disturber of the peace. By this time, Victor and Adèle had left the banquet hall and were unaware of what had taken place.

A physician who was one of the wedding guests was asked to give Eugène a sedative, and it was he who first realized that the young man had gone mad. Eugène had to be bound hand and foot before the sedative could be administered, and he was taken immediately to a hospital, then removed at dawn, by Abel, to a private sanitarium for the insane in the countryside near Paris. There he remained for the rest of his days, never recovering his wits, never recognizing any of his relatives or friends.

It was Biscarret's unpleasant duty to tell Victor what had happened, and he went early in the morning to the hotel. Victor was stunned, as was Adèle, and they left in tears, causing the hotel management to assume their union had failed.

General Hugo, now married to Catherine, had neither come to the wedding on his own initiative, nor, according to Abel, had he been invited. But the tragedy brought him to the city from Blois, and Eugène's fate was responsible for a reconciliation between Léopold and his youngest son. Adèle not only hit it off with her father-in-law, but established an immediate rapport with Catherine, too.

The elder couple stayed in Paris for more than a month, and Victor and Adèle saw them daily. Seeing Léopold for the first time through the eyes of an adult, Victor gradually realized that his father was a warm, sensible, and loving man, who was anything but the monster that Sophie had painted him. Catherine, too, was an intelligent and tender person, and Victor remembered the many kindnesses she had shown him as a child, gestures that his mother's violent hostility had driven from his mind.

When the young Hugos later established a home of their own, the elder Hugos frequently visited them, and Victor and Adèle accepted so many invitations to the quiet, three-story house in Blois that they came to regard it as their second home.

Victor managed to remain loyal to his mother's memory even while accepting and reciprocating his father's affection. But the reconciliation was more than personal. Of greater importance was the influence that General Hugo exerted on his son's career.

The older man often reminisced about his life, and the fascinated young author listened avidly. Over a period of time he gained a new view of Napoleon Bonaparte, far different from anything he had ever heard from his mother. Gradually he gained an appreciation of Napoleon's administrative, diplomatic, political, and military genius. At his father's suggestion he read Goethe, and began to understand that it was Napoleon who had codified and cemented the personal freedoms won by the people in the French Revolution. Always patriotic, Victor's feelings were inflamed by the accounts of Napoleon's exploits.

When he realized that French law had changed for the better because of Napoleon, that freedom of speech, religion, assemblage, and the press owed a permanent debt to the Emperor, he began to comprehend the repressions fostered by the restored Bourbon monarchy. Thanks to General Hugo, his youngest son was transformed from an ardent, conservative royalist into an ardent Bonapartist.

The change was not evident for some years. When it finally burst into the open, Victor had become so renowned that repercussions were felt throughout Europe.

Four months after Victor's marriage he reached his twenty-first birthday. He was now a handsome, self-possessed young man, and his dress and manner gave him the appearance of a successful merchant. Nothing in his outward life even suggested the flamboyant nature that would assert itself in later years. Aside from self-confidence in his talents, an attitude that vocational reverses could not alter, Victor probably did not think of himself in unusual terms. He was a middle-class husband, solid and conservative, and he soon discovered he was to become a father.

Léopold, named after Victor's father, was born in July 1823, and died two months later. A girl Léopoldine, was born on August 28, 1824, to be followed by three other children: Charles, born on November 9, 1826; François-Victor, born on October 21, 1828; and Adèle, born on July 28, 1830. Léopoldine was her father's favorite, and she always remained close to him. According to some students of Victor Hugo, the relationship was too close, but careful scrutiny of all evidence reveals no truth in the hints of sensational biographers. It is undeniably true that Victor turned more and more to his eldest child as a confidante when his own marriage became increasingly sour and strained, but his relationship with Léopoldine was never overtly incestuous.

It is mildly surprising to discover that neither Adèle nor Victor appeared particularly upset by the death of their first-born. During the few weeks of the infant's life Victor took great pride in him, and wrote a long letter to Abel "for the sake of posterity," in which he described the baby at length.

The naming of the lost first-born and the infant daughter who followed him into the fold of the family was nonetheless significant. Little Léopold spent his last days at Blois and died there. Sickly from birth, Léopold failed to respond to the prescriptions of the family's physicians, and Catherine Hugo suggested that country air might help both mother and child. So Adèle journeyed to the house at Blois. Catherine made every effort to save her husband's grandchild, and in the process won Adèle's eternal gratitude. The two women remained close as long as Catherine lived, and she was one of a very few persons toward whom Adèle displayed genuine, consistent warmth. Victor did not know he had married a woman of limited emotional response. The passing of little Léopold left both parents relatively unmoved. Adèle put the infant out of her mind and became pregnant again within weeks of the baby's death. Both she and Victor looked forward to the birth of another child.

In the early months of 1823 Victor Hugo was concentrating on the very real problems of earning a respectable living for himself and his pregnant wife. Not yet experienced in the ways of publishing, he made a deal with a former marquis named Persan, who contracted to bring out a new edition of the *Odes* and publish a mammoth, four-volume novel called *Han d'Islande* (*Han of Iceland*).

The new printing of the *Odes* sold out. A thousand copies of *Han d'Islande* were bought, although it was not a good book, and would be forgotten today if it had not come from the pen of Victor Hugo. The young author quickly learned the vicissitudes of the publishing industry of his day. After he had received five hundred francs in royalties, out of two thousand francs due him, Persan conveniently declared himself bankrupt. Before Victor could sue him, the publisher launched a ferocious attack on the integrity of the young author, claiming, in a series of letters to the newspapers, that Victor was a scoundrel and a cheat.

These assaults attracted far more attention than did the novel itself. Burdened by a confusing and complicated plot, it was a horror story abounding in murders and executions, the supernatural, tortures, and every other sensational theme that the author had been able to dredge from his lively imagination. Only the love story rings true, and as Victor said in later years, he recounted his own romance with Adèle.

The odes and later poems that Victor contributed to a new magazine, *Muse française*, showed the influence of his father. Napoleon was still a tyrant, but the poet hailed his military genius, and applauded the glory that French regiments had won under his banner.

The appeal of this work was immediate. The public had been smarting under the anti-Bonaparte attacks of the restored Bourbon regime. Tens of thousands of Napoleon's veterans recalled their exploits at war, and were proud of the part they had played in history. Victor's poetry reflected their mood.

He began to write literary criticism, too, although he considered it the lowest form to which an author could descend. But he was learning what kept the pot boiling, and he took money from any source that would pay him. It was during this period that he wrote at some length on the work of Lord Byron, probably in translation, as his own

c

command of English was negligible. Whatever the reason, his writing was superficial, but did him no great harm. Certainly he was influenced by Byron's romanticism, whether or not he recognized it in this formative period.

Goaded by Adèle, whose interest in her husband's writing was limited to his income, Victor spent the final months of 1823 working on his poems, and completed enough for another book. A bookseller, Ladvocat, agreed to publish them, and paid an advance royalty of two thousand francs for the privilege. The crown, obviously hoping for additional praise, added a new purse to Victor's holdings, and gave him a pension of one hundred francs per month.

The young husband was achieving a degree of financial respectability that not only satisfied him, but placated his wife, who was buying furniture, linens, and other household goods for their own future home. Victor, who could live amicably with anyone if he was allowed to work without undue interference, was comfortable in the home of his parents-in-law. Adèle endured her lot stoically, except when alone with Victor, and then she complained that her mother tried to dominate her. Like countless young wives throughout the centuries, she yearned for a dwelling of her own.

The rapport of General Hugo and his son continued to grow, and all at once their positions were reversed. Léopold wanted to be restored to active military duty, and dreamed of winning a promotion to the rank of lieutenant general. Victor offered to help him, and went to the Bourbon court to plead his father's cause. There he learned a lesson in practical politics. The crown was delighted to be praised by an author of growing popularity, but had no intention of granting power of any sort to one who had served under the flag of Napoleon. Victor was treated politely; his request gathered dust in the Bourbon archives.

The year 1824 was a busy one for Victor and Adèle. In June they finally moved to a small apartment on the second floor of a building on the rue de Vaugirard, above a joiner's shop, and there they remained for three years.

The *Nouvelles Odes* was published in March 1824, and was an immediate success. The entire edition was sold out within two weeks, and Ladvocat brought out a new printing, paying the poet an advance royalty of an additional thousand francs. Victor was now a man of consequence in the literary world. Colleagues who gathered at his home for cheese and wine listened to him with growing respect. He was one of a very small band who could earn his living with his pen, and he developed a variety of theories, most of them shallow, that were suitable to his new station. They are regarded as gibberish in a later age, chiefly because he appeared, as yet, to have no idea that he stood in the vanguard of a new romantic movement. At this time the young authors were apolitical, still feeling their way in a movement that was—and would be—informal and informed.

The young Hugo's first home was more than adequate, but Victor showed the first signs of developing grandoise gestures. Adèle, whose second baby was due in August, had already purchased solid, sensible furniture of the sort her parents used. Victor saw a mammoth divan in a shop window. It was covered in white velvet, trimmed with gold, and the proprietor assured him it was a twin of one the Empress Joséphine had at Malmaison, her country house. Victor wanted it, even at the cost of three hundred francs.

Adèle protested that the price was equivalent to six months' rent and would look ridiculous in their tiny sitting room.

Victor replied by buying the divan and supervising its installation.

Adèle had no further cause to complain. As she soon discovered, the divan had many uses. Unexpected overnight guests could sleep on it, she stretched out on it when nursing her baby, and sometimes one or another of Victor's literary friends used it for an assignation, provided he knew his hostess had gone to sleep for the night. Victor's ideas were more practical than she had supposed.

When Léopoldine was born, Victor immediately lost his heart to his daughter. Some of his most delicate lyrics, all of them dedicated to the baby, were written in the months immediately following her birth.

In mid-September the ineffectual Louis XVIII died, and was succeeded by Charles X, one of the most reactionary, short-sighted monarchs ever to rule France. He had the foresight, however, to heap honors on influential supporters, and Victor Hugo stood high in the ranks of that elite group. The new king immediately made him a member of the Legion of Honor, doubled his pension, and invited him to the coronation at the ancient Cathedral of Rheims.

Victor attended the event and was disturbed when he heard King Charles formally reassert the ancient principle of the divine right of kings. Several of Victor's colleagues were also present, among them the venerable Chateaubriand, and although they were royalists, they were more than upset. Later Léopold Hugo put the declaration in its proper perspective for one of his sons, explaining that the people had been granted a voice in their own government, first by the Revolution, then by Napoleon, and that no monarch could revert to the laws of Louis XIV. The people of France, he declared, were not dumb sheep.

At the time Victor accepted the validity of the king's policy, and probably agreed with it. But he was still required to pay for the royal favors he had received, and wrote a long ode, *The Coronation of Charles X*, which praised the sterling qualities (presumed) of the new monarch. It was one of the dullest, flabbiest, and least inspired works he ever wrote. His heart wasn't in his work.

All the same, *The Coronation* paid off. On the personal order of King Charles, it was published by the Royal Press. Members of the court obediently purchased copies for themselves, their relatives, and their friends. And members of various royalist organizations understood the broad hints of the king, who said he would look with increased favor on those who had copies of the book in their homes.

Victor was richer by another fifteen hundred francs, and he celebrated by taking his wife and daughter on a tour of Switzerland. The snow-covered Alps provided him with the inspiration for scores of poems, which eventually earned many times the cost of the journey. The trip was made in the company of a fellow author, Charles Nodier, and his family. Nodier was the editor of the *Muse française*, and also held an important post as a librarian, so his house was a focal point for aspiring authors of the day, among them

Alfred de Vigny, Soumet, Alphonse de Lamartine, Honoré de Balzac, and the elder Alexandre Dumas, who subsequently became one of Victor's close friends and followers.

This group was the first with which Victor was associated, and although they later became identified as romantics for a number of years, they were at this stage of their development, more properly, pre-romantics. They stood for no positive set of standards, but were even now in rebellion against the prevailing formality of classicism.

A later group of Victor's professional associates became known as the Cénacle. It was equally informal, but took a more vigorous and direct stand in favor of the romantic approach to both prose and poetry.

In the late autumn of 1824, after returning from Switzerland, Victor took his family to Blois. There he displayed a tact and talent for diplomacy that previously had been missing from his makeup. Although he and Catherine had become friendly, his step-mother remained somewhat uneasy in his presence, remembering how thoroughly Sophie Hugo had hated her. Victor showed how much he admired her in her own right by asking her to become Léopoldine's godmother. The gesture was perfect, and tightened his ties with Catherine. Thereafter her beloved Victor could do no wrong.

In the next five years Victor continued to prosper. His family grew, the list of his published works lengthened, and almost everything he wrote made money. The year 1826 saw the publication of two major books: *Odes et ballades*, an immediate success, and a revised version of his first novel, *Bug-Jargal*.

The novel dealt with a revolt of blacks in Santo

Domingo and, together with a conventional love story, featured a theme of miscegenation, the love of a black leader for a white woman. Romantic in the extreme and solving the problem by having Bug-Jargal sacrifice himself for his love, Victor was one of the first authors since Shakespeare to use the theme. *Bug-Jargal* was over-plotted, far too violent, and filled with scenes of blood and melodrama. One of its most important characters, the twisted, ugly Habibrah, died when he fell into a deep chasm. With appropriate changes, this character later appeared as the notorious hunchback, Quasimodo, in *Notre-Dame de Paris.*

In spite of its obvious faults and the refusal of the critics to deal with it seriously, the novel was an overnight success. Men of literary pretensions, including all the members of Victor's own circle except Nodier, considered the book to be trash, too, but the reading public loved it. Three printings were rushed through the printer's presses in as many months. Never again would Victor be in dire need of funds. His success was so great that his father, in a rare gesture, wrote him a letter apologizing for his refusal to believe that his youngest son could earn a living as a writer.

Victor accepted the tribute calmly. "I agree that few are able to do what I am accomplishing," he wrote with his growing lack of humility. "But there are few in France or elsewhere who are endowed with my versatility or my ability to make my words come to life. The Abbé de Rohan says I have been given a gift by God, but he is wrong. My colleagues spend their days visiting each other, sitting and posing in cafés, and talking about writing. But I am not like them. I write. That is my secret. What I achieve is done by hard work, not through miracles."

There was no question that he worked furiously. Every morning of every day in the week Victor retired to his private room promptly at 8 o'clock. By this time he had prepared a simple breakfast of coffee, bread and jam for himself, had fed the babies and gone out for a long, brisk walk. He rarely saw Adèle until later in the day.

His workroom was furnished in a manner conducive to steady concentration. The drapes and rugs were plain, without patterns, there were no paintings on the walls and no bric-a-brac on the tables. Victor's desk was a slab of plain, polished wood which he hooked to a wall, and he stood in front of it, writing. "When an author sits at his work," he said at one of the literary gatherings, "the blood sinks to his arse when it should remain in his head, and there are too many who write with their arses instead of their minds."

He wrote so rapidly that he wore down several quill pens every week, and regardless of whether he was composing poetry or prose, he was rarely at a loss for words. "I believe in the inspiration of concentration," he said, "so I revise no more often than is absolutely necessary. Writing becomes stiff when it is not spontaneous, and changes make a composition wooden."

He took no respite until 2 o'clock in the afternoon, when he appeared for dinner with Adèle. Now that they could afford to eat well, Victor insisted they dine accordingly. The meal began with a light first course, usually seafood, which was followed by a rich soup. Then came fish and meat courses, each with its own appropriate vegetables and potatoes. There was a large salad, cheese, a dessert, and fresh fruit. At least four or five different wines were served, and Victor drank copiously, but always remained sober.

"I dislike the feeling," he told his step-mother, "that alcoholic spirits can take command of me. I want to remain in total control of my own destiny."

After dinner it was impossible to return to work immediately, so Victor played with the babies, not hesitating to awaken them if they happened to be asleep. When they became older, he told them stories every afternoon. These were continuing tales, and he always remembered the point at which he had stopped at the end of the previous day's installment.

He also used the after-dinner period to look through his mail, and soon fell into the habit of dictating his replies to Adèle. Later in his life, when he was no longer living with his wife, any mistress who happened to be sharing his dwelling with him had to take dictation. It was one of his requisites.

Promptly at 4:00 P.M. Victor returned to his study and resumed his writing. On a nearby mantel he kept a small, enameled clock that had belonged to his mother, and when it chimed the hour of 8:00 P.M. he stopped work for the day, regardless of what he happened to be writing. It did not matter if he was in the middle of a sentence. He wiped his pen and put it aside, knowing he would pick up the manuscript the following morning and begin with the next word or sentence.

After changing his clothes he settled down to a few hours of reading, usually for vocational purposes and rarely for pleasure. He could read as rapidly as he could write, and often went through two or three complete books in as many hours. People who saw him leafing through the pages of a book refused to believe he was doing more than surface skimming, but he permitted skeptics to test him. He was able to prove to their bemused satisfaction that he could read several pages, remembering every detail, in the time it took an ordinary person to digest a single paragraph.

By 11:00 P.M. Victor was ready for a social hour or two, and sometimes friends dropped in for a light supper of cheese, an omelette, a roasted chicken, and a fruit tart or a soufflé. On the nights when he and Adèle did not entertain, he went to the house of Nodier or one of his other friends for supper. Adèle did not go with him. Ladies went abroad after dark only when they accompanied their husbands to the theater or the opera.

By 1:00 A.M., perhaps 2:00, Victor was ready for bed —and lovemaking. Having discovered the joys of sexual intercourse, his appetites were insatiable, and Adèle, who soon tired of pregnancies, suffered his advances but did not enjoy them. Later she became bored and depressed by this great bear of a husband who not only dominated her, but demanded more—and still more—until she feigned sleep in order to escape from him.

Victor, however, required no more than three or four hours of sleep. No matter how late he dropped off, he was wide awake at 6:00 A.M., ready for another grueling day.

He changed his routine on Sundays by stopping work after dinner and going out for a second walk, usually accompanied by his wife and children. Six hours of work on a Sunday was enough to satisfy him. On Sunday mornings Adèle went regularly to mass, but her husband did not bother to accompany her. Although still considering himself a loyal, practicing Catholic, he was bored by the liturgy and thought the sermons stupid. The Abbé du Rohan, who sometimes delivered provocative sermons solely for the sake of arousing his friend's intellectual ire, could not persuade him to come to church more than four or five times each year.

It was during this period of Victor's life that he discovered his artistic talent. He had done pen and ink sketches since he was a small boy, but had never studied art, and did not know he had any talents in the field until he became involved in a dispute one night at Nodier's house. Trying to illustrate a point he was making, he took pen and paper, and drew a sketch of a man's head and torso that delighted his friends.

So, in his spare time, he began to draw, and sometimes amused himself by doing the frontispieces for his own books. But oils annoyed him, and he soon abandoned the medium. "I lack the patience for such work," he told Nodier, "and if I cannot achieve perfection, I prefer not to draw."

He kept up his work with pen and ink, however, and some of his sketches were sold for high prices during his lifetime. One, acclaimed as a romantic masterpiece, was called "The Dream" and showed a man's hand and bare forearm groping upward into space through a sea of dark, forbidding clouds. Certainly Victor's contemporaries regarded him as potential master of painting, and later authorities have been inclined to agree.

Only when the young author was in the grip of the strange melancholia that sometimes overcame him did he vary his routine. When his depression took hold of him, he did no work whatever, and usually locked himself in his bedroom for periods of a few hours to two full days and nights. At such times he could not eat, drink, or sleep, but slouched in a chair, usually attired in his nightclothes, stared listlessly into space.

He had no way of knowing when these attacks would strike, and his depression usually lifted as swiftly as it had come, without reason. The tragedies that erupted so frequently throughout his life were in no way responsible for his bouts of melancholy. Often he was at his strongest during times of adversity. But when everything seemed to be going well he would buckle, and would remain in the grip of the depression until it lifted.

It has been suggested that Victor suffered from a touch of the madness that had destroyed the mind of his brother Eugène. Certainly a strain of insanity ran through the family, and probably had been inherited from Sophie, whose paranoid attitudes made her noticeably unbalanced. The fate of Victor's two daughters substantiate the theory that there may have been insanity in the Trébuchet genes.

Whether the dark, weird thoughts that crowded Victor's imagination and fill so many pages in his works indicate a strain of madness is a moot question. The *Ballades* of 1826 dealt with the realm of fantasy, and some of the wild, chilling figures and blood-curdling events that take place in these poems were the work of someone who was either a little mad or very shrewd.

A number of German authors had been writing poems and novels of the genre later to be known as Gothic, and Mme. de Staël had initiated the cult in French. Victor's brother Abel displayed a great interest in a similar strain to be found in Spanish literature, and as early as 1822 published a long, learned treatise on the subject.

Victor discovered, long before 1826, that spine-tingling concepts paid handsome dividends. Like all professional authors he showed an enduring curiosity in the sales his work accumulated. He knew that a book containing romantic horror-fantasy sold as fast as copies appeared on the bookstalls of Paris.

The publication of the *Ballades* openly placed him in the ranks of the romantics, as he himself indicated in a preface. Classical literature, he said, was artificial, and resembled the sculptured, pruned gardens of Versailles. But romantic literature was as natural as the wild and primitive forests of the New World.

The *Ballades* became an overnight sensation, thanks in part to a criticism in the most influential newspaper of the day, *Le Globe*. The paper's literary editor and critic, Charles-Augustin Sainte-Beuve, hailed the author as a genius, and praised his work as it had never been before.

Victor did not know Sainte-Beuve, sought him out, and discovered he was a neighbor who lived with his aged mother. Sainte-Beuve was a pedantic, precise young man, slender of build, with a delicate face that reminded Victor of Eugène in their childhood. Although the critic was shy and somewhat aloof, he quickly responded to Victor's gestures of friendship, and the two soon became intimates.

Himself a romantic, Sainte-Beuve exerted a great influence on Victor. As an enthusiastic devotee of the English Lake poets, he aroused Victor's interest in them, and may have translated their work for the benefit of one whose English was limited. The two men like to think they were intellectual twins, and Sainte-Beuve moved still closer to the Hugo household, taking an apartment for himself and his mother in the building adjoining that of the Hugo home. In time, this caused one of the greatest upheavals ever to occur in the lives of Victor and his family.

The critic was in part responsible for the formation of a new intellectual and social circle that met most frequently at Victor's new dwelling on the rue Notre-Dame-des-Champs. It included the young romantic poets and novelists opposed to the classical school of literature and art, the latter dominated by such figures as Louis Boulanger, the painter, and David d'Angers, the sculptor. The group called itself the Cénacle de Joseph Delorme, after the pseudonym under which Sainte-Beuve had published a book of somewhat better than mediocre poetry.

The beauty of the Cénacle was its informality. These young men came together principally to eat, drink, and chat. It was no coincidence, to be sure, that their thinking was similar, that they rejected rigid classicism and its prophet, the critic Boileau.

It was not accidental, either, that they loved life. Like their colleagues in England—Wordsworth, Coleridge, Byron, Shelley, Keats—they were forming a new kind of literature. The beauty of their efforts is that their movement at the outset was not deliberate, but was, in essence, the spontaneous outgrowth of the feelings of exuberant youth. And no one was more exuberant than Victor Hugo, at this stage of his career no conscious intellectual.

The year 1827 was one in which Victor made his strongest moves away from the conservatism of the Bourbons and began to lean heavily toward Bonapartist romanticism. A seemingly minor incident provided the spark. Three of Napoleon's marshals, Soult, Mortier, and Macdonald, were among the prominent Frenchmen invited to a ball given in February at the Austrian embassy. All three, who had fought with distinction against the armies of Imperial Austria, had been made dukes by their Emperor.

The major domo, who announced each guest as he appeared at the entrance to the grand ballroom, elected to ignore the noble titles of the three old soldiers. Still angry over the affair many years later, Victor wrote in *Victor Hugo raconté*, "Austria, humiliated by titles which recalled her defeats, publicly repudiated them."

Soult, Mortier, and Macdonald refused to accept the insult, and immediately marched out of the embassy. The next day Paris buzzed with the story, and no one was more outraged than Victor, who had been listening for years to his father's tales of the glory won by Napoleon's armies.

He went straight to his desk, and in a heat of passion wrote one of his most famous poems, the "Ode à la colonne de la Place Vendôme." Every line rang with a blazing, patriotic fervor, and the ode created a sensation when it was published two days later by the *Journal des débats*.

Victor's feelings precisely mirrored those of a vast majority of his fellow countrymen. The poem won him national recognition and praise on a scale he had never before known. The conservatives, although Bonaparte-haters, could not criticize him for the nationalist sentiments he expressed. Equally important, the so-called "liberal" press, which was devoted to Napoleonic principles, for the first time expressed admiration for the poet. Until then he had been regarded as a typical reactionary who fawned on the

Bourbons. The opening of doors by this group overnight transformed Victor from a partisan to a national literary figure.

By 1827, Victor had become increasingly interested in theater, which he attended frequently, sometimes with Adèle and sometimes with various male friends. Although he had no experience in the field, he decided to write a play in the heroic, romantic mold of Shakespeare, whom he admired. He chose Oliver Cromwell, the British Lord Protector who had sent the Stuart kings into exile, as his subject. Victor had read dozens of books on Cromwell, and was proud of his research. But the central figure in his play bore less resemblance to the Lord Protector than to the Emperor Napoleon. In the Hugo version of history, a dynamic leader dedicated to the freedom and welfare of all the people drove the decadent and reactionary Stuart monarchs from the throne of England and ushered in a new era of prosperity and hope.

The play was not produced, much to the relief of Victor's friends, to whom he read it at some of the evening meetings of the Cénacle. Many of them had seen some of their best work refused theatrical production or book publication by the Bourbon censors, and they knew the same fate would befall *Cromwell* if Victor persisted in his attempt to have it presented on the stage.

He, however, had never known censorship, and laughed at their fears. At the same time he remained cautious, and rather than take unnecessary chances, he did not press for a production. Instead he published the play, writing a preface for it that was far more important than the drama. In these pages he launched a vigorous attack on the classical school of writing, declaring that it was stultifying. He issued a call to all writers to rally to the flag of romanticism, which he equated with freedom and natural human emotions. In this appeal he wittingly made himself the leader of the romantic movement, enhancing his importance on the French literary scene.

No doubt Victor was sincere and intellectually honest, but at the same time he saw an opportunity and seized it. Intuitively he knew that classicism was dead and that the public would follow the writers of romanticism. Other poets may have been impractical, but Victor Hugo never allowed himself to forget his year of near-starvation, and had no intention of going hungry again. His family was still growing, and so were his tastes for expensive food, wines, and clothing. There were two full-time servants in the house, and he was paying the considerable rent of 1250 francs per year. At the age of twenty-five Victor was enjoying his prosperity, and had not yet gained the inner stature that would enable him to take a stand against reaction.

His position seemed secure, and 1828 promised to be a year of even greater success. Léopold and Catherine had taken winter quarters in Paris to be closer to their sons and grandchildren, and the Cénacle had already become the most famous literary group in France. Abel Hugo, who was now one of its leading spirits, discovered a restaurant where the food was excellent but inexpensive, the wine robust but cheap; members of the Cénacle formed the habit of eating at the place at least one or two evenings each week. They were young and high-spirited, so it was inevitable that they should consume large quantities of the good wine. Victor quickly learned to hold his own, but no one ever saw him become intoxicated.

One evening in late January Victor and Adèle paid a call on his father and step-mother. The general was his usual, robust self, full of reminiscences and sound advice, which Victor sought. The young couple returned home shortly before midnight, and no sooner reached the house when a messenger from Catherine arrived. Léopold Hugo had been stricken, probably with apoplexy, and died within moments.

The loss of his father was the most serious blow Victor had yet sustained, and left him far more grief-stricken than the death of his mother. He mourned in private for months, and although he soon forced himself to resume his normal social life, Adèle and his friends noticed that he rarely smiled and never joked.

He worked harder than ever in order to assuage his sorrow, but few of the results showed that year. He brought out a final, revised edition of the *Odes et ballades*, and wrote a play, *Amy Robsart*, an adaptation of Sir Walter Scott's *Kenilworth*, that was produced in mid-year with his young brother-in-law, Paul Foucher, listed as its author. It was a bad play, hastily conceived and sloppily executed, and the critics treated it as unmercifully as the opening night audience, which hissed.

Victor immediately admitted that he was the real author and that Paul was blameless. This act of courage enabled young Foucher to launch his own literary career without a blight on his name. At the time, Victor thought he would become the laughingstock of the theater, but he refused to let anyone else take the blame. As Abel said, "Victor is growing up."

As it happened, the admission did Victor no harm; his reputation as a poet was already too great. The following year the faith of the public in his talents was justified by the publication of what he called in the preface "a useless book of pure poetry." *Les Orientales* often has been called one of his finest collections of poems.

The title was somewhat misleading, as was his claim that he had written only "pure" poetry. Most of his scenes were laid either in Greece or in the Arab lands that bordered the Mediterranean, and although he wrote many lyrics, he could not avoid the political themes that so often preoccupied him. In fact, one entire section, called "Lui," was devoted to the subject of Napoleon Bonaparte's career, which he treated with sympathy and understanding, although portions appeared on the surface to be critical. General Hugo would have found nothing objectionable in "Lui."

The immediate success of *Orientales* poured money into Victor's purse, and late in the year an incident increased his fame as a compassionate humanitarian. When walking near the Hôtel de Ville, he saw the public executioner preparing the guillotine for his next day's grisly work. The man's callousness horrified and angered Victor, who hurried home and wrote a scathing denunciation of capital punishment called *Le Dernier Jour d'un condamné* (*Last Day of a Condemned Man*). A hot-headed diatribe, it cannot be classified as one of his major works, but it had a sensational effect.

The subject of capital punishment was introduced in

the Chamber of Deputies, and the old Marquis de Lafayette, a national hero, read the entire text into the record.
The public at large applauded Victor more vigorously than
ever before, too. The people hated the guillotine and all it
represented, and the poet had become the champion of a
particularly popular cause.

Victor Hugo was riding high. He was financially successful, his reputation continued to grow, and he was living
the life of a model husband and father. But forces were at
work beneath the façade of respectability that soon would
erupt and make him one of the most notorious rakes in
Western history.

Chapter IV

*W*HEN no scandal can be unearthed in the life of a great man, rumor goes to work. William Shakespeare may or may not have been in love with Anne Hathaway. Julius Caesar may have been subjected to a protracted homosexual experience in his youth. Alexandre Dumas, the elder, may or may not have had seventeen mistresses.

Conjecture regarding the private life of Victor Hugo is unnecessary, however; the facts speak for themselves. His marriage failed, and he became the most indefatigable —and successful—woman chaser in an era when women chasing was elevated to the level of a high art.

Hugo's activities in this sphere appear, at first glance, to defy reason. The year 1829 was the busiest of his life up to that point. He enjoyed success and financial independence greater than he ever had before. The new Hugo apartment, on the rue Notre-Dame-des-Champs, was located in Paris's most elegant residential district. A group of devoted followers imitated the poet's free-flowing, romantic style. At the age of twenty-seven, Victor Hugo had already reached the pinnacle of his profession.

His critics have blamed the libertinism that overtook him soon after on his association with the theater, long regarded as even more of a moral cesspool in France than in other countries. But an examination of the record reveals some remarkable contradictions.

It is true that Victor had been fascinated by the theater since his youth, and in 1829 he fulfilled a lifelong ambition by completing a play, *Marion Delorme*, that the Comédie-Française promptly agreed to produce. The theme, that of a courtesan's regeneration through love, had long been in Victor's mind, appearing repeatedly in his poems. But there were implications in the theme far beyond the personal.

King Charles X, completely misjudging the temper of the times, was failing in his attempt to turn back the clock to the era of absolute monarchism. Short-sighted as well as stubborn, the king was just beginning to realize that France stood on the thin edge of a new revolution. What he and his advisers did know was that *Marion Delorme* struck close to the royal core. Charles, like all mortals, suffered from a weakness; his was a predeliction for ladies of the evening.

Victor's play opened at the Comédie in July, and was wildly acclaimed by the audience. But the censors, believing that mockery of the king rather than an appreciation of the drama's merits was responsible for the hearty applause, ordered the play withdrawn. For the first time in his distinguished career, Victor was forced to suffer the stigma of official displeasure and a heavy financial loss.

Stung in pride, Victor immediately fought back by retiring to his study and, in a single month of furious effort, writing another play. On August 29 he started to work on *Hernani*, and on September 30 he electrified the members of the informal Cénacle by reading it to them. A month later he read it in the Green Room of the Comédie, whose staff gave him a standing ovation and instantly agreed to produce the drama.

Set in the Spain of the early sixteenth century, *Hernani* was devoted to the theme of honor. On the surface the honor was that of the Spanish nobility, but anyone who cared to dig deeper might see that he was writing about royal honor. The melodrama was violent and in today's terms sometimes absurd, but the poetry was soaring and frequently lyrical.

Victor spent the better part of the autumn at rehearsals. The theater of the Comédie became his second home, and actors, directors, and members of the production staff often adjourned to the Hugo apartment at the end of the day. Victor was completely captivated by the excitement of show business.

Hernani opened at the Comédie on February 25, 1830, and received a welcome that made the rafters tremble. Paris hadn't known such a reception since the plays of Voltaire had made theatrical history almost a hundred years earlier. The censors recognized the possibility that the honor of Charles X was being questioned,

but the revolutionary fervor of France was rising. This time the government was afraid to crack down on a play that had been received with such enthusiasm.

Victor could afford to be smug. He himself had organized a claque to make certain that *Hernani* was applauded. Members of the Cénacle sat in a body, and Théophile Gautier, a dashing young drama and literary critic whose flamboyantly colorful manner of dress outraged the conservatives, held a copy of the script in his lap to make certain the friends of the playwright applauded in the right places.

It soon developed that *Hernani*'s success did not depend on a clacque. The reception given the play at succeeding performances was equally tumultuous, and Victor found his reputation as a dramatist as great as that which he had achieved as a poet.

Not satisfied with his accomplishments, he soon turned to yet another field, the novel. Obviously influenced by the romantic work of Sir Walter Scott, he completed the historical novel, *Notre-Dame de Paris*, in a scant four months. Never losing his objectivity, he knew that a central character, the hideous Quasimodo, would win immortality as the hunchback of Notre Dame. This grotesque character, who conceived a pure love for the gypsy heroine, Esméralda, captured the imagination of France, and subsequently of readers throughout the civilized world. Victor's imagination was breathtaking, his style was superb, his poetic images were verbal gold.

"Hugo," Gautier wrote, "is the greatest of living French poets, dramatists and novelists. He has no peer."

Other critics agreed, and only one, Sainte-Beuve,

either remained silent or damned Victor with a trickle of very faint praise. The attitude displayed by the man whom Victor had considered his best friend was not surprising, under the circumstances.

These circumstances were clouded in mystery for more than a hundred years. Sainte-Beuve and Adèle Hugo fell in love with each other, but were so clever in concealing the facts that not until 1939 was conclusive evidence found in their correspondence that they had actually become lovers, and had not merely been indulging in platonic mutual admiration.

Posterity may have been fooled for over a century, but Victor Hugo assuredly was not. He was the first to guess the truth, if not to know it, and he reacted with all the explosive violence that seethed beneath his well-mannered surface.

The situation had been developing for a long time. Adèle was too placid for her passionate husband, whose ego demanded an absorbed, continuing interest in his work as well as a ravenous physical appetite that matched his own. Adèle knew and cared no more about poetry than she had at the time of their marriage. Her mind drifted when she tried to read novels, including her husband's, and the theater bored her. Strictly middle class in her attitudes, she was content to surround herself with pretty things in her home, to cook substantial, unimaginative meals or to supervise their cooking, and to go through the motions of rearing her children.

As her surreptitious correspondence with Sainte-Beuve clearly indicates, Adèle Hugo was not particularly fond of children. Five times within a few years she gave birth to an infant. As she told her husband in a complaining letter soon after the birth of their last, it seemed to her that every time she went to bed with Victor, they had another baby.

There were nursemaids on hand to look after the children, but Adèle felt that her youth was being wasted in one pregnancy after another. She yearned for freedom, but was tied down by four living children and a husband who brought home hordes of men devoted to the cause of literature. Rather than listen to the interminable talk with a fixed smile, Adèle preferred to withdraw to her own sitting room or bedchamber.

It was in the latter that Victor invariably found her, and demanded what were known as his marital prerogatives. It did not cross his mind that her joy might be more confined than his. Just as one dined every evening and slept every night, one indulged in the pleasures of the flesh with one's mate before retiring. This was the natural order of life to Victor, and the best of all possible lives.

He was content. He had gained weight, still looked like a young boy, and every portrait made of him prior to the early 1830s shows him in a smiling pose. Thereafter all was changed. Deep circles appeared beneath his eyes, his clothes seemed to hang on him, his lips were drawn together so tightly they seemed to disappear altogether into his face. His eyes resembled those of a Huguenot clergyman preaching damnation.

Until his discovery of his wife's affair, Victor led a model middle-class life. Unlike his fellow poets, playwrights, and novelists, he never drank to excess during evenings at the cafés, and always returned home sober. On occasions when women were present, he saw to it that Adèle was at his side, unlike his colleagues who enjoyed being seen in public with their attractive mistresses. In fact, there is no record of any kind to indicate that Victor was previously unfaithful to his wife. He not only believed in the sanctity of marriage, but lived in accordance with his convictions.

By 1829 he was an exceptionally busy man. Until that time he was usually at home, and received Sainte-Beuve when the poet called at the Hugo apartment. Sainte-Beuve himself, in his *Volupté*, confesses that for years he looked covertly at Adèle, and, for reasons he did not comprehend at the time, went out of his way to avoid conversing with her.

Sainte-Beuve had fallen into the habit of stopping off at the Hugo house each day, and his host's absence did not deter him. Adèle had become his friend, too, and he found it increasingly easy to chat with her. When he admired a dress or shawl she was wearing, they had long discussions of women's fashions. Adèle found this particularly pleasant, as her husband rarely noticed what she wore. Sainte-Beuve also could discuss another of her favorite topics, religion, which bored Victor, and the critic-poet was full of fascinating information on such subjects as needlework and tapestry-making.

Frequently Sainte-Beuve arrived to find Adèle in tears. She was developing an infinite capacity for feeling very sorry for herself, but the man sympathized with the plight of this young wife whose bear of a busy, successful husband failed to understand her sensitive nature.

In any event, the critic's friendship with Victor went

through a profound change. Sainte-Beuve was annoyed by the interest in the theater that the successful poet was developing, thinking it beneath him. He had tried to dissuade Victor from associating with the production of *Marion Delorme*, and objected even more vigorously to the new friendships formed during the rehearsals of *Hernani*.

Sainte-Beuve's protests found expression in a remarkable letter he wrote to Victor in February 1830, a few days before *Hernani* was scheduled to open:

In truth, when I see what has been happening to you for some time, your life forever a prey to all, your leisure lost, the redoublings of hatred, the old, noble friendships drifting away, the fools and madmen who are replacing them, when I see the wrinkles and clouds on your brow which do not come from the travail of great thoughts alone, I can only feel afflicted, I can only regret the past, salute you with a gesture and go off to hide myself, I know not where.

His jealousy became even more virulent in the next paragraph, which referred to Adèle:

And Madame? She whose name should resound on your lyre only when people listen on bended knee to your songs? She is exposed to profane eyes every day, distributing notes to more than eighty young men hardly known before yesterday. This chaste and charming familiarity, the true prize of friendship, forever sullied by the crowd; the word devotion prostituted, the useful appreciated above all; materialistic combinations dominating everything! ! ! !

Victor was irritated by his friend's carping, and because he found Sainte-Beuve's company unpleasant began to avoid him. There appears to be no basis for the belief, however, that the Hugo family made its move to the rue Notre-Dame-des-Champs because Victor tired of Sainte-Beuve's daily visits. Victor's landlord disapproved of the presence of actors and other persons considered low quality, and refused to renew the Hugo lease. Victor wanted a larger dwelling, so he was happy to leave.

Sainte-Beuve, undaunted, began to make daily calls at the new apartment, and it is significant that he timed his visits carefully, arriving when he knew Victor would not be at home. Adèle would have been blind to be unaware of her admirer's growing interest in her.

Whether Sainte-Beuve confessed his love to Adèle prior to the birth of her last child is a matter of conjecture. According to their correspondence, Adèle did not admit to him that she loved him while she was still carrying her baby.

The new baby, Adèle, was born in July 1830, and at her mother's instigation, Sainte-Beuve became the infant's godfather. At about this same time Adèle made preparations for the new life she intended to lead, and informed Victor that she would not resume intimate relations with him. Her pregnancy had been very difficult, she told him, and she didn't want another. She was tired of bearing children.

The young, middle-class husband was stunned. He did not want her health ruined, to be sure, but there were remedies that women used in order to prevent childbirth. Every French housewife had her own collection of herbs and medicines, and while they weren't completely effective, they helped. Adèle said she would never use any of these measures, and that ended the matter as far as she was concerned.

In the period that followed, Victor began to see his marriage in a new light. His wife's greed for the good things that money could buy became more apparent to him. So did her lack of interest in his work, her inability to understand anything he wrote. He had begun a new book of poetry, *Les Feuilles d'automne*, subsequently to be celebrated as one of his most enduring, but Adèle was indifferent to the excerpts he tried to read to her.

France continued to move rapidly toward a new revolution. Discontent and ferment were spreading through Europe. Napoleon's conquerors, who tried at the Congress of Vienna to reestablish the pre-war order, were failing everywhere as the Industrial Revolution expanded. Workers yearned for the personal freedoms and the material comforts of the growing middle class.

The situation became especially critical in France, where the goals of the great Revolution of 1789—liberty, equality, and fraternity—had been kept alive during the Napoleonic era. According to one of the jokes current in Paris, Charles X was endowed with the innumerable faults of his Bourbon ancestors, but none of their virtues. Unfortunately for Charles as well as his countrymen, the humor was not far from the mark.

Charles was mean, suspicious, and narrow, with no sympathy or understanding of commoners or of the times in which they were living. Having spent his entire life in the company of aristocrats, he sincerely believed that the rights, prerogatives, and authority of the crown were divinely inspired. Without exception his ministers shared his reactionary views.

Revolutions and insurrections broke out all over

Europe in the summer of 1830. In July, the working class of Paris mounted barricades, supported by liberals of every class, including a surprising number of merchants, traders, and businessmen. Victor Hugo wrote that his youngest child came into the world while bullets whined across the fields near the family's new apartment.

Victor was also responsible for the observation that if Charles X did not know how to rule, he at least had the good sense to know when he wasn't wanted. Before the month ended, he abdicated and fled the country.

The forces that wanted to proclaim France a republic were in command. By acclamation the Presidency was offered to the aged hero who had made a name for himself on the far side of the Atlantic, Marie-Joseph, Marquis de Lafayette. But Lafayette wanted no power for himself, and handed the revolutionary Tricolor to the most unlikely of candidates, Louis-Philippe, Duc d'Orleans.

One of the most curious figures of French history, Louis-Philippe was a Bourbon by birth. As a boy he had taken part in the French Revolution on the side of the people against his own relatives, but had been forced to go into exile a few years later when he was suspected of conspiring against the Republic. He had become a college professor, and still had the soul of an academic pedant. His heart, strangely, was middle class. Although he held the rank of Lieutenant General of France under Charles X, he rarely wore his uniform, admitting that it made him feel conspicuous. He was more at home in modest civilian clothes. Horseback riding he found too dangerous and uncomfortable, and carriages too expensive to keep, so he usually walked from one place to another in Paris.

On August 7 the Chamber of Deputies voted to give Louis-Philippe the crown, and the Senate concurred, but the new monarch did not become the King of France. His official title was King of the French, a slight but significant difference. The forces of republicanism had won a victory.

Victor Hugo, who was already acquainted with Louis-Philippe because they frequented some of the same unfashionable, inexpensive cafés, saluted the new regime with a poem, *Ode to Young France*. It was not one of his inspired works, but had the virtue of being an honest expression of his political sentiments, which is more than can be said for his poems extolling Louis XVIII and Charles X. The *Ode* was dull, but Victor had pressing domestic matters on his mind.

The dignity of the new king's office made it necessary for him to buy several coaches now. He refused to permit royal crests to adorn the doors, a move that won him increased popularity with republicans. In another gesture calculated to please the public, he opened to the public the Palais-Royal, the home into which he moved with his wife and eight children. Only the rooms in which he and his family actually lived were out of bounds.

Louis-Philippe could be seen on the streets daily, taking a constitutional alone in civilian clothes, and, wonder of wonders, he continued to stop in at the cafés he had frequented. At one of these he joined Victor Hugo for an hour of convivial conversation on the state of the world's literature, and invited the poet to dinner the following week.

This was no command appearance, but a simple, family meal. Nevertheless, Adèle Hugo attended with

Victor, and together they had the dubious pleasure of watching Louis-Philippe carve the roast himself. Victor subsequently commented in a note to his brother Abel, "I hope he reigns better than he carves. I could not refrain from shuddering when I saw how gracelessly our new monarch hacked that beautiful roast, which cost a pretty penny. But no matter. He calls me 'Victor,' and insists that I address him, in private, as 'Louis-Philippe.' One would almost think we were brother republicans."

The new king, however, was far more shrewd than Victor or virtually anyone else realized. Louis-Philippe's genes were Bourbon, and they soon went to work for him. A love of power for its own sake was the family curse, and the new king discovered he enjoyed wielding it. He had no intention of becoming a figurehead while other, lesser men actually ruled the country. Canny and cautious, he had no desire to lose either his throne or his life, so he gathered the reins into his own hands very gradually, imperceptibly. A number of years passed before it became apparent that their elected representatives had become the figureheads.

During the eighteen years that Louis-Philippe ruled, nevertheless, the spirit of the middle class reigned supreme in France. Victor Hugo became the living personification of the bourgeois dream, the bourgeois success story; he was the author whose work struck a responsive chord in the psyche of every bourgeois reader and play-goer.

The influence that Victor exerted was remarkable. In April 1831, he published *Notre-Dame de Paris*. Thanks to its enormous success, he single-handedly was responsible for a popular revolution in French architecture. People seemed to realize, for the first time, that Notre Dame was a magnificent cathedral. Medieval styles were copied in the construction of new homes, offices, and public buildings, and every newly rich citizen insisted that his house be decorated with gargoyles.

Even Victor's personal tastes set new styles. Unlike Gautier and some of his other new friends in the theater, he could not force himself to wear garish clothes. But one day he saw a waistcoat of pale gray in the window of a tailor's shop, and bought it. Within a short time thousands of Parisians were appearing in pale gray vests.

In spite of his fame, his growing wealth and influence, however, Victor Hugo was a desperately unhappy man. In November 1830, Sainte-Beuve had come to him while he was hard at work in his study, and although it was his inviolable rule that he could not be interrupted there, particularly when writing poetry, he paused to learn of his friend's crisis.

Sainte-Beuve, not completely lacking in honor, felt compelled to confess that he was in love with Adèle.

Victor felt sorry for him. Adèle's husband, the father of their four surviving children, was able to imagine his friend's torment. According to what he subsequently wrote to Abel, he gave Sainte-Beuve good, sound advice. He told the critic to control his emotions, find someone else he could love, and prevent his sentiments from spoiling a friendship with a man who admired and respected him.

Sainte-Beuve promised that he would try, but the effort was too great. Early in December he sent Victor a pitiful note:

My friend, I cannot endure it. If you knew how my days and nights are spent, and to what contradictory pas-

sions I am a prey, you would have pity on the one who has offended you, and you would wish me dead.

Victor responded with the dignified nobility of a middle-class husband who had no idea that his wife's feelings might be involved:

Time will heal all of your wounds. Let us hope that some day in the not distant future we shall find in this unfortunate situation only reasons for becoming more fond of each other. Come to see me often. Write to me always.

Sainte-Beuve lacked the strength, and wrote that he could no longer visit the Hugo house.

Again Victor showed great understanding. If personal visits were too painful, at least his friend could correspond.

For three weeks Sainte-Beuve did not reply; then he sent New Year's gifts to the children.

Adèle, who had played no part in the drama up to this point, entered the situation as an active partner rather than a passive object by dutifully inviting Sainte-Beuve to dinner.

He declined.

For several months there was no communication between the Hugo family and the critic. The publication of *Notre-Dame de Paris* in March spurred Victor to action. Always loyal to his friends, he sent a note to his old associate, asking him to write the review of the novel for the *Globe*.

By this time Sainte-Beuve's waspish, feline nature had reverted to normal. He not only declined, with a surprising lack of graciousness, to write the review of the book, but he became abusive. He could not express his views of *Notre-Dame de Paris* in print, he declared, because he

found it a mere travesty that lacked any literary qualities.
Also:

> *However guilty I may have been toward you, how-
> ever guilty I may have seemed to you, I thought, my friend,
> that you were then, in view of our intimacy, guilty of
> wrongs toward me, wrongs of lack of confidence and
> candor.*

Victor's reply, which he dispatched within twenty-
four hours was not only generous, but says a great deal
about his character:

> *I did not believe that what has passed between us,
> what is known to us two alone in the world, could ever be
> forgotten, especially by you, by the Sainte-Beuve I have
> known. You must remember what occurred between us on
> the most painful occasion of my life, at a moment when I
> had to choose between her and you. Remember what I told
> you, what I offered you, what I proposed to you with the
> firm resolution, as you well know, to keep my promise and
> to do as you would wish; remember that, and think that you
> have just written me that in this affair I was lacking in
> confidence and candor toward you. I will forgive you for
> that from this moment. Perhaps, alas! a day will come when
> you will not forgive yourself. I am the true friend who has
> trusted you and who trusts you yet, as you shall see.*

Two or three weeks later Sainte-Beuve answered in
what appeared to be a carbon copy of his old friend's mood.
He was truly contrite, he declared, and his most earnest
desire in all the world was to shake Victor Hugo's hand.

Victor immediately invited him to the house and insisted that their former relationship be resumed. All would

be as it had been before Adèle's beauty and charm had robbed the critic of his sense of balance and propriety.

Still lacking in worldly experience, Victor obviously believed what he wrote. Not only was Sainte-Beuve welcome when he was at home, but also when he was absent. Adèle, although persisting in her refusal to share her husband's bed, was showing him unprecedented kindness and compassion, and Victor seemed to think that normal marital relations soon would be resumed.

It did not occur to him that Adèle might have her own reason for treating him so pleasantly.

Sainte-Beuve's daily visits were resumed. Most of the time, of course, he showed up at the apartment on the rue Notre-Dame-des-Champs when Victor was visiting his publishers, stopping in at 'the Comédie, or was otherwise engaged. As often as two days each week, however, the men met face to face, and both found the ground beneath their feet treacherous. Conversation was difficult, there were long, silent pauses, and both felt embarrassed.

By mid-summer of 1831 Victor not only knew the experiment had failed, but had heard that Sainte-Beuve was deriding him to many of their mutual friends. Why? Logic, rather than sentiment, indicated that Adèle might be having an affair with the critic.

Although lacking experience in extra-marital escapades, Victor was no fool. The possibility that his wife was interested in someone else crossed his mind, and he decided to keep a close watch on her activities. It was not long before she supplied him with the evidence he sought.

Some of Victor's biographers have hinted that he resumed the friendship with Sainte-Beuve in order to trap Adèle and her lover. This is unlikely, as Victor was never devious in his dealings. In his correspondence with Abel, the one person he took into his confidence during this trying time, he repeatedly expressed the hope that Adèle would come to her senses and would treat him as a loving, dutiful wife should.

In any event, by mid-summer of 1831 Victor's patience with Sainte-Beuve and the situation in which they found themselves was exhausted. The strain was beginning to interfere with Victor's work, and this was a situation he could not permit. Something had to be done, and he did the obvious, sending Sainte-Beuve a letter that was a masterpiece of diplomacy, yet was firm and unyielding:

What I must write to you causes me deep pain. This three months' trial of a half-way intimacy, badly resumed, badly patched over, has not succeeded. Our friendship of the present is not our former, irrevocable friendship. When you are not present, I feel in the depths of my heart that I love you as I formerly did; when you are present, however, it is a torture. Let us cease for a time to see each other in order that we will not stop caring for each other.

Sainte-Beuve was not slow in understanding the import of the letter. No matter how delicately Victor had chosen to express himself, he was directing his former friend not to come to the Hugo dwelling again.

Adèle also understood, and treated her husband with less kindness.

From that moment life became more difficult for Madame Hugo and her admirer. Denial of the right to meet under Victor's roof and moon at each other spurred them to action. According to a poetic narrative Sainte-Beuve later wrote, they arranged a rendezvous at the Hôtel St. Paul, a hostelry for commercial travelers, where they registered as man and wife under assumed names. There they spent long hours talking, gazing at each other, and, occasionally, going to bed together.

In the main their affair was not sexual. The desires of the feminine Sainte-Beuve were not strong, and he was content, as a rule, to look at Adèle and chat with her. She, of course, was delighted to have found a lover who made few physical demands. They were an ideally mated couple.

For more than a hundred years neither historians nor literary detectives could find any concrete evidence, other than Sainte-Beuve's poetry, to indicate that the affair had been more than platonic. The critic, they contended, had been engaging in a form of wishful thinking, and the meetings at the Hôtel St. Paul had been the product of his daydreams.

A few months before the outbreak of World War II, the truth was revealed in a magazine called the *Mercure de France*. The author, Léon Deffoux, presented incontrovertible proof that Adèle and Sainte-Beuve engaged in an adulterous physical affair over a period of several years. They had written each other scores of private letters, long concealed, that left nothing in their relationship to the imagination.

The important question is whether Victor Hugo knew of his wife's literal infidelity. Scarcely a year has passed, down to the present day, without the discovery of new masses of Hugo correspondence, but it is impossible, as yet, to answer the question definitively.

There are hints, to be sure, but these are open to a variety of interpretations. For instance, he made a brief trip to Rouen in 1832, and while there sent a brief note to Adèle in which he declared, "My broken heart will not heal." The previous year he had written to Sainte-Beuve, "I no longer know where I stand with the two beings I love most in the world. You are one of them."

The case can be argued either way, but in view of the events that followed, it appears likely that Victor knew.

He had other matters on his mind during this difficult time. *Les Feuilles d'automne*, devoted to the themes of nature, love, and the innocence of childhood, was a book of romantic lyric poems, and the French critics agreed they were the best Victor had written. Three large editions were sold out within a short time.

Other ventures were less successful. Collaborating with Louise Bertin, the intellectual daughter of one of Paris's most influential newspaper editors, Victor wrote an operatic version of *Notre-Dame de Paris*, which was called *La Esméralda*. It failed to capture either the dramatic qualities or poetic values of the novel, and was Victor's most disappointing work.

In 1832 he tried his hand in the theater again, and wrote a poetic drama, *Le Roi s'amuse*, in which the central character, a hunchback and jester, was similar to a character in Verdi's opera *Rigoletto*. The play opened in late November, and the author enjoyed a triumph reminiscent of *Hernani*'s success.

Unfortunately, however, Victor had portrayed King Francis I as a man of many vices. He was confident that the regime of his bourgeois friend, Louis-Philippe, would not object, but soon learned otherwise. The new king was a Bourbon, after all, and shared with other members of his family the sensitivity to any criticism of past monarchs, particularly those who had been his direct ancestors.

The opening-night audience was still cheering when the official censors posted a notice on the front door of the Comédie. *Le Roi s'amuse* could not be performed again until its status had been reviewed by a royal board. Less than twenty-four hours later all performances were permanently prohibited.

The most distinguished young author in France had been doubly humiliated. Not only had censors closed his play, but he had taken the unprecedented step of investing a substantial sum of his own money in it, and that money was lost. Furious, he blamed the Comédie-Française for not fighting hard enough on his behalf, and foolishly brought suit against the theater, one of the few rash moves he ever made in a long business career.

Hoping to overcome his disappointment, he immediately went to work on yet another play. It was a historical drama, called *Lucrèce Borgia*, and he refused to allow the Comédie to produce it. Every theater in Paris wanted the play, of course, and Victor decided in favor of the Porte-Saint-Martin, which did not hesitate to hire talented actors and actresses, regardless of the importance of their names.

A relatively minor role, that of the Princess Negroni, was given to a totally unknown actress, Juliette Drouet. Victor was present at the auditions, had the right to veto all casting, and was asked whether he agreed that Mlle. Drouet should be given the part.

He and the young woman had already exchanged a long glance, and for once in his life Victor Hugo was speechless. He could only nod, and at this critical, lonely period, Juliette Drouet entered his life, never to leave it again until her death a half-century later.

Chapter
V

In several of the many poems that Victor Hugo wrote about Juliette Drouet or dedicated to her, he called her, quite simply, the most beautiful woman in France. He was prejudiced in her favor, to be sure, but dozens of his contemporaries agreed with him. His friend and colleague, Alexandre Dumas the elder, a collector of beautiful women, pronounced himself dazzled. Théophile Gautier wrote that he swooned at the sight of her. Even women were impressed, and George Sand wrote that she agreed with Hugo's estimate.

Juliette had long hair of such a deep, rich black that it looked blue in the gaslight that was beginning to replace candles. Her eyes were black, too, but when a bright light struck them at an angle, they appeared to have a violet cast. Her profile was classical and flawless. Her figure, according to the standards of any era, was perfect. The portraits made of her as a young woman reveal that she was truly a spectacular beauty. She lived into the age of photography, and her photos as an elderly lady in her seventies show her as still lovely, with great dignity and charm.

Her real name was Julienne-Josephine Gauvain, and she was born in Brest on April 10, 1806, so she was four years younger than Victor. Her parents died when she was a small child; she was adopted by an uncle, René-Henri Drouet, whose name she took. Juliette displayed precocity very early in life. By the time she was five she could both read and write, accomplishments that were particularly remarkable in an age when few members of her sex, especially those who lived in the provinces, were literate.

Her devout uncle sent her to Paris when she was ten, and she entered a convent school on the rue du Petit-Picpus. It was taken for granted that she would become a nun. Devouring books at a rate that alarmed the good sisters, she showed an aptitude for French literature that astonished them. Her ability to appreciate and analyze poetry filled them with wonder.

By the time Juliette was sixteen it became evident that she was not suited for a religious life. She was too lively, too curious about the world, and males, already attracted by her beauty, were too curious about her. The nuns were relieved as well as regretful when she left the convent.

Juliette immediately drifted into the bohemian world of artists, authors, and actors. Earning a living presented her with no problems. Showing no hesitation, she became the mistress of a succession of well-known actors, theatrical directors, and painters, and her lovers paid her bills. As a courtesan, she took care to live with only one man at a time. And she was expensive. Very early in her career, she developed a love of luxuries that cost large sums of money. She also demanded far more than wealth. Her lovers had to be men of charm, wit, and, above all, intelligence. Juliette Drouet lived with a man only if he could carry on a stimulating conversation with her, who, in her own words, "fertilized my mind." The dull, like the ugly, were dismissed with an indifferent shrug of her exquisite shoulders.

At the age of nineteen, after becoming the mistress of a distinguished sculptor, James Pradier, Juliette reached a turning point in her life. She gave birth to a daughter, whose paternity Pradier recognized, and became a surprisingly good and attentive mother. Wanting to make something of her life, she decided to embark on a stage career, and although she knew her beauty would win her small parts, she wanted to learn her trade. So she went off to Brussels, where she served an apprenticeship for two years, and then returned to Paris. In 1830, at the age of twenty-four, she obtained a small part in a play at the Porte-Saint-Martin. She attained a measure of technical proficiency, and, although her talent was limited, her appearance was still breathtaking.

That beauty, combined with her effervescent personality, won her a degree of renown, and she set up housekeeping in a large, sumptuously furnished apartment, where she had a cook, a personal maid, and a nursemaid for her daughter. Her wardrobe was extensive, she rode through the streets of Paris in her own carriage, and her collection of jewels was the envy of other young actresses.

In 1832 she became the mistress of an exceptionally

wealthy Russian nobleman, Prince Demidoff, and for the first time in her life she began to save money. Still ambitious, she sought larger roles in the theater.

On January 2, 1833, a New Year's reception was given at the Porte-Saint-Martin by its managing director, Félix Harel, and in the Green Room of the theater Victor Hugo met Juliette Drouet. Their eyes lingered for an instant, Victor bowed and Juliette smiled; that was all, and they did not speak.

Victor was stunned, subsequently describing her as a "bird of flame," and was actually afraid to address her. Juliette, who had read most of his published work, was equally stricken. He was the leading author of France, and the presence of such a genius numbed her.

The couple became better acquainted during rehearsals. Victor treated her with the respect accorded a queen. He always addressed her as Mademoiselle Juliette, he held her chair for her, and he bowed low over her hand. Other members of the cast were astonished by his attitude.

Juliette, who knew men, quickly realized she was making a notable conquest. Much later she confessed to Victor that she flirted outrageously with him, deliberately played mischievous pranks on him, and aroused his jealousy by playing up to other men.

The play opened on February 2, 1833, and although it was a rather crude melodrama well below the usual Hugo standard, it was an immediate, solid success. Juliette won a minor personal triumph, and all of the critics, Gautier included, praised her.

There was no reason now for Victor to appear at the

theater any more often than he wished, but Juliette was the magnet that drew him there every evening. He no longer had a home life of any consequence. He either knew or suspected that Adèle was seeing Saint-Beuve on the sly, and if anyone was ever ripe for a romance that would restore his wounded ego, soothe him, and give his passionate nature a satisfactory outlet, that man was Victor Hugo.

On the night of February 16, he stood outside the theater after the performance and watched Juliette drive off in her carriage. By his own account, he could no longer "tolerate the suspense" she created in him, and followed her to her elegant apartment on the rue Sainte-Denis. What followed was inevitable: Victor stayed for the night.

The life of Victor Hugo was changed for all time, as was that of Juliette Drouet. A great passion, which both had anticipated at their first meeting, had been born. Thereafter they saw each other constantly, and became inseparable. Juliette, who had always been a one-man-at-a-time woman, dismissed her Russian nobleman and evidently moved to another expensive apartment at rue de l'Echiquier. Victor, still a good father, took time from his work each day to spend a few hours with his children, but he dined every evening with Juliette, and spent every night at her apartment. Adèle undoubtedly knew of her husband's liaison, but was in no position to protest.

Juliette, as much in love as Victor, was in a delicate position. Her pride made it impossible for her to tell him that her living depended on the favors of her lovers, and she purposely led him to believe she was a woman of independent means. For the better part of a year and a half she was able to maintain the deception, still living on the same grand scale, and using her savings to augment her slender earnings as an actress.

The Hugo household moved again, this time to one of the most elegant squares of Paris, the place Royale built by Victor's hero Henry IV. Victor rented two floors of a white and rose brick building at 6 place Royale (later to become the Place des Vosges). The dwelling was a mansion with a slate roof, huge French windows that extended from floor to ceiling, and superb hardwood floors. The square was thick with chestnut trees, and all of the Hugo neighbors were wealthy aristocrats who, wonder of wonders, were flattered that a famous young author had elected to live in their midst.

There was only one thing about the location. The cafés and shops of the neighborhood were first-rate, it was true, and Victor, to whom food had become important, had passed favorably on the quality of the merchandise sold by the greengrocer, the butcher, the fishmonger, and the baker. But, alas, Juliette's apartment was located on the far side of the city! A man might boast that he lived around the corner from the honest poor of the working class, and might even pretend to himself that he was one of these laborers. But it was very inconvenient for him to dash through the streets, more often than not unable to find a carriage for hire, when he was going from his own house to Juliette's, or vice versa.

There was only one solution. Obviously, he had to find Juliette a new dwelling in the rue Saint Anatase, nearer his own. Perhaps he was afraid she might renew some of her old, questionable friendships. Whatever the reason,

Victor went apartment-hunting on her behalf. Adèle learned what he was doing and protested, but Victor heard her voice far less than he did the wind, which he extolled in his lyrics. Adèle made a scene, and Victor went for a walk; Adèle wept, Victor yawned. Soon Juliette had a cozy new apartment, located only five minutes' walk from the home of her lover. Victor was happy, Juliette was ecstatic, and no one cared what Adèle felt or thought.

Early in the summer of 1834 Juliette was forced to tell Victor the truth about her financial situation. She had intended to reveal no more than was necessary, knowing that in his remarkable innocence he would be repelled when he discovered how she had lived for years. Precisely as she had anticipated, he became upset, and they quarreled with increasing bitterness over a period of many weeks.

Unable to tolerate the situation any longer, Juliette gave her furniture, her carriage, all of her belongings except her clothes and jewelry, to her creditors. The first Victor knew of the matter was that she was gone. She sent him a brief note of farewell before fleeing from Paris with her daughter. She left no forwarding address, and Victor had to question a number of her friends before he finally learned she had gone to Brest to make her temporary home with a respectable married sister.

Although determined to put the wayward woman out of his mind and heart, Victor could not forget her, and after torturing himself for a week, he followed her to Brest. Juliette had been equally miserable, and they were reconciled immediately, but they had to solve some serious problems.

Juliette owed her creditors approximately fifty

thousand francs, a considerable sum of money, and Victor agreed to assume the obligation. Though he was earning an extremely comfortable living, the burden was a heavy one, and he worked out a system for paying off the debts that was both practical and romantic. He agreed to give Juliette seven hundred fifty francs per month, and she, in turn, would use half of the sum for her living expenses, while applying the other half to her debts.

This made it necessary for her to live modestly, and she took a small apartment for herself and her daughter in the rue de Paradis, where she enjoyed none of the luxuries she had formerly known. In fact, on chilly days her apartment was bitterly cold, as she had to watch her pennies so carefully she was forced to economize on fuel.

The remarkable part of the bargain was that Juliette agreed to give up all of her former friends and associations, to stop frequenting the cafés and shops that had been so important to her. She promised to see no one but Victor, to accept no invitations unless he, too, would be present, and to ask no one to her apartment unless he was also there. Their love was to be the purge that would purify her and wash away the stains of her former life as a courtesan.

Only a romantic author could have dreamed of such a situation. It was not accidental that Juliette would spend her life in accordance with one of her lover's favorite literary themes, which he had used only a few years earlier in his play *Marion Delorme.*

It is a tribute of sorts to Juliette that the scheme succeeded. Even her theatrical career fell away, although that was neither her fault nor Victor's. He made half-hearted efforts to obtain roles for her in the plays of others, but she did not get the parts. And when he was later in a position to do something for her himself and gave her a role in his own play, *Ruy Blas*, Adèle intervened, threatening to create a national scandal if Juliette became a member of the cast. So Juliette Drouet devoted the rest of her life to Victor Hugo, and for a half-century her entire existence revolved around him.

Their arrangement was unique in other ways. In the autumn of 1834 Victor and his family went to Les Roches as the house guests of Éduard Bertin, the editor of the *Journal des débats*, and spent six weeks in the valley of the Bièvre. Juliette made the journey separately, and took a room a few kilometers from Bertin's house. She and Victor arranged a secret rendezvous in the woods, and spent their afternoons together.

The couple also made more conventional journeys together, and beginning in 1835, they went off on prolonged holidays. They visited Normandy, Picardy, and Britanny, they went to Belgium and Holland, the German states of the west, and with him she discovered the glories of the Swiss Alps and the French fishing villages on the Mediterranean. Their tastes were similar; both loved hiking in the open countryside, and both enjoyed a long tramp along a deserted beach or a climb into the mountains.

Victor spent so much time at Juliette's apartment in Paris that she had to move into larger quarters in the same building so there would be a room he could use exclusively as his studio. He paid for the difference in the rent, and she thanked him for his generosity! Juliette developed a talent for cooking. Victor loved the meals she prepared, and for the rest of his life he dined, more often than not, under her roof. She became an expert needlewoman, too, mending his socks and darning his shirts—tasks that were either beneath Adèle or beyond her capability. Over a period of years the mistress became, in effect, the middle-class wife whom the bourgeois Victor had always wanted.

Victor had no cause for complaint, to be sure, but life was not easy for Juliette. With time hanging so heavily on her hands, she found it necessary to occupy herself when her lover was absent, and she soon found employment— as his secretary. She copied his manuscripts for him, answered his letters from readers and handled portions of his other correspondence. Eventually she placed herself in charge of his files, too, and even organized his research materials for him. When she had nothing else to do, she wrote letters to Victor, sometimes sitting down at her desk only moments after he left her. The result of these labors was a remarkable, almost one-sided correspondence. Victor saved her letters, fortunately, and they have provided posterity with an astonishingly complete record of Victor Hugo's life.

Juliette's letters quite naturally, however, made no mention of one subject, Victor's relationship with his wife.

Adèle, who had driven her husband into the arms of a mistress, had no cause for complaint. Although she was aware of his affair—as was all of Paris—she kept her own counsel for a long time. No one knows for certain when her own affair with Sainte-Beuve came to an end. By 1837, Victor and his former friend no longer spoke to each other. When they happened to meet in public at a café, or less frequently at the theater, Victor's faint nod of greeting indicated there was no love lost.

Nothing in Victor's own correspondence indicates whether he forbade Adèle to see Sainte-Beuve, but by 1837 she did stop seeing him. Thereafter she remained close to her own hearth, living quietly, acting as her husband's official hostess when he found it necessary to entertain at home. She accompanied him on social or semi-business occasions when he found it discreet or desirable to be seen in the company of his wife rather than that of his mistress.

There are hints in Victor's correspondence with Abel that he never resumed intimate relations with Adèle. He was content to dwell under the same roof with her, but they slept in separate bedrooms even when they made joint journeys. Presumably Adèle was more or less content with this arrangement, as she was spared the love-making that had always been anathema to her. But, like it or not, she was in no position to alter it, and for the rest of her life would spend her nights alone.

Victor, for his part, having tasted the forbidden joys of extramarital love, was launched on a way of life that would have won him notoriety even if he had not been a great author. He found many women attractive, and when he was drawn to one, he immediately besieged her. As he himself subsequently confessed, actresses, courtesans, and other women by the score became his mistresses, some for a single day or night, others for periods of up to a month or two. He had only one reservation: under no circumstances would he make love to a married woman who lived under her husband's roof. Perhaps he was avoiding complications, but probably he had no desire to inflict the sort of pain on any other husband that Sainte-Beuve had caused him to suffer.

Physically as well as emotionally, his exploits were little short of astonishing. It was not unusual for him to see an attractive prostitute on the street in the morning and bed her before lunch, then go to a rendezvous with an actress, leave her in time for a very private meeting with a courtesan, and hurry to Juliette's apartment for dinner and a night of love-making with the woman he came to regard either as his principal mistress, his unofficial wife, or both.

His appearance was very much in his favor, and women found him magnetic. He was putting on weight, so his body better matched the huge head about which he had once been so sensitive. His hair was long and thick, and he lost very little of it as he grew older. At Juliette's instigation he tried a variety of beards, finally settling on a luxurious facial growth that, combined with his deep-set, penetrating eyes, made him irresistible to the ladies and demimonde who found that the great Victor Hugo's appearance matched his glittering reputation.

He did not hesitate to use the tricks of a Don Juan if they served his purposes. On a number of well-documented occasions, after he had written a poem for Juliette and had dedicated it to her, he pretended he had written it to someone with whom he was seeking an affair, and presented her with a copy. As many as five or six copies of a single poem each with a different dedication in the margin in Victor's own hand have been unearthed. More often than not the same poem appears in print dedicated to Juliette.

The overwhelming majority of the women in Victor Hugo's life were brunettes, and many of them bore at least a passing resemblance to his mother. So Victor spent most of his adult life, after Adèle had been unfaithful to him, seeking the love his mother had never given him. Inasmuch as he was no ordinary mortal, he conducted no ordinary search.

Victor's colleague, Balzac, is the authority for a frequently quoted comment on the subject of women. They were standing together in the foyer of the Comédie, and a lovely young woman strolled past them.

"You spoke to her," Balzac said, "so it appears you know her."

"Oh, yes," Victor replied. "She makes no secret of the fact that I slept with her last month."

A second young woman waved from the far side of the lobby, and Balzac said, "I suppose you have slept with her, also?"

"Not yet," Victor said, and consulted a little notebook he carried in the inside pocket of his swallow-tailed coat. "I have a dinner engagement with her on Wednesday, and a supper engagement the following Tuesday, so it will be Tuesday next before I sleep with her."

Alexandre Dumas the elder, who offered Victor competition as a ladies' man, knew when he had met his match. "I refuse to be seen at a restaurant or a café with Victor Hugo," he complained to Théophile Gautier. "I can spend many days in the preparations for love with a lady. I sigh, I send her gifts, I inscribe tender sentiments in copies of my books, I dance attendance on her. Then she sees me sitting with Hugo. He smiles. He bends over her hand, and when he kisses it, she believes she is the only woman in all the world for him. She is not only captivated by him, but she forgets that I exist. So I must wait until he is done with her before she remembers, suddenly, that Dumas has been courting her for a long time. I have tried Hugo's technique, but for me, it is not effective. He weaves a spell of magic, but for the life of me, I cannot understand what it is that all these women see in him. Is he so much more tender and compelling than any other man? I doubt it, but the ladies know no better, and compete for the favors of a man whose novels are somber and whose plays are ordinary. Only in love—and in his poetry—does he excel!"

Meanwhile, no matter what the complications in the life of one whose poetry excelled, he was required to support his family and pursue his vocation.

Victor's exploits with women would have been a full-time occupation had he not possessed drives and stamina that were denied lesser men. What is truly remarkable is that he led an extraordinary literary life, churning out poetry, novels, plays, literary criticism, political essays, and even articles on travel. Juliette quotes him as saying:

Every thought that has ever crossed my mind sooner or later finds its way onto paper. I do not engage in random or useless thinking. Ideas are my sinews and my substance. I must use them to earn my living and to make my continuing mark in the world, so I husband them, and never fritter them away. An observation, a feeling, even a fleeting sensation, all these are the precious marrow which compels me to stand at my writing desk.

Victor was happy, and his muse smiled. *Les Chants du crépuscule*, published late in 1835, was hailed as his masterwork by all the critics except the mute Sainte-Beuve, and contained some of his finest poetry. His work was growing more mature, more solid, as *Les Voix intérieures*, published in 1837, and *Les Rayons and les ombres*, published in 1840, amply testified.

But Victor was no longer satisfied, and needed still more worlds to conquer. It was not enough to be known as the greatest author of his age, to have an adoring mistress, a docile wife, and children who worshipped him. Other men, such as Chateaubriand and Lamartine, were playing major roles in the great world. They were active in political affairs, they were recognized as men of influence.

"I wish," Victor said in a brief note he wrote in 1836 to Juliette when she was visiting relatives to Brest, "to be recognized as an Influential Force."

A man of letters could, if he chose, run for public office, become a member of the Chamber of Deputies and determine the fate of his fellow countrymen. One could, if sufficiently distinguished, be elevated to the peerage, but that was easier said than done. A man of letters was not eligible to hold a title until he was elected to the Academy. Like Voltaire almost precisely one hundred years earlier, Victor showed no interest in becoming a member of the French Academy until other ambitions sparked him; then, suddenly, his election to the prestige-laden organization obsessed him.

There were advantages to membership other than becoming eligible for a title. One was always identified as a member of the Academy whenever one's name appeared in print. One always had a convenient soap-box from which to make his views known, too. Speeches made at Academy meetings were reported extensively, the newspapers devoting great space to them, no matter how dull they might be. When one made a significant address, it was printed verbatim by the newspapers.

Certain disadvantages counterbalanced the advantages, of course. Most of the "Immortals" who made up the membership of the Academy were very mortal, very dull, and very prosaic. Membership was limited to forty, and most of the seats were held by academicians who perpetuated the spirit of an antiquarian society by voting for their own kind to fill vacancies. They looked with deep suspicion at the so-called popular writers, who, by virtue of their success, could not write anything that would live longer than this year's sales. Voltaire, who had been elected only when his exclusion had become a public joke and national scandal, had fought for years to get in.

Now Victor Hugo faced the same problem, which was made even more embarrassing because one had to announce himself a candidate. Victor was far too successful and far too proud to beg, but in this matter he had no choice, and in 1836 he made his first application.

If the members had laughed at him, he would have had cause to become indignant, but they treated him even more condescendingly, and rejected him by an overwhelming vote, without discussion. Scarcely able to believe he had been subjected to such summary treatment, he applied a second time that same year. The members demonstrated that their first response had not been accidental. No one arose to defend the candidate, no one extolled his record or read from his works. The vote against him was a crushing 34 to 2.

Victor was so abashed that he waited three years

before trying again. According to tradition, any man who had been turned down three times accepted the verdict as final and did not try again. But Victor Hugo cared nothing about tradition when his own reputation was at stake, and later he overcame lethargy and prejudice to win a smashing triumph. For the present, it seemed, he had nothing to do but work, make love to an ever-increasing circle of women, and lay the groundwork for a political career by seeking the friendship of men who were prominent in public affairs.

The lyric quality of his two great books of poetry written during the mid-1830s was not materially different from that found in the poems immediately preceding it. His technical skills were greater, to be sure, and his writing had become more polished, more urbane. What distinguishes *Les Chants* and *Les Voix* from his earlier work is his subject matter.

In a prelude to *Les Chants*, Victor wrote that he wished to explore the "strange twilight condition of the human soul and of society in the period we live in," and he succeeded admirably in achieving his goal. Man, he was discovering, was a contradictory creature, one who found happiness eluding him, no matter what he accomplished. The ambivalence of human nature was evident in political affairs, too. Man dreamed of establishing a perfect society, but every system of government and administration he devised was flawed; no sooner did he eliminate past failures and their causes than he invented new and more subtle shortcomings.

By this time Victor had decided that the greatest of all rulers had been Napoleon, who had established the best of all governments and governmental systems. An author had to exercise care in his expressions of admiration for Napoleon, however. Louis-Philippe might be a friend who displayed many democratic tendencies, but he was still a Bourbon, a member of a royal house that loathed the mere mention of Bonaparte's name. His censors had already shown their teeth, what was more, and Victor had no desire to suffer their bite again.

So he invented a flimsy but effective literary device. His many poems about Napoleon were written within a carefully constructed framework of history. He wrote about a past era almost as remote as that of Henry IV, whom he also admired, and it did not matter that a scant two decades had passed since Napoleon had been sent into exile at St. Helena by his conquerors. Readers accepted the stratagem, knowing what the poet meant. The censors also realized what he was doing, but preferred to half-close their eyes; their somnolence stirred none of the tempests that would have arisen had they cracked down on the poet this time.

The influence of Juliette Drouet was manifest in the Twilight Songs of *Les Chants*. A number of literary authorities agree that twelve of the thirty-nine poems in the collection were inspired by her, and an additional five were dedicated to her, too.

Some of the poems in the collection expressed the author's growing spirit of humanitarianism, a theme that was not evident in an earlier novel destined to be regarded as one of his minor works. *Claude Gueux*, published in 1834, explored the theme of the death penalty and the miserable state of life in French prisons. The reading public believed that Victor could do no wrong, and the book had earned enough money to enable him to continue living in the style to which he had happily accustomed himself. But he knew, as did his serious critics, that *Claude* was not one of his best.

What caused far greater criticism, both in his own day and later, was the inclusion of work inspired by Adèle in *Les Chants*. Three of the poems were not only written for her, but applauded her quiet grace and solid domestic virtues. Several of his contemporaries attacked him, saying he was guilty of indiscretion, because a gentleman did not write about his wife and his mistress in the same book.

It is not surprising that the most waspish of the critics was Sainte-Beuve, who wrote that Victor included Adèle only as an excuse to write about Juliette. "He throws a handful of lilies in the eyes of the public," the critic said. It is possible, perhaps probable, that Saint-Beuve was still Adèle's lover at this time, so he had to exercise caution. He was so careful that he did not write his criticism under his own name, but used a pseudonym.

Victor was not fooled, immediately recognizing his former friend's style. "My imagery is sound," he wrote with a shrug, "and the book is selling rapidly. So it matters little what this flea who lives upon the body of French literature may think of it."

Théophile Gautier, to whom the remark was written, saw to it that all of literary Paris knew of the comment. Soon Sainte-Beuve was greeted in the cafés with so many snickers and droll observations that he found it more comfortable to remain at home, and for the better part of a year appeared in public only when his vocation demanded it. He had more reason than ever to hate Victor Hugo, but he was powerless to retaliate. It did not pay to betray the friendship and trust of a person who was universally admired as an author and liked as a man.

The year 1837 was one of the most difficult Victor had yet encountered. In the early months the new regime completed the construction of the Arc de Triomphe, and everyone in Paris except Victor Hugo rejoiced. The poet was outraged when he discovered that the name of his father had been omitted from the distinguished roll of Napoleonic generals inscribed on the arch. Retaliating in the way he knew best, he dedicated *Les Voix* to General Hugo, and explained his reasons in several pithy newspaper articles, in which he dared to throw sharp barbs at the short-sighted Louis-Philippe.

In the spring, Eugène Hugo died in the madhouse to which he had so long been confined. Even at the end he did not regain his reason, although his physicians had predicted that he would recover his wits for a time before he expired. Victor grieved for his lost brother and could not be consoled.

Then, before he had recovered from his brother's death, his eldest living child, Léopoldine, fell ill. She was the victim of a deep melancholy from which it was impossible for the best physicians in France to rouse her, and Victor was afraid she was heading down Eugène's path. Before the year ended the girl made a strong recovery on her own, and Victor was able to convince himself that her ailment had been minor.

But the various strains, combined with the long hours he spent at his writing table each day, sapped his own health. His eyesight was impaired, and for a time it was feared that he would go blind. His physicians prescribed complete rest, advice he would have ignored had it not been for Juliette.

She demanded that he take her to Switzerland for a long holiday. Victor demurred, saying he had already lost too much time and could not afford further delays in his work schedule. But Juliette, who knew how to handle him, threatened to return to her former way of life. At the age of thirty-one she was still lovely, and in Victor's eyes she was spectacularly beautiful, so he capitulated. For six weeks he did no writing and no reading. Juliette made certain he did not see a short story, *Mme. de Pontivy*, that Sainte-Beuve had just published, and that was a thinly disguised account of his affair with Adèle.

Victor spent hours walking in the mountains with Juliette each day; he ate heartily and slept ten hours every night. By the time they returned to Paris, he was restored both physically and spiritually, and forever indebted to his mistress. He was also heartened to learn that *Les Voix*, which he regarded as the best poetry he had ever written, had been received with enthusiasm by the critics, and that the book was already in its third printing. He could afford to thumb his nose at the Academy, and Léopoldine's return from a sanitarium afforded him great relief.

For the moment, all was right with Victor Hugo's world.

Chapter
VI

THE theater was a never-ending source of fascination for Victor Hugo in the 1830s and early 1840s. His temperament still required action, sound, and fury, and he enjoyed being in the center of a storm that never stopped raging. The theater was a perfect outlet for his emotions as well as his talents. One of the advantages to him was his proximity to attractive actresses. It became a standing joke in the cafés that any young woman seen in public with him was either seeking a role in a Hugo play or had just been awarded one.

Posterity has chosen to regard most of Victor's plays as minor works, and certainly none better deserves that classification than *Marie Tudor*, which was produced at the Porte-Saint-Martin in 1833. Outrageously melodramatic, it was a version—a very warped version—of the years that Queen Mary, the eldest child of Henry VIII, spent on the

E

throne of England. Victor's Mary was even lustier than her father, and far more bloodthirsty. The play abounds in love affairs, executions, and murders, with history twisted beyond recognition.

Victor, who had always taken pride in the historical accuracy of his work, reacted angrily when the critics rightly accused him of altering the facts of the past for his own theatrical purposes. He wrote indignant letters to the newspapers, and cited the sources of his research: two Italian plays and another that had been produced in France. The public did not care. *Marie Tudor* was a splendid evening's entertainment for the middle-class Parisian whose life lacked excitement, and the theater sold out every night.

An unfortunate by-product of *Marie Tudor* was its startling similarity to a play by Alexandre Dumas the elder, called *Christine*, that was produced at approximately the same time. Dumas thought that Hugo, whom he had regarded as a close friend, had stolen portions of his plot, and refused to speak to him. Bertin, the editor, tried to end the feud by pointing out to both that they had taken their material from the same sources, which had made the similarities inevitable. The two were not reconciled until 1837, when Victor, in a rare gesture of friendship, used his influence at the court of Louis-Philippe to win Dumas the award of the Legion of Honor.

Another play by Victor was presented in 1835, and marked his return to the Comédie-Française. *Angelo, tyran de Padoue*, was a very bad play that owed its tremendous success to the fact that the two leading roles, those of a wicked courtesan and a lady of great virtue, offered spectacular playing possibilities to the stars who won the assignments.

It appeared that Victor could do no wrong in the theater. The Théâtre de la Renaissance offered him exceptionally attractive terms for the right to produce *Ruy Blas*, which appeared there in November 1838, and achieved a triumph even greater than that won by *Hernani*. The critics thought it was by far the best theatrical work Victor had ever written, and this judgment has been confirmed by most scholars. The theme was that of the love of a commoner for a queen, and the play attracted considerable additional attention in its own time because of the author's close friendship with the Duke and Duchess of Orléans.

Victor did nothing to discourage the whisperers who said he was in love with the Duchess, a handsome young woman with dark hair, very much the physical type he admired. The near-scandal caused business to boom, but the truth of the matter was that Victor, who never completely lost his sense of balance in dealing with women, was too sensible to conceive a passion for a member of the royal family. He well knew that Louis-Philippe was guided by a strict middle-class morality, and an affair with the duchess would have led to certain banishment.

The last of Victor's plays, *Les Burgraves*, did not appear until 1843, and is significant principally because it was Victor's farewell to the theater. His principal character was the medieval ruler, Frederick Barbarossa, and the plot concerned the machinations of the lords of the Rhine against him. By this time romantic plays were losing popularity, and the critics regarded melodramatic antics as absurd. So did the public, which actually laughed at a Hugo play.

Victor was so incensed by the ridicule that he publicly abandoned all connection with the theater, and for many years thereafter kept his promise.

By that time his love for the dramatic had found an outlet far broader in scope and infinitely more exciting. Victor had discovered politics, and dreamed of himself as a member of the Chamber of Deputies, as a Senator, and even as a cabinet minister. Gautier and others in whom he confided laughed at his ambitions, but he shrewdly went to work. He would have to give politics more time than he could afford if he sought a seat in the Chamber, so he decided to concentrate on the Senate. Knowing he would not be eligible until he held a seat in the French Academy, he turned first to that aspect of the problem.

The support of the wealthy and socially prominent would be helpful, and he was assiduous in cultivating them. Victor found that he enjoyed playing the role of the social lion. His home long had been a literary center, and such friends as Gautier, Dumas, and Balzac came there frequently. Gradually he expanded the circle to include prominent politicians, distinguished scientists, newspaper and book publishers, and eventually, members of the aristocracy.

The best description, perhaps, of an evening at the Hugo apartment on the place Royale is given by a contemporary, Théodore de Banville, who recreates the aura:

In the rear salon, around an enormous bank of flowers, were seated the young women, beautiful, smiling, magnificently dressed, happy to be present at the home of the great poet, and there Mme. Hugo did the honors with her sovereign grace.

Then came the grand salon, where a crowd of men and women—not one of whom was banal or mediocre—moved about. Dressed in the height of fashion, their conversation stimulating, they discussed all manner of subjects, from the arts to the great events that shake the world.

The two manteled fireplaces at each end, decorated with rare mirrors and golden candlesticks, the immense curtains of red damask, the antique furniture, lent great character to the room, and the window recesses were so wide and deep that each one became a kind of small salon where one could avoid the crowds and talk freely with one's companion.

In the dining room, ornamented with old armor, there was a still greater crowd, many sampling the generous and delicious buffet of cold meats, smoked fish and salads laid out for their delectation. One saw there men who have become famous, as well as the young and eager, coming and going, sometimes writing or sketching in their open notebooks.

It was charming, particularly in the summertime. The great door of the apartment remained open; the perfume of flowers and foliage came in through the windows, and the party invariably spread to the Place Royale, for the young men went to smoke their cigarettes in the paths around the statue of Louis the Chaste, then returned, intoxicated with the night, the deep blue of heaven, into the dazzling light of the torches and of fair ladies who resembled goddesses.

The center of attention, always, was the unfailingly well-mannered Victor, whose charm and wit, grace and old-fashioned courtesy overwhelmed the guests. Invariably he wore a black frock coat, dark gray trousers, and the pearl-gray vest he had made famous. He could discuss any subject, often with great authority, or seeming authority, and always with wit. This quality frequently surprised those who found his work ponderous and solemn, and he himself often remarked on it.

"My writing is my profession," he said, "so I do not make light of it. But, when I speak with my friends, I do not try to curb my sense of humor."

The stamp of ultimate success was placed on the Hugo salon in 1838, when the Duke and Duchess of Orléans appeared, unannounced, and mingled with the guests. Thereafter every door of Parisian high society was opened to Victor, and he received far more invitations to dinners, suppers, and informal evenings that it was possible for him to accept.

Ever aware of the proprieties, he took care not to step beyond them. When he went out for an evening, Adèle occasionally accompanied him, but when she remained at home, he went out alone. Juliette Drouet would have been welcome in many salons, but never went with him. Lesser authors and artists may have flaunted their mistresses in public, but Victor was far too conscious of his stature. So, when he was otherwise occupied for an evening, during which he frequently arranged liaisons for the following day, Juliette waited patiently for him at her apartment, knowing that sooner or later he would appear.

The Duke of Orléans became one of his sponsors when twice he applied for Academy membership in 1839.

In 1840 another vacancy occurred in the membership of the Academy, and Victor made an unprecedented fourth application for the place. The Duke of Orléans made no secret of his intervention on behalf of his friend, and others, including aristocrats and influential politicians, added their insistent voices to the clamor.

Victor was elected by a vote of 17 to 15.

On June 3, 1841, he was inducted, and the Duke and Duchess of Orléans sat in the visitors' gallery to watch the ceremony and listen to his speech of acceptance. It was the first time in the history of the Academy that members of the royal family had ever attended a session of the Academy.

The duke and duchess heard an extraordinary address. Victor began by paying glowing tribute to Napoleon, and there were many in his audience who were shocked by his seeming lack of tact. One simply did not mention Bonaparte, no matter how popular he might be with the masses, in the presence of Bourbons. But the royal family came in for its share of adulation. The Revolution of July 1830 had placed the representative of a great tradition on the throne, Victor said, "thereby transforming into a young dynasty, an old family, monarchical and popular at one and the same time, full of the past through its history, and full of the future through its tradition."

Then, completely casting aside precedent, Victor launched into a full-blown political theme, his concept of the future of France. He was opposed to new revolutions, he declared, just as he was opposed to reaction. Both were anathema to him. Instead, France should follow the example of Napoleon Bonaparte, whose policies were being fitted to modern times by Louis-Philippe. All persons, regardless of their religious or political beliefs, should be granted complete personal liberties. All men should be equal under the law, and the administration of justice should be impartial, fair, and fearless. Yet, in her dealings with her own citizens and with other nations, France should be prudent, never stepping beyond the bounds of common sense. The ideals of the French Revolution should be maintained, and the poor should be given every opportunity to improve their lot.

The newspapers were thoughtfully provided with complete copies of the address, made by Juliette in her flowing longhand. The speech created a minor sensation, and wise politicians suspected that Victor Hugo might become a force in the land beyond the limits of literature.

Victor was so intoxicated by his success that he followed his induction speech with something even more remarkable. In 1839 and 1840, he and Juliette had spent their long annual holiday together touring the Rhine River. An author who hated to waste any experience, Victor published, in 1842, a book called, *Le Rhin, Lettres à un ami.*

This was a travel book, so colorful, so full of descriptions, and so packed with information that it soon became a classic. In fact, it inspired a host of imitations. Dumas, who had never visited North Africa, sat down and wrote a bestselling travel book about the region.

Le Rhin was far more than it appeared on the surface. It was Victor Hugo's way of throwing his hat into the political ring. Already infatuated by the sound of his own words, he was beginning to think of himself as an expert in international relations, and the Rhine offered him the opportunity to expound on his concept of the way to attain permanent peace in Europe.

France and the German states, he said, together formed two cores of a central sphere of influence. If they worked together they would be more powerful than the nations on the periphery that forced their separate and joint will on the Continent: Great Britain and Imperial Russia. So far, few would have disagreed.

The elaboration of Victor's thesis was novel, to say the least. In order to reduce frictions between France and Germany, he said, the French should occupy the left bank of the Rhine. He was realistic enough to admit that the Germans might be unwilling to accept this idea voluntarily, so he proposed they be given the wealthy state of Hanover and the free city of Hamburg as a consolation prize.

There was still another string to his bow. Since the days when Napoleon had been the master of Europe, other nations had been made uneasy by the French doctrines of liberty, equality, and fraternity. Less advanced and far more provincial than France, other governments still considered these principles wildly radical. So, Victor said, France had to exercise patience. In due time these governments would become aware of the will of their people, who yearned for rights that all true Frenchmen already took for granted. Until that day arrived, France would be wise to practice her own brand of freedom quietly, without trying to export it.

Louis-Philippe could not take Victor's visionary ideas seriously, nor could his ministers, and most practical politicians laughed. The Duke of Orléans, the king's eldest son and heir to the throne, was the only person of prominence who publicly agreed, and he was rebuked by his father for holding forth on subjects about which he was ignorant. But the duke, who liked to think of himself as an intellectual, was impressed by everything his friend said.

Victor, for his part, was hitching his wagon to the star of Orléans. When the young prince succeeded his father, it was inevitable that Victor Hugo would become one of his closest counselors, and undoubtedly would be offered a cabinet post.

In the late winter of 1842, fate intervened, and Victor's hopes were dashed. While the duke was riding through the streets of Paris, something frightened his horses, and the animals began to gallop madly. The duke tried to jump from his carriage to save himself, but was mortally injured and died before the end of the day.

The next in line was the king's second son, the Duke of Nemours, an anti-intellectual who was bored by Victor Hugo. But the duke's lovely young widow soon was urging her father-in-law to see more of Victor so the Orléans influence remained strong. She was persuasive enough to win Victor occasional invitations to the Tuileries. It was an unexpected tragedy in the poet's life, however, that brought him and Louis-Philippe closer together.

Several years earlier, in 1839, Victor's daughter Léopoldine was becoming one of the beauties of Paris. Victor, who had less in common with Adèle each year, had grown closer and closer to the eldest of his children. Léopoldine accompanied her proud father to dinner parties and the theater, to salons and cafés and shops. Everyone who saw them together commented on the obvious depth of their mutual affection.

It was in either 1839 or 1840 that Léopoldine began to pay surreptitious visits to Juliette Drouet. Victor, of course, was responsible for the initial meeting of the two people he loved most, but after Juliette and Léopoldine came to know each other, they formed their own friendship. The woman would have responded to anyone Victor loved, and the girl, starved by her own mother's austerity, thought Juliette was the most wonderful person she had ever known. They not only saw each other often, but corresponded, and Juliette's letters were filled with warm, maternal wisdom.

Victor could see no flaws in his brilliant daughter. She wrote poetry, much of it in a style similar to his, and he saw to it that her slight efforts were published. In his opinion she was a genius.

In 1842 Léopoldine met a young businessman of a shipping family from Le Havre, Charles Vacquerie, who bore a strong physical resemblance to Victor, although he was fast losing his hair. The young couple fell in love. Charles was a sober, responsible person, well able to take care of a wife, and Victor approved of the romance, as did Juliette, to whom Léopoldine brought the young man on private visits. Inasmuch as Charles was fairly wealthy and his family background was impeccable, Adèle also approved.

The young couple were married in mid-February 1843. Much has been made of the fact that the ceremony was private, and that none of Victor's friends received invitations. Victor and Léopoldine, according to gossip that will not die, had been incestuously attracted to each other, and Victor was supposed to be furious when his daughter found someone to marry.

The facts do not substantiate this vicious canard. Victor would not have encouraged a friendship between his daughter and his beloved mistress, nor would he have allowed Léopoldine to marry had his feelings been incestuous. The truth was simple. The girl wanted a quiet wedding. Knowing that all Paris would appear at the church and that her father would insist on giving her a reception worthy of a princess of France, she preferred to be married without fanfare in a private ceremony.

The rules of propriety made it impossible for Juliette to attend the wedding, and she sent a pathetic letter to the bride. Léopoldine, she hoped, would not forget her, and she begged the girl for a memento of the occasion: a slice of wedding cake, perhaps, or a snip of material from the bridal veil. Léopoldine replied by sending both, with a letter that summed up her feelings:

"How I wish you had been my mother, dear Juliette."

Victor's mistress could have wished for little more than that.

The father of the bride, like countless others before and after him, was depressed. The young couple knew so little about life. Charles, although experienced in business, might not know how to handle his affairs, now that he had a wife. Worst of all, Le Havre was a two-day journey by coach from Paris, and Victor would see his dear daughter infrequently. He sent the young couple a steady stream of advice, bought them furniture without the knowledge of Adèle, and hinted broadly that he hoped they would name their first son after him.

By the end of summer Victor's life had returned to normal, and he went off with Juliette on their annual holiday, this time to southern France and Spain. Adèle, who always resented these excursions, protested even more vigorously than usual, but Victor paid no attention.

On the night of September 4 Victor was awakened

from a sound sleep, and went out onto the balcony of the small inn in the Pyrenees, where he spent hours staring at the pine forest. His feelings of deep foreboding, which he could not shake off, subsequently formed the hard core of his belief in the occult.

Juliette was sleeping, but his pacing awakened her, and she wanted to know what was wrong. Victor's fears were so illogical that he dissembled, and ordered her to go back to sleep. She complied.

Finally he turned to the greatest solace he knew, and sat down, in the dark, at the crude little desk in the inn bedroom. There he wrote portions of a poem, some parts of which later made no sense, so he threw them away. But the opening line revealed his state:

O Death! Obscure mystery! Somber necessity!

The following morning his fears were forgotten, and, putting away his notebook, he continued his journey with Juliette. On the night of September 7 they took lodgings at an inn in the little village of Soubise. It was there the following morning, while reading a newspaper as they ate breakfast that he learned Léopoldine and Charles had been drowned in the Seine when the small racing boat in which they were taking an outing capsized.

Victor and Juliette left immediately for Paris. The journey was a nightmare of carriages breaking down, connections missed, and other mishaps, and four days passed before Victor reached home. He was crushed, his whole world shattered as it had never been when his mother, father, or Eugène had died. Juliette could not console him, nor could his relatives and friends.

Uncounted words have been written about Léopoldine's death. For the better part of fifty years it was common for rumor-mongers to hint that the girl, unable to enjoy normal relations with Charles because of her love for her father, had taken her own life and that of her husband. No concrete evidence exists to support this horrible and spectacular theory.

The possibility of suicide, even of dual suicide, cannot be completely discounted, to be sure. Certain lines in unfinished poems that Léopoldine wrote can be interpreted as hints that she, perhaps in concert with Charles, was contemplating self-destruction, though such lines might be no more than the morbid thoughts of a very romantic girl.

Yet Léopoldine had spent time at a sanitarium when suffering from a bout of melancholy, and her uncle, Eugène Hugo, was robbed of his reason. Was this a streak of madness in the family?

Historians can only take the tragedy at face value, as an accident. Members of the Vacquerie family and friends of the young couple, both in Le Havre and Paris, described Léopoldine and Charles as ecstatically happy, in a manner befitting honeymooners who had been married a scant eight months. Léopoldine's letters to her father and to Juliette revealed her to be sublimely, sometimes inarticulately, happy. Neither she nor Charles had any known cause to take their own lives.

The tragedy left a permanent scar on Victor, and he grieved for his lost daughter to the end of his own life. Until Léopoldine's death he had looked young for his forty-one years, but now he aged overnight, his manner became somber and studied, and he rarely bothered with the witticisms that had enlivened so many social gatherings.

He took refuge in poetry, but the first drafts were so garbled that he was forced to put them aside and rewrite them at a later date. These poems, which included some of the loveliest and most tender verses he ever wrote, were not published for thirteen years, when, in 1856, they appeared in a collection, *Les Contemplations*.

Louis-Philippe, who had just lost his son in a tragic accident, felt closer to Victor, and the widowed Duchess of Orléans, the poet's guardian patroness, continued to urge her father-in-law to see more of Victor. Invitations to the Tuileries became more frequent.

Victor had remained something of a recluse, refusing to see his friends, to frequent the cafés, or to visit salons. He went to Juliette no more than once or twice each week, and at home he locked himself in his study, eating most of his meals there. He refused to see anyone except his two sons and surviving daughter.

But an invitation from the king was a royal command, and could be neither rejected nor ignored. With increasing frequency Victor donned his frock coat and pearl-gray vest to go to the Tuileries. Usually he and Louis-Philippe were alone, and spent long periods closeted in the king's private sitting room. They dined together, huddled at one end of a long table, and neither had any appetite for the splendid dishes that batteries of servants placed before them.

Victor and Louis-Philippe were pathetic, grief-stricken figures. Two middle-aged, middle-class men sharing their inarticulate loneliness. Each found a small measure of consolation in knowing that the other suffered, too.

On April 13, 1845, the third anniversary of the Duke

of Orléans's death, King Louis-Philippe demonstrated his own friendship and that of his late son for the premier poet of France by naming Victor a peer. From that time forward, Victor could call himself Vicomte Hugo. So, at a time and in a manner least expected, for reasons that had driven him to despair, Victor became a member of the Senate.

His elevation to the peerage caused something of a political sensation. The adherents of the house of Bourbon rejoiced, believing that the nation's most prominent man of letters was firmly in their camp. The Bonapartists protested very mildly; they knew that Victor was a devoted admirer of Napoleon's, and reasoned that if their group should come to power again, Vicomte Hugo would be in a position to help their cause. The *National*, a republican newspaper, published a cartoon showing Victor as a hideous Quasimodo, with the forces of democracy, a long row of stone gargoyles, laughed raucously at him. Some Republican groups were pleased, however. They knew Victor was a champion of the working man and that he was devoted to the cause of international peace, so they believed his presence in the Senate would be beneficial to them.

For the moment, however, politics were of secondary consideration to the grieving father, who took no pleasure in his elevation. Adèle enjoyed being called the Vicomtesse Hugo. Their social life had been the one tie that had bound them together, and now that they were seeing no one, receiving no guests, and going nowhere, even that slender bond had been at least temporarily severed.

Always conscious of his tendency toward melancholy, and mindful of Eugène's fate, Victor knew that he should take active steps to overcome his depression. His work offered him only a partial solution. He had started work on an ambitious new novel, which he was calling *Les Misères*, and was also writing considerable poetry that he knew was the best he had ever done. Yet, the harder he worked, the more isolated he became.

He knew that he could forget his desolation only in the throes of passion. His relationship with Juliette Drouet no longer sufficed for the purpose; they had been living together for a decade, and she had become his wife, for all practical purposes. Visits to prostitutes were dull, courtesans were easy marks, and those ladies happy to go to bed with Vicomte Hugo, Peer of France, bored him to distraction.

What he needed was the challenge of an intricate new affair with someone whose passion was as great as his, someone difficult to tame. He looked around, then deliberately selected a partner who, through no coincidence, happened to be available and eager to play the role he wanted to assign her.

Chapter VII

*A*NY modern woman who met Léonie d'Aunet Biard unhesitatingly would label her a bitch. Her only friends and constant companions were men, whom she gathered like a collector, and she was never seen in the company of another woman.

Born Léonie d'Aunet, she was an aristocrat brought up in Parisian society, which she considered stultifying. Her social position meant little to her. A brunette at birth and throughout her childhood, she was bored by her own appearance, and at the age of seventeen she bought a compound, a mixture of lemon juice and various chemicals, that transformed her into a blonde. She remained so for the duration of her brief, spectacular career. She was very short, and although physically well endowed, was exceptionally slender, almost bird-like.

Léonie was painfully shy, a quality that men found

attractive; other women noted that the glances she sent shooting around a crowded room were bold and coldly speculative. Her voice was sweet and very soft when she addressed a male, but laden with malice on the rare occasions when she deigned to drop a remark to a member of her own sex. Léonie was ambitious on her own account, and yearned for an association with a man who would achieve great things and take her with him to the heights.

At the convent school Léonie attended, the nuns were worried by her unorthodox daydreams, which she did not hesitate to repeat to them.

In 1840, when she was nineteen years old, she left home to become the mistress of a prominent young painter, François-Thérèse-Auguste Biard, and lived with him openly in his studio in the place Vendôme, a notorious artists' center. Her family thought of bringing her home by force, but preferred to avoid the scandal when they discovered she was pregnant.

Three months before Léonie's baby was born, Biard married her, and in a flush of enthusiasm, bought a large house, with a garden, on the Seine outside the city. The couple occasionally entertained artist friends there, but the ambitious girl found herself cooped up in a country house with her baby, and was expected to find her relaxation on board a boat that her husband bought her. Thoroughly dissatisfied, she found excuses to visit the city, and accepted every invitation, including those proffered by the aristocrats she had always despised.

Léonie had first made the acquaintance of Victor Hugo at a salon late in 1842, and was immediately attracted to him. He was politely gallant, but she wasn't his physical type, and he forgot her. Then, the following spring, Léonie invited him to a costume party at the Biard country house. The idea of spending an evening in a different way amused him, so he went, and discovered that the party was even more unusual than he had anticipated. Léonie was not only more vivacious and charming than he remembered, but late in the evening she took him aside to complain about her husband's angry moods, mercurial temperament, and violent fits of unfounded jealousy that made her life miserable.

During the next year Victor occasionally saw Léonie at various social gatherings, and was mildly attentive, but developed no serious interest in her. He was being true to his own principles, which prohibited him from approaching married women. After the tragic death of Léopoldine, Léonie wrote him a letter, offering her condolences and telling him that she knew unhappiness, too. She was planning to obtain a legal separation from Biard as soon as her second child was born.

If Léonie actually brought such a suit, there was no record of it in the courts, and if she went as far as to consult an attorney, no member of the legal profession came forward to announce the fact during her later troubles.

Presumably Victor's affair with her began about six to eight months after the death of Léopoldine, but none of the facts are known. His first poem presumably referring to her was written in the late autumn of 1844.

It was at almost precisely this same time that trouble developed in his relationship with Juliette. In November 1844, or thereabouts, Victor learned that Louis-Philippe intended to elevate him to the peerage. The idea had no appeal for Juliette, and she protested vigorously. Her daily letters hammered away at the subject—Victor had enough honors—a title would remove him from the people—his popularity would decline. He would waste himself on trivial matters, and be unable to devote energy to the one thing that mattered, his work.

What Juliette did not mention was her own fear. Vicomte Hugo would be so far above her that he would want no more to do with her. Victor sensed her apprehension and tried to allay it in soothing notes, but she refused to be reassured. She fought the very idea of his elevation.

Her opposition hurt him, and Léonie offered him consolation. Inordinately ambitious, she saw in Victor the fulfillment of her own aspirations. She would become the lifelong intimate of the greatest author of the age, who would rank higher in the nobility than her own father and uncles. She encouraged Victor, flattering him, and the balm healed his wounded vanity. Certainly he found some measure of relief from his grief over Léopoldine in his new relationship with Léonie.

Victor's liaison with Juliette suffered. She was no longer required to remain alone, seeing no one else, but she had formed a habit pattern over the period of a decade that was hard to break. She lived only for Victor, and wanted to be on hand whenever he came to her apartment, which now he infrequently did. She had long known of his brief flings with other women, but wisely considered them insignificant and chose to ignore them. Apparently it did not cross her mind that he might have become involved in a serious romance.

A letter she wrote to him on December 29, 1844, revealed her desperation:

For more than two months, literally, I have not set foot in the street, except the day when we went together to buy a new lamp. You tell me you will take me out, but I can't agree to go out at midnight in this frightful weather. You have acquired the habit of coming to see me at one or two o'clock in the morning.

Why are you always so late? Do I offer you nothing but a pillow and a mattress? And even when you arrive, you are so tired and preoccupied that you have no time for conversation, but go straight to bed and fall asleep.

What can I do? Suffer. Always suffer from this terrible torture which no one sees and no one pities. If only you felt sorry for me, it would help, but you do not. God alone knows what strength I must find within me to suffer this new kind of sequestration. There are moments when it weighs down on me like a stone cover, and when I would be capable of anything in this world in return for a little air and liberty.

Victor had no intention of permitting Juliette to slip away from him, but he did feel sorry for her, and urged her to go to cafés and shops, to visit friends and resume her life in the world. She had no more friends, and had lost all interest in the outside world. Her daughter, Claire Pradier, was attending a boarding school, with Victor paying the costs, so she was even denied the company of her child. Nevertheless, she wanted only Victor, and had to be satisfied with crumbs.

Auguste Biard was less innocent than Juliette, and

suspected that his wife was having an affair with someone. He believed her lover was connected with the theater, but she swore to him that she would have nothing to do with any actor. Biard pretended to accept her word, and bided his time.

Following her on a number of occasions, he saw her go to a quiet apartment building in the passage Saint-Roch in the Vendôme quarter, not far from his studio. When she disappeared into the building on July 5, 1845 (some say July 2), Biard went straight to the Commissary of Police for the district, and swore out a warrant for the arrest of his wife on charges of adultery.

Regardless of the licentiousness prevalent in artistic circles as well as other classes, France clung to the standards of bourgeois morality, and adultery was a grave charge. The accused frequently were kept in jail for as long as a year before being brought to trial and sentenced to still longer imprisonment. So Biard truly was seeking vengeance.

He was not disappointed. A squad of policemen broke into the apartment, and found Léonie in the act of sexual intercourse with no less than Victor Hugo. Both of the guilty parties were placed under arrest, and after scarcely being given the time to dress, were hauled off to the Saint-Lazare prison. Had Biard chosen to drop the charges, his wife and her lover would have been released, but the disgrace was not enough for the outraged husband, who was determined that they should both languish in jail.

The mortified Victor, who had been ennobled only three months earlier, immediately took advantage of an ancient French law, and demanded that he be released at once. A Peer of France could be tried only by his fellow noblemen, sitting as a star court in the Senate, or Chamber of Peers.

The law had not been invoked in a case of this sort for many years, and the authorities hesitated for several hours. But Victor was persuasive, and they finally allowed him to depart. He made every effort to obtain Léonie's release, too, but the officials remained deaf to his pleas.

According to an apocryphal story, Victor went to Adèle and, dropping to his knees, begged her forgiveness. The story makes it clear that he was not apologizing for the affair itself, but for the embarrassment caused by its public disclosure. No one knew what the new vicomte and his vicomtesse said to each other.

The reaction of the rest of Paris—with one notable exception—is no secret. The furor was almost unprecedented. Even the most distinguished and conservative of newspapers printed the story, and although they did not mention Victor by name, they described him in such complete detail that no reader was left unaware of his identity. The republican press enjoyed a field day at his expense, and his personal enemies were elated.

Sainte-Beuve's comment was the most malicious. "As I have remarked about his work in recent years, it is a clumsy matter, and is clumsily done."

Victor's friends also could not resist making jokes at his expense. "He needs practice," Dumas said, "in drawing on his trousers more quickly." Alphonse de Lamartine observed, "France is elastic; one rises even from a divan." And Théophile Gautier remarked, "I thought my dear friend was more experienced. He should have been found in the throes of composition, or, at the very least, in the act of reading to the lady on the subject of morality."

The uproar continued to grow worse. Léonie was still behind bars, and her vengeful husband hired an attorney and instructed him to bring formal suit against Vicomte Hugo in the Chamber of Peers. The situation resembled that of a bad French farce, and the country itself was becoming the laughingstock of Europe. Louis-Philippe decided to intervene personally.

Biard was summoned to the Tuileries, where he was told that he was allowing the clearing of his own name to blot the honor of France. The king finally persuaded him to drop any thought of bringing charges against Victor, but not even the royal persuader could influence him in his desire to obtain vengeance against his wife. Léonie remained in prison.

Now it was Victor's turn to be called to the palace. The audience was brief and, presumably, mortifying. Louis-Philippe ordered his newly created Vicomte to leave the country until the gale subsided, and suggested that he go to Spain.

Victor's wife and friends believed he was obeying the king's wishes, but instead he went to Juliette Drouet's small apartment and stayed there for a month, hidden away from the world. Although it is almost beyond credence, Juliette knew literally nothing about the notorious incident. She read no newspapers, she saw no friends, and she had no acquaintances with whom to exchange gossip. Her isolation was so complete that she may have been the only adult in Paris who had not heard of the affair.

All she knew was she had Victor to herself, and she was content.

Gossip continued to simmer as long as Léonie remained in prison. Then a Mme. Hamelin, a wealthy widow, came to the younger woman's rescue. She worked out a deal whereby Biard dropped the charges against his wife, while she, in return, agreed to give him permanent custody of their children and to file for an uncontested legal separation. Léonie finally left prison after being incarcerated there for eight weeks, and found shelter under the roof of Mme. Hamelin.

There were hidden angles that made the entire matter more ridiculous than anyone realized, and that would eventually, cause still more complications. Mme. Hamelin had briefly been a mistress of Victor's, and still felt very fond of him. Victor's relations with Juliette, meanwhile, continued to improve. The bond that held them together was strengthened by a fresh tragedy in 1846, when Juliette's melancholy daughter, Claire Pradier, celebrated her release from boarding school by attempting suicide, lingering for a while before her death.

For all practical purposes, Victor had been her father. He had paid all of her bills at school, had given her an allowance, and purchased all of her clothes. During her childhood, he had never made an appearance at her mother's apartment without bringing her a gift, and he told her innumerable stories. At the girl's funeral he stood beside Pradier, her own father, while the casket was lowered into the ground.

The deaths of Claire and of Léopoldine were remarkably similar. For a time mutual grief brought Victor and

Juliette closer than they had ever been, and he wrote a poem to Juliette the next day, and another later in which he linked the names of the two dead girls, their "angels."

Adèle now became his accomplice in weaving a web of intricate relations. Encouraged by Mme. Hamelin, Victor and Léonie resumed their affair, usually meeting under the Hamelin roof. Victor no longer concealed the truth from Adèle, who preferred to see a discredited aristocrat to a former courtesan and actress as her husband's principal mistress.

The Vicomtesse Hugo actually invited Mme. Biard to the place Royale for tea, and Léonie accepted. Victor was banished from the premises for the afternoon, and the two women discovered they had more in common than a mere man. Both were ladies, both had the same sense of social values, and both were pleasantly surprised to find they enjoyed their feminine chat.

In the months that followed, the two women became friends, and the relationship endured for several years. Victor, who not only wrote poems to Léonie, but also corresponded with her, now allowed himself to be seen in public with her. She sometimes went to dinner with him, more frequently spent an idle hour or two with him at a café where the literary lights of the city gathered, and on a few occasions he escorted her to the theater. They suffered no further interference from Biard and the public scandal had subsided completely.

Léonie was pleased, believing that her mortification and sacrifices had not been made in vain. She considered herself Victor's semi-official mistress, and her lifelong ambition had been obtained. Her joy was flawed, however, by the realization that Victor continued to see Juliette Drouet, and to spend several nights each week at her apartment.

Finally, in 1848, after Léonie had been unable to obtain a decision from Victor himself, she decided to solve the problem in her own way, and sent Juliette a packet of their mutual lover's letters.

The receipt of these letters was the first that Juliette knew of her rival's existence. Though prematurely white-haired, with a lined face, and knowing she would never find another man who would support her, Juliette immediately offered to release Victor from his relationship with her.

In this supreme hour of crisis she made no scenes, stooped to no recriminations or vituperation. If Victor no longer loved her, she said, he was free to depart, and she wished him well.

Although Victor was not aware of the extent of his dependency on Juliette, he had no intention of losing her, and proposed an arrangement that, at first glance, appears to be no more than an arrogant expression of his vanity. Only he could have proposed what, in effect, would be a contest. He would continue to see Juliette, he would continue to see Léonie, and love would tip the scales in one direction or the other. By this he did not mean his love for one or the other, but the love they showed for him.

Adèle, whose position was different, was exempted from the contest. She was secure, being his wife, and there was no pretense of love or anything resembling it on either side. She may have felt qualms, her children having reached maturity, but it was impossible for Victor to dislodge her, so she became merely the interested bystander.

In his own devious way, Victor knew what he was

doing, and loaded the dice in favor of Juliette. An impartial observer, unfamiliar with the background, would have said that Juliette stood no chance. Her figure had thickened, her face was that of a middle-aged woman, and there was no longer a sway to her walk. Léonie, however, was still young, vibrant, and exuded the sexual aura that Victor Hugo found necessary to his happiness and well-being. The odds were in her favor.

Juliette, who could have demanded a showdown, quietly accepted Victor's idea. Certainly she had strong masochistic tendencies, and in her life with Victor she must have enjoyed punishing herself, but she was no fool. She knew Victor better than he knew himself, and the calculated risk she took was slight.

Léonie, however, objected to being humiliated again by the man for whom she already suffered so much. On the other hand, she was in no position to reject Victor's suggestion. She was no longer accepted in respectable society, the possibility of a reconciliation with her husband was remote, and there had been no opportunity to seek another protector. Having no alternative, she swallowed her pride.

Juliette made no change in her way of life. Whenever Victor sought her company, her advice and solace, or the comfort of her bed, he knew where to find her. She was familiar with his foibles, his habits, his likes and dislikes. When he wanted to talk, she listened. When he was silent, she did not annoy him. When he retreated to the tiny study at one end of her apartment, she did not open the door, and left him to work in solitude.

Léonie chafed under the restrictions. She had no intention of spending every day and every evening sitting with folded hands under Mme. Hamelin's roof, waiting for the sound of Victor's approaching footsteps. She tried to accede to his absurd demands, but the strain was too great. She made active efforts, without her lover's knowledge, to find someone else who was wealthy, prominent, and wanted a full-time mistress.

Victor's activities during this period can best be described as maniac. Two mistresses, each of whom awaited his pleasure, were not enough to satisfy him. In his spare time he had scores of brief affairs with other women, among them courtesans, actresses, unmarried ladies of quality, widows and wives who were separated from their husbands. Among them was the beautiful actress Alice Ozy, but he lost out to his son Charles. From her diary, Juliette later estimated that, between 1848 and 1850, he went to bed with at least two hundred women. Her statistics admittedly were incomplete, as Victor must have forgotten some of his affairs when he ultimately confessed the truth to her.

His sexual exploits during this period gave him no peace of mind, and Victor sought other outlets. He developed a great interest in the supernatural, which had been sparked by his presentiment on the night of Léopoldine's death. A man named André Weill, the self-styled "king of the occult," introduced him to such esoterics as séances, table-tapping, and fortune-telling. He read omnivorously on the occult, with considerable skepticism, but later, as events proved, became a devotee.

Until this period in his life, Victor's achievements had been numerous. But one accomplishment was still lacking: he had not yet earned a dignified political reputation based on his principles. The scandal that erupted over his affair with Léonie Biard had stifled his political ambitions for a time. Not until the late winter of 1846 did he say a single word in the Senate. By then, to be sure, the furor had died down. No true Frenchman held the amatory exploits of another against him, and Victor was regarded as the unfortunate victim of very bad luck. His personal past was forgotten, and his fellow countrymen were once more willing to listen to his views on national and international matters.

In the next two years he delivered a number of major speeches. He addressed the peers on the partition of Poland, on France's relations with the Pope, on the future place of the Bonaparte family in the nation, and on the preservation of the French seacoast. His concern over the erosion of the coastline caused by the tides foreshadowed the conservation movement of the future.

These speeches are significant in revealing Victor as the humanitarian he was, a liberal in the best sense of the word. He sought equality and freedom for all, and his speech on the Bonapartes was particularly to the point. It was cruel and short-sighted, he declared, for France, the most enlightened of nations, to force the relatives of her most illustrous son to live in exile. It was Napoleon who had consolidated the country's liberties, but those without gratitude were preventing his relatives from dwelling in their homeland.

The address did not endear him to the king, but Louis-Philippe had other, far more important worries. His attempt to gather the reins of government into his own hands was rousing the nation, and France again stood on the brink of revolution. The working classes had not been granted the equality they demanded, the voice of the

1. The house, no. 140, where Victor Hugo was born, February 26, 1802,
Besançon, where his father, a major, was garrisoned.

2. Joseph Léopold-Sigisbert Hugo, Victor's father, reached the height his career as a Napoleonic general.

Mme. Hugo, née Françoise Trébouchet, Victor's unfaithful mother.

4. Eugène, Victor's olde brother, who went insane o Victor's wedding day.

5. Alfred de Vigny, the poet and close literary friend of Victor, his stand-in or "best man" at his wedding. *Photo Hachette*

6. The Hermitage of the Feuillantines, former convent in Paris, where in the enormous enclosed garden Victor and his brothers played in a wonder world of childhood.

Photo Roger-Violet

7. Victor Hugo shortly before his marriage at
the church of Saint-Sulpice in Paris, October 22,
1822.

8. Adèle Foucher, the childhood companion
and his bride.   *Photo Hachette*

9. News drawing of Hugo's Romantic followers fighting jeering Classicis
at the first performance of Hugo's *Hernani*, 1830.   *Photo Roger-Violl*

10. The Théâtre Française (Comédie Française) where most of Hugo's dramas were performed.

11. Juliette Drouet, Victor Hugo's mistress of fifty years, whom he m
when she was reading for the part of Princess Negroni in his drama, *Lucrè*
Borgia. *Lithograph Léon Noël.*

12. Sainte-Beuve, the poet, critic, and secret lover of Adèle Hugo, Victor's
fe.

NOTRE-DAME

DE PARIS.

PAR VICTOR HUGO,

TROISIÈME ÉDITION.

PARIS,
CHARLES GOSSELIN, LIBRAIRE,
RUE SAINT-GERMAIN-DES-PRÉS, N° 9.
M DCCC XXXI.

13. Cover of the 1831 edition of Victor's enormous Romantic success, the novel *Notre-Dame-de-Paris*, illustrating the hunchback of Notre Dame, Quasimodo, and the goat girl Esmeralda.
Photo Hachette

14. Number 6, Place Royale, Victor's home, now the Victor Hugo Museum, here he moved when his great novel *Notre-Dame-de-Paris* was published. he original name Place des Vosges was restored after the downfall of apoleon III.

15. Caricature of Victor Hugo's successes, which appeared in the journal *Le Charivari*, showing him leaning against the Cathedral of Notre Dame, his right foot on the Théâtre Française, his left foot on the Académie Française.

16. Victor Hugo revealing his political ambitions in his daring address before the Académie Française, to which he was belatedly elected in 1841 in his fourth try. Watercolor by Hermann Vogel. *Photo Hachette*

VICTOR HUGO'S GREAT CONTEMPORARIES

(*Facing Page*)

17. Chateaubriand, author turned statesman, top left.

18. Lamartine, poet who became President of the Provisional Republic of France in 1848, top right.

19. Alexandre Dumas, père, Hugo's rival in authorship and women, below.

(*Above*)

20. Caricature of three others: Balzac, Théophile Gautier, and Lemâitre.

21. Léopoldine, Hugo's daughter, married to Charles Vacquerie. They drowned in the Seine at Villequier in his boat six months after their marriage in February 1843. *Photo Hachette*

22. Charles Vacquerie, brother of Auguste, the young man who became
Victor Hugo's most trusted follower and his first biographer.

Photo Hachette

VICTOR HUGO

A SES CONCITOYENS.

Mes Concitoyens,

Je réponds à l'appel des soixante mille Electeurs qui m'ont spontanément honoré de leurs suffrages aux élections de la Seine. Je me présente à votre libre choix.

Dans la situation politique telle qu'elle est, on me demande toute ma pensée. La voici : Deux Républiques sont possibles.

L'une abattra le drapeau tricolore sous le drapeau rouge, fera des gros sous avec la colonne, jettera bas la statue de Napoléon et dressera la statue de Marat, détruira l'Institut, l'Ecole polytechnique et la Légion-d'Honneur, ajoutera à l'auguste devise : *Liberté, Egalité, Fraternité*, l'option sinistre : *ou la Mort;* fera banqueroute, ruinera les riches sans enrichir les pauvres, anéantira le crédit, qui est la fortune de tous, et le travail, qui est le pain de chacun, abolira la propriété et la famille, promènera des têtes sur des piques, remplira les prisons par le soupçon et les videra par le massacre, mettra l'Europe en feu et la civilisation en cendre, fera de la France la patrie des ténèbres, égorgera la liberté, étouffera les arts, décapitera la pensée, niera Dieu; remettra en mouvement ces deux machines fatales qui ne vont pas l'une sans l'autre, la planche aux assignats et la bascule de la guillotine; en un mot, fera froidement ce que les hommes de 93 ont fait ardemment, et, après l'horrible dans le grand que nos pères ont vu, nous montrera le monstrueux dans le petit.

L'autre sera la sainte communion de tous les Français dès à présent, et de tous les peuples un jour, dans le principe démocratique; fondera une liberté sans usurpations et sans violences, une égalité qui admettra la croissance naturelle de chacun, une fraternité, non de moines dans un couvent, mais d'hommes libres; donnera à tous l'enseignement comme le soleil donne la lumière, gratuitement; introduira la clémence dans la loi pénale et la conciliation dans la loi civile; multipliera les chemins de fer, reboisera une partie du territoire, en défrichera une autre, décuplera la valeur du sol; partira de ce principe qu'il faut que tout homme commence par le travail et finisse par la propriété, assurera en conséquence la propriété comme la représentation du travail accompli et le travail comme l'élément de la propriété future; respectera l'héritage, qui n'est autre chose que la main du père tendue aux enfants à travers le mur du tombeau; combinera pacifiquement, pour résoudre le glorieux problème du bien-être universel, les accroissements continus de l'industrie, de la science, de l'art et de la pensée; poursuivra, sans quitter terre pourtant, et sans sortir du possible et du vrai, la réalisation sereine de tous les grands rêves des sages; bâtira le pouvoir sur la même base que la liberté, c'est-à-dire sur le droit; subordonnera la force à l'intelligence; dissoudra l'émeute et la guerre, ces deux formes de la barbarie; fera de l'ordre la loi des citoyens, et de la paix la loi des nations; vivra et rayonnera, grandira la France, conquerra le monde, sera en un mot, le majestueux embrassement du genre humain sous le regard de Dieu satisfait.

De ces deux Républiques, celle-ci s'appelle la civilisation, celle-là s'appelle la terreur. Je suis prêt à dévouer ma vie pour établir l'une et empêcher l'autre.

VICTOR HUGO.

IMPRIMERIE DE JULES-JUTEAU ET C°, RUE ST-DENIS, 345.

23. Victor Hugo's campaign poster, written by himself, as a candidate for the National Assembly in the election of 1848, after the revolution of that year. He became a Deputy.

Photo Hachette

24. Louis-Napoleon, the modest Republican nephew of Napoléon Bonaparte, elected President of France in 1848 with the friendly support of Victor Hugo.

25. Napoléon III, self-proclaimed Emperor of France, three years after his election as President. In defiance, Victor Hugo went into hostile exile for 19 years.

26. La Conciergerie, which Victor visited daily to see his sons and Auguste Vacquerie, all editors of the Republican journal *L'Évenément,* imprisoned here by Napoléon III.

(Facing Page)

27. Charles Hugo, upper left.

28. François-Victor Hugo, upper right.

29. Auguste Vacquerie, bottom.

30. Victor in exile, 1852, posed on the Rock of the Out-
laws on the Island of Jersey, presumably looking toward
France, photographed by Auguste Vacquerie.

31. Victor (in later years) on the balcony of Hauteville House where his
cold morning showers in the nude shocked tourists. Juliette watched from
her little villa nearby.

32. Hauteville House, on the Island of Guernsey, where Victor Hugo spent 15 years of his exile-vendetta against Napoléon III. The conservatory to the left on the second floor was his studio, where he wrote most of *Les Misérables*.

33. Victor's garish bedroom at Hauteville House. No home of his escaped his passion for ornate furnishings.

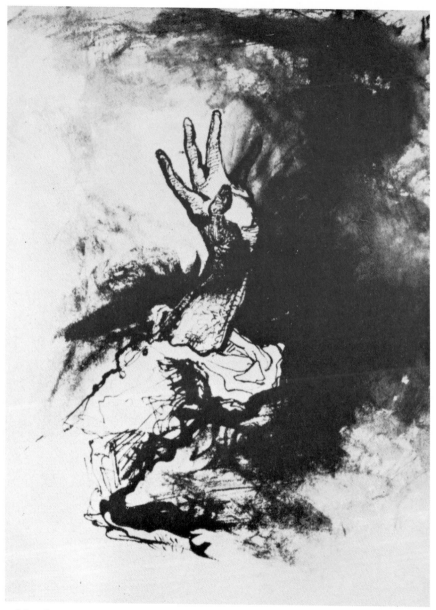

34. The Dream—drawing by Victor Hugo, one of many reflecting his melancholy and sense of foreboding. He drew hundreds of pictures, including the frontispieces for many of his novels. *Photo Hachette*

35. Mme. Hugo, the unwelcome mistress of Hauteville House. When she departed for France, Juliette Drouet moved in.

36. Adèle, Victor's daughter, who, after an elopement from Guernsey with a ne'er-do-well, was deserted, went mad, never recovered, died 1915.

37. Victor Hugo carried in triumph as a Deputy at Bordeaux in the elections of 1871, after the downfall of Napoléon III.

38. Drawing by Vierge of Victor Hugo following the funeral cortège of his son Charles through the streets of embattled Paris, March 1871, when the National Guard of France was fighting the Communards. *Photo Hachette*

CONQUESTS OF DISTINCTION

39. *Left*, Mme. Auguste Biard (née Léonie D'Aunet), Victor's famous second mistress, cause of a major scandal when they were caught together in April 1845, three months after his elevation to the House of Peers.

Photo Hachette

40. *Right*, Judith Gautier, daughter of Théophile, who led the crowd welcoming Victor back from exile at the Gare du Nord in 1870 and became his lover in 1872. *Photo Chéri Rousseau*

41. *Below*, Sarah Bernhardt in her role as the queen in the revival of Victor's drama *Ruy Blas*. She was his lover in his seventieth year.

42. Victor and his grandchildren Jeanne and Georges, for whom he wrote the enchanting stories in *The Art of Being a Grandfather*.

43. Drawing of the black-draped Arc de Triomphe, where Hugo's body lay in state. More than two million people attended his funeral. The next day, June 1, 1885, he was buried in the Panthéon.

middle class was only faintly heard, and the people became dangerously restless. The Revolution of 1848 exploded in February, and in turn it sparked other uprisings all over Europe.

Through sheer happenstance, Victor Hugo was walking through the streets of Paris when mobs formed and descended on the city's important public buildings. Swept along by a crowd, he found himself in front of the ancient Bastille, the center of the day's storm. A regiment of soldiers loyal to the crown tried to disperse the throng by firing over the heads of the people, and several citizens were injured in the crush.

The Revolution succeeded as rapidly as it had begun, when the troops changed sides, the soldiers being the sympathetic sons of farmers, workers, and merchants. During the excitement Louis-Philippe and his wife escaped from the Tuileries in disguise, and managed to leave the country. Various government ministers also made their way into exile, and the founders of the Second Republic met at the Hôtel de Ville and the Chamber of Deputies convened to organize a new government.

Victor Hugo, peer of France and budding politician, saw his chance to influence events, and could not turn away from an opportunity as golden as it was dramatic. The greatest crowds again gathered in front of the Bastille, and he joined them. Working his way through the throng, he was determined to make a speech that would win him political glory. According to his own dramatic account, he climbed onto a carriage that had been overturned, but he merely mounted the steps of the Bastille.

He was recognised, and the people applauded him,

F

then grew quiet. The revolution had been won at a cost of remarkably little bloodshed, and the citizens of Paris wanted to be amused. Who could better entertain them than the nation's foremost author?

Victor's address was an incredibly naive blunder. The crowd had just learned that Louis-Philippe had been deposed, and he agreed that the monarch had to leave. Loyal to the friends who had helped him, however, Victor proposed that a regency be established, and that the regent be none other than the attractive Duchess of Orléans.

The crowd laughed as hard as it applauded. The people of France, having rid themselves of a Bourbon, wanted no Bourbon in-law as regent, much less a woman —and a German princess by birth. Victor's attempt to influence history failed ignominiously, and he went home to nurse his injured pride.

But there were compensations. The poet Lamartine, now Premier of the provisional government, offered him the Ministry of Public Instruction, which he declined, but he was appointed mayor of the district of Paris in which he had lived. His friend Louis Blanc became Commissioner of Labor. Victor, to be sure, wanted to be elected to the new Assembly in June, where he would have a platform to speak. The campaign would start in April.

Victor did not hesitate, and plunged into the thick of the fight. He wrote his own campaign poster, one that was far more literate, more dramatic, than that of any other candidate. He stood as a candidate of no party, but said he wished to represent the common people. Describing these citizens, he was sufficiently ambiguous to appeal both to the conservatives of the middle class and to the laboring class.

Sixty thousand of his fellow citizens voted for him, but he lost the election. As a number of candidates had not won pluralities, the losers were entitled to run again. Victor did, and two weeks later he was elected to the Assembly. At last he was in a position to influence the affairs of France from the political rostrum.

A few days later he made his maiden speech in the Chamber of Deputies. In the immediate past the laboring classes had succeeded in establishing National Workshops, which were a form of unemployment relief. The conservatives were opposed to these organizations, calling them socialistic. Victor cast his lot with the right wing, saying that the laboring man would prosper if he trusted the capitalist system. Thanks in part to his efforts, the National Workshops were voted out of existence, and the bourgeoisie breathed more easily.

The result of this vote was a series of the worst riots in the history of Paris. The insurrection broke out on June 23, and in the next three days scores of people were killed, hundreds were wounded, and many buildings were burned by the incensed mobs. Anarchy ruled Paris, and for a time the clock was turned back to the insane era of 1793.

Victor was worried about his family, concerned about Juliette, and spent most of his time scuttling back and forth between the house on the place Royale and Juliette's nearby apartment in the rue Saint Anatase. It took courage for any well-dressed man to be abroad, particularly in those parts of the city infested by mischief-hunting mobs, but Victor felt no regard for his safety, and his conduct verged on the reckless. "It did not occur to me," he said at a much later date, "that I might not be safe in the company of my fellow Parisians."

On the third day of the struggle he went to the barricades that had been erected in front of the Bastille, and when he saw two large crowds facing each other across a barbed wire fence, he lost all patience. Mounting a box only a foot or two from the wire, he harangued the crowd on behalf of the new government. Respect for the sacred institutions of France, he shouted, was of paramount importance if the nation was not to fall into utter chaos. It was the duty of all men of good will to put aside their firearms, knives, and clubs, and to work together for the welfare and benefit of all.

His heroism on June 25 was authentic. Few other members of the new Assembly dared to show their faces in public, much less make speeches when they might have been stoned or shot to death. But Victor was no longer posing, and thought nothing about his own skin. His unselfishness in the face of genuine danger was giving him political stature and winning the respect he had always wanted.

When the insurrection ended, Victor was the first to rise in the Assembly and propose an amnesty. No Frenchman had committed treason, he declared, and no Frenchman should be punished for acts performed during the mad three days and nights of terror.

Although committed to the principles of observing the law and maintaining order, Victor wanted to see for himself why the laboring classes were so upset. He went, unaccompanied, to some of the worst slum districts in the city and to some of the new industrial suburbs, where he was horrified by living conditions. To assure himself that these conditions were not merely local, he made a trip to the old citadel town of Lille, in the northeast, and there saw slums that rivaled the worst in Paris.

On August 1, 1848, a new newspaper, *L'Événement*, made its appearance in the city. Among the members of the editorial staff were Victor's two sons, Charles and François-Victor, the poet Paul Meurice, and Auguste Vacquerie, the young brother-in-law of the late Léopoldine. Victor Hugo had contributed the newspaper's slogan, "Vigorous opposition to anarchy; tender and profound love of the people." Privately, without fanfare, Victor Hugo was one of the newspaper's four principal financial investors. Quietly, using his influence in literary circles, Victor Hugo was responsible for the appearance of the bylines of Théophile Gautier and the distinguished liberal poet, Gérard de Nerval.

An article by Victor Hugo himself appeared in the first issue, and in it he pulled no punches. Writing with candor and deep emotion, he described in detail the slums he had seen. He ended on an impassioned note: "These dwellings and the kind of life they create must be destroyed. Poverty in France must and will be eliminated."

Although Victor did not yet know it, his voice was becoming that of the French people. His political judgments were still vague, however, as he showed by his friendship with another recently elected member of the

Assembly, Prince Louis-Napoleon Bonaparte, who had recently returned to France from exile. Louis-Napoleon was the son, presumably, of Louis, King of Holland (Napoleon's brother) and his queen, Hortense Beauharnais, daughter of Empress Joséphine by her first marriage. As Hortense hated her doltish husband and refused to become intimate with him, it was a well-established fact that Louis-Napoleon was not Louis Bonaparte's son. His paternity had been the subject of intense speculation since the time of his birth, and it was possible that Hortense herself didn't know. It was generally believed that a famous Dutch admiral had sired him.

The identity of Louis-Napoleon's father was of no real importance, however. What mattered was that he bore the magic name of Bonaparte, and France was ripe for the change he offered. A mild-mannered, pleasant man who was at ease socially, he concealed his burning ambitions behind gentle, forward-looking conservatism. He sounded liberal in humanitarian ways, yet he expressed no radical sentiments, and he made it plain that he had no intention of rocking the French ship of state. Actually he was a shrewd and clever maneuverer, known as such only to a handful of intimates.

From the time of Louis-Napoleon's first appearance in the Assembly, he and Victor were friendly toward each other. The poet was impressed by the name of Bonaparte, which he had trumpeted for so long, and Louis-Napoleon, if he did not really enjoy Victor's company, knew that the Hugo name and the Hugo talents would be formidable aids if enlisted in his cause. The two men sat together in the

Assembly each day, dined together frequently, and often stopped at a café for a drink together when they had no time for a longer conversation.

Louis-Napoleon was an adventurer who had spent his entire adult life traveling from one place of exile to another, and had lived in Switzerland, England, the United States, and Belgium, among many places. He had exerted constant efforts to keep alive the mystique of the Bonaparte name, and he had participated in conspiracies that would have marked him as a bungler had there been a truly popular and strong government in France.

He had one ultimate goal: he wanted to become the absolute, undisputed monarch of France. He kept his ambition hidden, and his manners were so watery, his personality so unprepossessing that even those who hated the name of Bonaparte felt sorry for him. No one appeared to note that whenever he posed for one of the many portraits painted in 1848, he invariably held his hand inside his tunic, in the style of the famous Emperor.

In December 1848, an election would be held for the first President of the Republic of France, and there were many, Victor Hugo among them, who believed the country's prestige abroad would be improved if a Bonaparte occupied the office. Louis-Napoleon was specifically barred by a law against any relation of the late Napoleon I from the highest office. But it was universally believed that the forty-year-old former exile was harmless. A new law was proposed, ending the ban, and Victor Hugo made a stirring speech in support of the measure, which passed the Assembly by an overwhelming vote.

Two days later, in mid-October 1848, Louis-Napoleon Bonaparte announced his candidacy. Twenty-four hours later, *L'Événement* led the parade of newspapers that supported him. Its editorial, which argued passionately in his behalf, bore the signature of Victor Hugo.

In the election campaign that followed, no member of the Assembly, no literary personage was more ardent than Victor in Bonaparte's support. He directed the campaign in *L'Événement*, he made scores of speeches in Louis-Napoleon's behalf, and he spent many hours each week at the Bonaparte headquarters.

Most Frenchmen felt as he did. Louis-Napoleon Bonaparte was elected President of France in December 1848, garnering almost 5,500,000 votes as against less than 1,500,000 for his opponent, General Cavaignac, who had suppressed the resurrection under martial law. Victor had been one of the principal architects of a great victory, and he rejoiced.

Victor's activities as a politician, combined with the distractions of his love affairs, kept him so busy that it is astonishing that, he found time during this period for his writing. But he did, and though his output was reduced, it was still prodigious. He wrote poems for several collections; many others were included in works published in later years; and an even larger number were discarded. He completed a draft of the novel he was still calling *Les Misères*, but was not satisfied with it. Knowing that it would become his masterwork if he revised and expanded it, he put it aside for a time, thus setting himself a new work precedent. Never before had he been engaged in extensive rewriting;

he had always published poems and novels and sent plays into production as soon as he finished his first draft.

Victor was now also acting informally as editor-in-chief of *L'Événement*, directing the activities of the editorial staff, assigning stories to assistants, and recruiting the services of non-political writers of note, most of them his friends. He wrote many of the newspaper's editorials, and it was his sixth sense, so frequently in tune with the mood of the people, that was largely responsible for the newspaper's spectacular success.

Although conservative in tone, *L'Événement* had a liberal approach, stopping short of socialism. It appealed to the bourgeois, but also to the men in the street, who now leaned toward the radical. Most Paris newspapers lost money for their backers, and required continuing subsidies, but *L'Événement* was the exception. In its first six months of publication, it brought Victor the equivalent of the largest full year's income that he had earned to date. It also paid generous wages to his two sons, both of whom were developing into full-fledged liberals, and to Auguste Vacquerie, who was developing a romantic interest in the youngest of the Hugo children, Adèle. He was also something of a Boswell to Victor's Dr. Johnson.

Politics, the newspaper, his own writing, and the continuing affairs with both Juliette and Léonie made it necessary for Victor to limit his active social life. He felt, nevertheless, that the apartment on the place Royale was no longer large enough for his needs, and, shortly before the election, rented an entire house in the Montmarte district, at 37 rue de la Tour d'Auvergne. In accordance with his well-established tastes, he filled it with expensive bric-a-brac, silver and china, antique furniture, and a hodgepodge of exorbitantly priced odds and ends.

Juliette Drouet followed him, of course, and took a small apartment in the neighborhood at impasse Rodier. Léonie Biard, encouraged by Adèle, promptly did the same, and Victor was now the sole support of three households. Money did not concern him, however, any more than it had in the past.

He envisioned a lifelong political career for himself, and planned to publish a book of poetry or a novel every year or two. He had no idea that events, combined with his own political and social maturation, would bring about vast changes in his life, and would, in ways he could not have anticipated, give him the world stature he sought.

Chapter VIII

*N*EITHER Victor Hugo nor anyone else in France was aware of President Louis-Napoleon Bonaparte's intentions. To gain absolute monarchy he moved cautiously, lulling liberals and radicals while trying to build a conservative power base.

Although Victor had no idea what was taking place, he found himself in conflict with the President almost from the time that Louis-Napoleon took office. By the summer of 1849 he was openly opposed to the administration's major foreign and domestic policies. Editorials in *L'Événement* protested against the "reactionary tendencies" being displayed by the new government. Other newspapers were far more critical. Some of the President's supporters, perhaps with Louis-Napoleon's knowledge and assent, hired a gang of thugs. The offices of these newspapers were wrecked, and their printing presses were smashed.

Victor was outraged. The wanton destruction of

presses was a sacrilege to one who earned his living with words, and he paid a visit to the presidential palace to protest. No details of the meeting are known, but he made no secret of the fact that he and Louis-Napoleon argued bitterly, and that their relationship had chilled.

The following month he openly broke with the administration on the question of the alleviation of poverty. The wealthy Vicomte de Melun introduced a bill in the Chamber of Deputies proposing the establishment of a commission to study the slums and provide relief of some sort for the poverty-stricken. Victor thought the measure was far too weak, vague, and ineffectual, and attacked it in an address that was destined to bring together the humanitarians, liberals, and radicals of France:

The man of the masses suffers today from the twofold and contradictory feeling of his actual poverty and the greatness to which he knows himself entitled. And to them he is entitled, or the great ideals of the Revolution become a mockery!

We who sit in this Chamber bear a special responsibility, for it is we who represent the people of France. It is we who must take steps to rid this land of poverty, and set the poor on the road to greatness and enlightenment.

I am not one of those who believes that suffering can be suppressed in this world. Suffering may be a divine law, but I know of no law that prescribes poverty as a necessary cause of that suffering. I am one of those who think and affirm that poverty can and must be destroyed!

The newspapers that favored the administration dealt sarcastically with the speech, and Louis-Napoleon's supporters in the Assembly snubbed Victor as a sign of their displeasure. His activities in the next two weeks made the breach still wider.

The cause was the President's so-called Roman policy. Pope Pius IX, who had held office for two years, was one of the most liberal and progressive men in the history of the papacy, but the sentiments of the Italian people, ironically, far outstripped his ability to satisfy their desires.

Republicans led by the nationalist patriots, Mazzini and Garibaldi, occupied Rome in 1848, stripping the Vatican of its temporal powers in the city-state, and the Pope had fled to the countryside. France had sent an expedition to restore order, and a statement by Louis-Napoleon led Victor to believe that the freedoms of the Roman people would be assured. In July 1849, the city fell to the French column, the Pope was restored—and nothing was either said or done about preserving the briefly won liberties of the Roman people. Hugo angrily denounced the act as well as supporting a bill for relief of poverty, infuriating the conservatives.

Soon after, a World Peace Congress met in Paris, and Victor Hugo permitted the use of his name as a delegate. To his genuine surprise he was elected president, and therefore was required to deliver an address. That speech, far-reaching in its idealistic vision, seemed to underline everything that was wrong with the French actions in the Roman campaign and in opposing the workers in Paris.

The day was coming, Victor said, when all mankind would enjoy true freedom. This was the ultimate divine law, so it was inevitable that God would grant His greatest gift, liberty, to his sons everywhere. When the thunders of applause died away, Victor went on:

The day is not far distant when cannon will be exhibited in museums, just as instruments of torture are today. The day is not far distant when those two immense entities, the United States of America and the United States of Europe, shall be seen placed in the presence of each other, extending the hand of fellowship across the seas, exchanging their produce, their commerce, their industry, their arts, their genius, clearing the earth, peopling the deserts, improving creation under the eyes of the Creator, and uniting, for the good of these two infinite forces, the fraternity of men and the power of God.

The address created a sensation, and it was obvious to Louis-Napoleon and his supporters that Victor Hugo had developed into a statesman. What he advocated, however, was contrary to the President's intuitions—to take the throne and to restore the Empire of the first Napoleon. So the battle lines were drawn.

All through the summer and autumn Victor led the fight to grant the people of Rome the basic freedoms for which they had fought, and which had now been denied them by the force of French arms. More than a gadfly, he was becoming a political embarrassment to Louis-Napoleon, who temporized and evaded to conceal his real policy: granting nothing to the people of Rome.

Victor's humanitarian and liberal ideals became increasingly apparent in the following months. He was a firm advocate of universal suffrage. He made speeches in the Assembly against the use of the guillotine as an instrument of execution. And he regarded the policy of sending so-called political criminals—those who strongly opposed the administration—to penal colonies in the far-off tropics of the New World.

"The principles of the democratic form of government have become dear to me," he declared in an editorial he wrote for *L'Événement*, adding, "I am prepared to die for them." It did not yet occur to him that he might be required to prove his resounding words.

The constitution of the Republic prohibited a President from serving two consecutive terms, but Louis-Napoleon began a devious campaign in the autumn of 1850 to circumvent the proscription, even though the next election was as yet two years away. Victor, suspicious of the President's motives and partly aware of his machinations, wrote a strong editorial in *L'Événement*, denouncing his ambitions and calling them evil. The break was now complete, and the two men no longer spoke.

During the next year the administration moved repeatedly to silence the opposition press, which suffered constant harassment.

On Bastille Day, Victor concluded the debate in the Assembly violently attacking Louis-Napoleon for attempting to change the law preventing a second term. Soon after, Charles Hugo was sent to prison for writing an article denouncing the death penalty. The young man said no more than his father had already stated in several addresses on the Assembly floor, but Victor was immune to arrest because he was a Deputy. But it was now obvious that Louis-Napoleon was striking at Victor through his family, and he knew it would be only a matter of time before François-Victor was arrested, too.

In July 1851, Louis-Napoleon's supporters introduced a bill amending the constitution into the Assembly, that, in the unlikely event that it passed, would permit the President to succeed himself. His ambitions were out in the open now, and on July 17 Victor Hugo made the most fervent speech of his entire political career, an address that won international attention. At its climax he said:

What! because ten centuries ago, Charlemagne, after forty years of glory, let fall upon the face of this globe a sword and scepter so immeasurably great that no one since has been able or has dared to touch them. In the interval there were men named Philip-Augustus, Francis I, Henry IV, Louis XIV. Then, a thousand years after Charlemagne, another genius appeared. He picked up this sword and scepter, and stood erect over the continent. He accomplished the gigantic history whose brilliance still endures. He leashed the Revolution in France and unleashed it in Europe. He made his name synonymous with Friedland, Montmirail, Rivoli, Jena, Essling.

What! because after ten years of immense glory, he in turn dropped, through exhaustion, this sword and scepter which had accomplished so many colossal things, you come and wish to pick them up after him, even as he, Napoleon, had lifted them up after Charlemagne!

You want to take into your feeble hands this scepter of Titans, this sword of giants!

What for? after Augustus, Augustulus?

What! because we had had Napoleon the Great, must we have Napoleon the Little?

The scathing sarcasm struck its mark. The author-politician's name, *Napoléon le Petit*, became the rallying cry of the opposition. In France, throughout the Continent and across the Channel in England, the scathing name caught the imagination of the public. Until the end of his days Louis-Napoleon was known as *Napoléon le Petit*, and that is how posterity remembers him. Victor Hugo struck the single greatest blow anyone had yet delivered against the would-be tyrant.

There was little change in Victor's personal life up to this time. He wrote when he could, but was able to spend only limited periods at his writing desk. He continued to see both Juliette and Léonie, the "contest of love" not yet having been determined, but he gave up his habit of bedding other women indiscriminately. Not only would his new dignity not permit it, but he had no time for such frivolous affairs.

His political life absorbed him, and what energies he had to spare were devoted to his brace of mistresses. Victor's muse, if not silenced, spoke with a muted voice during this period, the only time in his life when he failed to write copiously.

The new house in Montmarte was large enough to accommodate seventy-five to a hundred guests at a time, but the famous salon had ceased functioning. Occasionally Victor played the host for fellow members of the Assembly who shared his growing sense of alarm, but he had no interest in entertaining literary and social guests.

Louis-Napoleon's supporters brought suit against *L'Événement*. Plainly the administration intended to halt the publication: the handwriting was on the wall. But by skillful defense, the editors won their acquittal.

Adèle viewed the situation with equanimity. Her later

correspondence with her husband reveals that she actively disliked the parties they had given for so many years. She enjoyed the respect that her husband generated, and that rubbed off on her, but she was always a shy woman and failed to enjoy the limelight. Juliette Drouet was still the bane of her existence, and though she actively encouraged Victor's affair with Léonie Biard, she lacked the strength and influence to terminate his liaison with his original mistress.

Events, and the role Juliette played in them, would strengthen her ties to Victor for the rest of her long life, and would terminate the "love contest" in her favor. If the issue had been in doubt, the wild upheavals that began on December 1, 1851, resolved them.

By this time Victor knew that a climactic clash with the administration was inevitable. François-Victor had been taken into custody, so both of his sons were now in prison. Juliette, who had renewed many of her old theatrical friendships, learned from influential men that Louis-Napoleon was waiting for the right moment to strike. Allegedly he told several of his intimates that when Victor Hugo was sent to prison, he would be kept there for many years.

Late in November 1851, Auguste Vacquerie and Paul Meurice of the *L'Événement* staff were sent to join Victor's sons at the old Conciergerie Prison. The charges against them were flimsy, but each received a sentence of six months.

Juliette was fearful for Victor's safety, but he was amused by her attempts to warn him. So she made her own complicated arrangements for him, and it was these precautions that preserved his freedom and probably saved his life when the storm broke in December.

Louis-Napoleon had made a careful analysis of his situation, and had concluded that a coup could not fail. The industrialists and bankers of Paris were supporting him, so he had all the funds he needed. The middle classes were apathetic, and the liberals, radicals, and unaligned working people had few strong leaders. Most of the army's best regiments were loyal to the President; Louis-Napoleon took the additional precaution of bribing key officers and sergeants.

Late on the night of December 1, trustworthy troops rounded up the liberal and radical leaders, including important members of the Assembly, and imprisoned them. This left the people without forceful leaders, although others tried to step into the breach before they, too, were hunted down and arrested.

December 2 was a day of considerable confusion; the forces of Louis-Napoleon consolidated their gains. Before dawn the next morning the loyal regiments erected barricades at key points in Paris. Disorders broke out in four or five places, but the crowds were dispersed. December 4 was known thereafter as the Day of the Massacre. The middle class joined the workingmen in organized opposition to the regime, but their opportunity for rebellion was given no chance. At least four hundred citizens, including women and children, were shot down indiscriminately, while many hundreds of others—possibly two thousand in all—were wounded.

The resistance was halted, the forces of reaction were in complete control of the city, and with the provinces displaying indifference to the events, the President proceeded with his plans to restore the Empire and declare himself Napoleon III.

The part that Victor Hugo played during these excruciating days was truly heroic. On the morning of December 2 he learned that a number of his colleagues had been arrested, and set out from his house to assess the situation for himself. An hour later he met with a group of staunch republican deputies, and took the lead in forming the Committee of Resistance to demand that the coup be met with firm, armed resistance. At first the majority of his colleagues still hoped that bloodshed could be avoided, but later they organized barricades at strategic points of Paris. Assemblyman Jean Baudin was one of the first destined to die on the barricades the next day, with a cry that became famous: "You shall see how a man can die for twenty-five francs (the nickname of the representatives)!"

Juliette Drouet was waiting for Victor when he left the meeting. Soldiers were watching his house, she told him, and another squad had stationed itself near her apartment. It was obvious that he would be arrested if he appeared at either place. That night he slept at the apartment of a theatrical couple, friends of Juliette's. Thanks to her precautions, he moved frequently during the next ten days. Juliette had made all of the necessary arrangements in advance, and her old friends, none of whom Victor had ever known, rallied to the cause. The police did not know where to hunt for him, and Juliette kept him one step ahead of them.

On the night of December 3 a police patrol pounded on the door of Victor's house. Informed that he was not at home, the men insisted on searching the house from attic to cellar. They smashed furniture, stole several items of bric-a-brac, and thoroughly intimidated Adèle and her daughter. Victor subsequently used all of these facts in his campaign against the dictator.

On the afternoon of December 3, he had gone to the Bastille, and horrified by the sight of soldiers and police standing guard at the barricades, had delivered a long, patriotic harangue, in which he had urged them to change sides and join the people of France in their fight against the tyrant.

No authentic account of his speech has survived. The story had been told many times, and Victor's biographers, the enemies of Louis-Napoleon, and many others have written their own versions of the incident. Few accounts tally, and none are identical. Words have been put into Victor Hugo's mouth by posterity. One incident is verified.

Juliette Drouet had been following Victor all day, hovering near him; and when he began his speech she rushed up to him, urging him to desist, crying out, "You'll be shot."

"I am willing to die for the cause of freedom," he shouted, and went on with his speech.

No one knows, down to the present day, why he was not killed. He was recognized, and that may be the clue. Officers in charge of the detachment stationed at the Bastille may have been reluctant to kill so prominent a man, and it may be the authorities were under orders from Louis-Napoleon not to harm him. The man who was about to proclaim himself Emperor had no desire to turn the rest of the civilized world against him. Although on political grounds he might explain away the arrest of Assemblymen and the killing of ordinary citizens, it would be far more difficult to do away with Victor Hugo.

On December 4, Victor ignored his own safety and spent the entire day wandering through the streets of Paris, noting brutalities and storing away the details in his mind. He saw the worst of the fighting at the Porte Saint-Denis, where at least forty people died, and where not one shot was fired at the authorities. Subsequently he told these facts in eye-witness fashion, in his book *Historie d'un crime* (*The Story of a Crime*), excoriating Louis-Napoleon. The death of a small child in the street, in the presence of the boy's grandmother, appeared in a poem, *Souvenir de la nuit du 4*, which achieved wide circulation.

Victor attended countless meetings on December 4 and thereafter, but the opposition had been smashed, Louis-Napoleon's troops were in complete command of the situation, his opponents were helpless. This knowledge did not forestall Victor from trying ceaselessly to organize the foes of the tyrant. Recklessly indifferent to his own fate, he cared only about preventing the coup d'etat.

Juliette tried to calm him, but he would not listen. Finally she made her own arrangements to ensure his safety. A few years earlier in the insurrection of June 1848, in one of his many unpublicized gestures of generosity, Victor had saved the life of a journeyman printer named Jacques-Firmin Lanvin, hiding him in Juliette's apartment.

Juliette remembered, sought out Lanvin, and the debt was repaid. She returned, on December 11, to the apartment in which Victor was hiding, carrying Lanvin's passport. She also brought a complete outfit of laborer's clothes. Victor thought it was cowardly to escape from France in disguise, but Juliette gave him no choice. For the better part of the two decades they had been together, she had seldom opposed him, but now she was adamant, demanding that he follow her instructions.

Unless he agreed, she said, he would never see her again.

Victor hesitated, then capitulated.

Juliette's bluff worked. She had sensed his deep dependency on her, and had used that to win her point. But, if had he refused, she told him in subsequent letters, she would have been forced to back down.

She had made all the arrangements for his future. He was to take a night train to Brussels, where he would be met the following morning. He would be hidden there for twenty-four hours, a week, or a month, however long might be necessary, until he could emerge again and issue a clarion call for freedom. She herself would follow him to Brussels within forty-eight hours.

There were many in Paris who assumed that Victor had died in the massacre on the fourth, and even the authorities seemed to be uncertain. Juliette argued that Victor was taking few risks, and it was unlikely that he would be arrested as he tried to depart.

That night a workingman in soiled clothes shuffled into the Gare du Nord, carrying a small bundle. His hair was graying, he walked with a stoop, there were smudges on his face and his fingernails were dirty, an authentic touch added by Juliette. His passport said that his name was Jacques-Firmin Lanvin, and he gave his vocation as typesetter. If questioned, he was to say that he was traveling to visit his elderly mother, a Belgian.

He bought a seat in the third-class section of the train, settled himself on the hard bench, and did not bother to look out of the window as the train left Paris. The police came through the cars at the border, and the shabby man, eating a sausage sandwich redolent of garlic, reached with a greasy hand for his passport. The official merely glanced at it before handing it back to him. The train crossed the border, and Victor Hugo was free.

It may be that Juliette's superb planning was responsible for her lover's easy escape, but there is another possibility, one that has been neither proved nor disproved in the past one hundred twenty years, although subject to considerable speculation. Victor may have been under surveillance, so that Louis-Napoleon knew he was trying to escape, and deliberately allowed him to leave. An imprisoned Victor Hugo would become a martyr, and the forces opposed to the new, self-proclaimed monarch would have a cause, a celebrated person around whom they could rally.

Victor Hugo in exile, Louis-Napoleon may have reasoned, would be relatively harmless, another puny voice crying out from the far side of France's borders. Louis knew from his own experience that few people and fewer governments paid much attention to impotent exiles.

If that was the new Emperor's tactic, it was one of his worst miscalculations. The pen of Victor Hugo, he would ultimately discover, could shake the world.

Chapter IX

*J*ULIETTE DROUET won the contest for Victor Hugo's affections by default; her fidelity and persistence were responsible for her victory. Certainly her thoughtful loyalty to her lover was remarkable. Thanks to a letter she had sent to Laure Luthereau, an old actor friend now managing a theater in Brussels, Victor was met on his arrival, and was taken to quarters Luthereau had found for him. Two days later, according to plan, Juliette herself reached Brussels, bringing with her several large suitcases that contained his most precious possessions, his unpublished manuscripts. Thousands of other republicans were also fleeing across the border, among them Louis Blanc. Alexandre Dumas was already there, in flight from his creditors rather than from the new dictator, Napoleon III.

Adèle, meanwhile, remained in Paris, and each day Léonie called on her at the elegant house in Montmarte.

There they wept together. Léonie because she had lost her campaign, and because, although she could only dimly peer into the future, she rightly suspected she would never see Victor again. Adèle's grief was more complicated: she had gloried in his political exploits, and felt that his flight into exile had disgraced her. In the months to come she would enjoy posing in a new role, that of the bereft and abandoned wife of a poverty-stricken refugee, and she relished the attention paid her by Victor's friends.

Victor gave up a great deal by leaving France. He had been earning royalties of sixty to seventy thousand francs per year, and new laws, quickly promulgated by Napoleon III, prohibited sending any sums to proscribed persons living abroad. Contrary to the impression that Adèle tried to create, however, he was far from penniless. He had invested large sums of money abroad over the years, and the interest enabled him to support two small households in Brussels, his own and Juliette's.

After trying several inexpensive hotels and finding them wanting, Victor settled in a comfortable suite on the Grande Place, by far the best address in Brussels. More conscious than ever of the proprieties of the time, he could not permit Juliette to live with him openly, and she agreed that his dignity would be impaired if his mistress resided with him. So she stayed with the Luthereau family, and, as compensation, Victor hired a lady's maid, one Suzanne, to look after her. Suzanne was a plain, energetic country girl, and she remained their devoted servant until the end of Juliette's life, many years later, when Victor retired her on a pension.

Having disposed of the social amenities, Victor returned to his writing with a vigor he had not demonstrated in years. But it was the political situation rather than the need to earn a living that preoccupied him. He regarded Napoleon III as a monster, and was eager to share his views with the world, particularly the people of France.

Writing with an impassioned fury, he started to work less than twenty-four hours after his arrival in Brussels. He wrote the story of the rise of Napoleon III, concentrating on the coup of December 2, and the words poured out of him in a torrent. In less than five months he completed a book so immense that, when finally published in later years, it required two volumes.

His immediate problem was that of finding a publisher. Imprisonment awaited anyone in France who accepted the task, so Victor deliberately refrained from trying to obtain a publisher there for the work he called *Histoire d'un crime* (*History of a Crime*). To his intense disappointment, he could persuade no publisher in Belgium, Holland, or England to handle the book, either. Many years would pass before the world would be treated to the remarkable prose poem that, in its intensity of feeling and sharply controlled language, was one of his finest exercises in self-disciplined composition.

Undaunted by his inability to find a publisher for this book, Victor promptly went to work on another, shorter book, which he entitled *Napoléon le Petit*. A diatribe that exposed the new ruler of France as a petty tyrant lacking any ability, it exposed Napoleon III as a grubby, scheming cheat. The most astonishing aspect of this predictable work is that Victor wrote it in a single month.

Making no attempt to find a publisher, he had the

book printed at his own expense in London. At his express demand it was issued on very thin paper, and a number of his fellow exiles in Brussels cooperated with him in disseminating the book. Copies were hidden inside hollow busts of Napoleon III, and were smuggled into France by the thousands before the ruse was discovered.

Napoléon le Petit sold openly in the Low Countries and Great Britain, and achieved considerable popularity. Victor's financial records show that the sale in these lands almost repaid the printing costs, and he was content. For the first time since he had become a professional author, he had not written for money.

Before the book was distributed, however, he felt it necessary to take steps for the protection of his family. Both of his sons had been released from prison at the end of their short terms, as had Auguste Vacquerie, and he was afraid they would be rearrested if they remained in the country after *Napoléon le Petit* appeared. A new law further complicated the situation: the property of an exile who fomented against the crown could be confiscated, and Victor owned considerable property.

So he wrote to Adèle, giving her specific instructions. She was directed to sell the lease on the house in Montmarte, and was to hold an auction in which she would dispose of furniture, bric-a-brac, everything that could be moved, in fact, except clothing and books. Loving his library of almost ten thousand volumes, Victor told his wife to give the books to several friends, ostensibly as gifts. Then, when he some day returned to France, he could reclaim them.

Adèle was delighted to get rid of ornate furnishings, suits of armor, and all the other bulky, expensive objects she loathed. Books meant nothing to her, so she sold the library at auction, too, an act that permanently deepened the marital rift in the Hugo household. She obtained comparatively little in her transactions.

Not until late July 1853, when Charles Hugo arrived in Brussels with word that the rest of the family had also left France and that all the property had been sold, did Victor permit the appearance of *Napoléon le Petit*. The Belgian authorities, several of whom were his great admirers, made it plain to him that he would become *persona non grata* in the country when the book appeared. No matter how great their personal respect for him, it was imperative that tiny Belgium remain on good terms with France.

So Victor left Brussels immediately and, accompanied by Charles, Juliette Drouet, and her maid, went to London. He remained there for only three days, and found the city "alien to me," as Juliette indicated in her journal. He did not consider himself a stranger in the English capital, but insisted that the city did not suit him. Even in exile, with his income limited, no new books bringing in royalties and many mouths to feed, Victor neither thought nor behaved like an impoverished refugee. In spite of the battering he had absorbed, his ego was intact.

After seventy-two hours in London, the little party went off to the Channel Isle of Jersey, located within sight of the French coast. The choice of a new home, Victor thought, was inspired. Once the summer residence of William the Conqueror, Jersey maintained a point of view that was unique. Her people were bilingual, in the main, and spoke, read, and wrote French as well as English. It was their conviction that they, together with some assorted compatriots from the French mainland, had conquered England in 1066 A.D., and they insisted that they were independent subjects of Queen Victoria, owing allegiance to her, but not as the monarch of Britain. Eventually Victor would also discover that they were a straight-laced people who lived rigidly moral lives.

At first glance, however, he and Juliette were delighted with what they saw. Winds swept clouds away from the island, and the sun shone most of the time. Vegetables, fruits, and flowers grew in profusion, and the natives were proud of their beef and dairy products, which the refugees found delicious.

Victor immediately rented a furnished house, called Marine Terrace, that overlooked the sea. It had a large sundeck on three sides, a greenhouse crowded with exotic plants, and, most important, enough bedrooms so that each member of the family could have his or her own chamber. There were several guest rooms as well, which meant that visitors from Paris could be accommodated.

Separate quarters had to be found for Juliette, in accordance with the time-honored formula she and Victor observed, and they rented an apartment about two hundred yards down the road. From her living room windows Juliette could see her lover pacing his sundeck—and engaging in eccentric activities there that soon made him the island's principal tourist attraction.

While the details of housing were being settled, Adèle arrived in Southampton, accompanied by François-Victor, young Adèle, and the ever-faithful Auguste Vacquerie. They had expected to go on to London, but instead found letters from Victor and Charles awaiting them, and it was from these communications that Adèle learned of Juliette's presence in Jersey.

The outraged wife decided the time had come to make a stand, and she wrote Victor a letter, telling him she would not join him as long as his mistress remained on the island.

Victor's reply was as brief as it was unruffled. He wrote:

I have provided you with a comfortable home here, and trust you will join me in it. If you choose otherwise, the responsibility rests solely with you. But I am compelled to inform you that, should you elect to absent yourself, I lack the funds to enable you to live elsewhere.

Adèle stubbornly stayed on in Southampton for the better part of a week, hating every moment of the sojourn. The weather was damp and muggy, and she found the English cooking unpalatable. Finally she capitulated, swallowed her pride, and went off on the twice-weekly packet boat to Jersey.

The need for money was obvious, and there was only one possible source, so Victor returned to his writing. Quickly establishing a new regimen, he followed it as though he had never known any other life. He arose each day at dawn, and took a quick dip in the sea, which astonished the natives and horrified the members of his own family, most of whom had hated and feared the water ever since Léopoldine had been drowned. Then he went to a study that he had established for himself on the top floor, overlooking the sea, and wrote unceasingly until noon.

Promptly at that hour he went to the sundeck, where he stripped, doused himself with several buckets of cold sea water, and massaged himself with a pair of rough gloves. Although the house was located on a relatively isolated section of the coastline, anyone who happened to be in the vicinity could watch him perform his strange ablutions, and word quickly spread.

The natives came to watch one or twice, and the tourists from England, who visited Jersey because of the sun and cheap prices, were fascinated. Victor literally didn't care who watched his bath. The English and Jerseymen were free people, he said, and it was their right to go where they pleased. "It is my right," he added in a note to Juliette, "to bathe where I please on my own property."

The Jerseymen were more amused than annoyed by Victor's idiosyncrasy, but were deeply perturbed by his open affair with Juliette. Each day, following his bath in the open, he went to the apartment of his mistress. There he dined with her, bedded her, and, before escorting her on a long walk along the seacoast, dictated correspondence to her and discussed the copying of his current manuscript. Juliette was now his only secretary, and performed the task so efficiently that, for the rest of her life, he never hired anyone else for the purpose.

Shortly before sundown, refreshed by his sojourn, Victor returned to Marine Terrace and retired to his study, where he worked for two hours before sitting down with his family to a long, leisurely dinner. He dominated the conversation, which was sometimes spiced with bitter quarrels with Adèle. The Hugo sons and Auguste took it upon themselves to act as peacemakers, and young Adèle, who seemed to become more morose and listless each day, usually burst into tears.

After dinner, a feast complete with several wines,

Victor returned to his study, and worked until midnight or later. Then he retired to his bedroom, which was carefully separated from Adèle's quarters by the rooms of his children and Auguste. Presumably he enjoyed a few hours of rest before returning to his labors.

In the autumn of 1853, a few months after the Hugo family settled in Jersey, they were visited by an old friend, Mme. Émile de Girardin, an ardent republican whom Victor had known as Delphine Gay, prior to her marriage. She brought with her a new parlor game that was popular in Paris, and this seemingly innocent pastime disrupted Victor's work schedules for months.

The game was table-tipping, or communing with the spirits of the departed, and at first Victor denounced the whole idea as rubbish. Mme. de Girardin could not persuade the spirits to cooperate with her, and one evening managed to induce Victor to join in the game. Auguste wrote about the incident in detail to relatives in France.

A spirit responded to Mme. de Girardin's summons, he said, but behaved crazily, refusing to reply to questions.

Victor took over the interrogation, asking questions that were witty, irreverent, and intellectual.

The spirit continued to reply erratically, and something in the nature of the table tipping convinced Mme. de Girardin that unplumbed depths needed to be explored. "Are you the spirit to whom we have been speaking?"

The table tipped sharply. "N-o."

"Who are you?" she asked.

"L-é-o-p-o-l-d-i-n-e."

The reply was so startling that Adèle fainted, and her surviving daughter became hysterical.

G

Victor put a hand over his eyes, bowed his head, and was so shaken he did not speak for at least five minutes. Thereafter he asked so many questions he kept the table tipping madly for hours.

That was the beginning of a mania that lasted for months. Victor spoke at length to the spirits of his father, his brother, his mother, and his step-mother. He summoned the shades of everyone he had ever known who was now deceased. His enthusiasm was so fierce, so contagious that the rest of the family was equally affected.

Now he began table-tipping immediately after eating a light breakfast. He forgot the existence of the long-suffering Juliette, and failed to keep appointments with her. Table-tipping was the sole pastime through the afternoon, and the family had to be forced to halt for dinner, then resumed the sport.

Adèle was the first to regain a healthy skepticism, and returned to sanity when her husband, tiring of communication with the dead, began to speak with the spirits of the living. This could be achieved, he claimed, when a living person was asleep. The climax came late one night when he talked at length with the spirit of Napoleon III, who was supposedly slumbering in his bed. Victor wanted to know what the dictator really thought of him, and the spirit answered that Napoleon felt great admiration and respect for him.

That finished Adèle.

But her husband continued to play the table-tipping game until the urgent need to earn a living intervened. Then he gave up the sport completely. Something had disillusioned him, but he refused to tell anyone what had happened, and not even to Juliette would he admit that he had been gullible.

The entire family was relieved when Victor gave up the childish game. He himself had been drained by the activity, which also imposed severe emotional strains on Charles and young Adèle. "My own sanity threatened to give way," the son wrote to a friend in Paris, "when my father held long dialogues on theology with the shade of none other than Jesus Christ."

Victor regained neither his perspective nor his sense of humor on the subject until the family left Jersey after a two-year sojourn. Then, finally, he told a friend:

I am probably the only person now alive who has discussed the nature of the Godhead with none other than the Holy Ghost himself. It was an edifying experience, principally because I discovered that He and I were in total agreement—in all of our views. Were I a devout man, relatively blameless in my private life, I believe I would qualify, at the very least, for the red hat of a cardinal. Alas, I am a sinner, so I must keep the gist of these talks to myself. No one would believe they were ever held, and, do you know, I strongly doubt their veracity myself.

The bread that appeared on the tipped table in Jersey was earned by a volume of poetry that Victor called *Les Châtiments.* Not yet finished with Napoleon III, he attacked the Emperor in satiric verse, and the volume soon became known as "six thousand lines of insults."

Probably no one but Victor Hugo could have written this extraordinary book. He concentrated on one subject, yet presented his case in almost innumerable ways, from separate and distinct angles and viewpoints, his mood varying from fiery denunciation to lofty, almost remote ridicule. He was writing in the great tradition of Rabelais, Molière, and Voltaire, and *Les Châtiments* compares favorably with the satiric verse of Victor's great predecessors.

The book ends on a note of hope. The French Revolution was not forgotten, Victor declared. He himself had not forgotten it, nor had millions of his compatriots, who still believed man was capable of achieving progress, and that liberty, equality, and fraternity were not idle words.

Victor had no difficulty in obtaining a publisher for the book, which was unaccountably deemed less offensive than a volume of prose. A fellow exile, now living in Brussels, paid him an advance royalty of seventy-five thousand francs. He was now sufficiently solvent to indulge in one of his favorite pastimes, that of publishing a newspaper, and provided the funds for a publication known as *Les Hommes de l'exil* that was written and edited by his sons and Auguste Vacquerie.

Copies of *Les Châtiments* had to be smuggled into France, but there were so many travelers willing to carry a few copies in their luggage and concealed on their persons that it was easy to outwit the customs agents at the borders. The French bought copies by the thousands, and although the methods of distribution were irregular and large sums of money were siphoned off, Victor eventually earned an additional fifty thousand francs in royalties.

International events complicated the life of the distinguished exile. In 1854 Napoleon III paid a visit to London, where he not only worked out a closer alliance with England, but succeeded in charming the naive Queen Victoria. Her government, pleased by the growing amity with France, arranged for her to make a return visit later in the year.

This infuriated Victor, as it did the sixty or seventy other prominent French refugees living in Jersey. The newspaper remained silent until the Queen actually left for Paris, and then Charles Hugo unleashed a violent broadside, attacking the British Crown.

This was too much for the authorities of liberal Jersey, and the publication was suspended. Its editors were told that it would be appreciated if they moved elsewhere, but the delicate hints were ignored.

Victor felt that he had been personally challenged, and he responded in kind, writing a declaration that attacked not only Victoria and her regime, but scalded the intolerant regime in Jersey.

The assault could not be ignored; on October 27, 1855, Victor received notice that he and his sons were required to leave the island within one week. Failure to reply to the demand would result in imprisonment.

Adèle wept and took to her bed. Juliette Drouet, always resourceful, knew how to solve the problem, and already had a solution in hand. She had been corresponding with the authorities of another nearby Channel isle under British jurisdiction, Guernsey. The lieutenant-governor there was willing to allow the Hugo family to take up residence on the island provided that neither Victor, his sons, nor Auguste Vacquerie took any action that might be construed as interference in either British or local politics.

On October 31, Victor sailed to Guernsey, accompanied by François-Victor, Juliette, and her maid. Word of his impending arrival had preceded him, and he was given some idea of the regard in which he was held everywhere when he came ashore. A crowd of about two hundred persons greeted him silently, the men removing their hats in tribute to him, the women curtsying. He and his son went to one boarding house, Juliette and her maid to another, and the task of finding a permanent dwelling began immediately, in earnest.

Victor was tired of living in rented quarters, and also reasoned that, if he became a property owner, it would be much more difficult to expel him. Also he had an unexpected cash windfall that made it easier for him to move into a home of his own.

Over the years he had been writing lyric poetry that had never been published, and he now proposed to bring out a two-volume book of more than eleven thousand lines, which he called *Les Contemplations*. None of the poems were political in nature, so there would be no reason for the French to ban the work. He and his publisher could earn legitimate royalties in that country.

The same publisher who had made such a success of *Les Châtiments* paid him twenty thousand francs, sight unseen, as a first advance payment for *Les Contemplations*. Therefore he had enough money in hand to buy a dwelling worthy of the style he loved. Hauteville House, a magnificent four-story dwelling, was the answer to his need. It was a manor overlooking the sea, with spacious grounds and a beautiful garden; there were eight or nine so-called public rooms, at least a dozen bedchambers, and best of all, on the top floor, a glass-enclosed solarium with a sea view. The surf pounded at the cliffs below the house, and Victor envisioned himself transforming the room into a study.

Hauteville House appeared to have been made for him. In the so-called Oak Gallery on the ground floor, for example, the paneled walls and pillars were of oak so intricately carved that it had taken skilled artisans several years to complete their task. The floor was inlaid with rare woods, and even the ceiling was carved.

Strolling with Juliette in the immediate neighborhood, Victor discovered a lovely little villa no more than a stone's throw from the manor house. It was called La Fallue, and Juliette fell in love with the place on sight. Victor immediately bought it for her, putting the deed in her name, and then returned to Hauteville House, which he purchased on the spot for ten thousand francs in cash.

When his son, Charles, reached Guernsey a few days later, Victor was already buying oversized furnishings and bric-a-brac, sending to London for the thousands of books that would make up his new library, and otherwise enjoying himself. He was installed in Hauteville House and Juliette had moved into La Fallue by the time that Adèle, her daughter, and Auguste arrived, bringing thirty-five large steamer trunks and uncounted crates of other belongings. Victor's unpublished manuscripts, notes, and other papers were loaded into one large crate, and he personally supervised the installation of these documents in his new study.

Hauteville House, which is maintained just as it was in Victor's own day, has become a shrine for all Hugo worshippers, and must be seen if one is to believe the incredible style in which the master of the written word lived. The baroque furniture is massive, there are rich tapestries and richer drapes everywhere; the rugs, imported from Turkey and North Africa, are of fantastically intricate design. Expensive paintings line the walls, gold and silver plate are on exhibit everywhere, and the bric-a-brac, ranging from inlaid porcelain peacocks to polished brass cannon four feet high, overflows in every room.

The wine cellar, when Victor lived in Hauteville House, contained more than five thousand bottles, all of them selected personally by the master. The dining room, redone according to Victor's instructions, was—and is—spectacular. A fireplace and the mantel above it are decorated with a magnificent design in Delft china, forming a mammoth letter H. At the opposite side of the room is a huge carved armchair, in Gothic style, which Victor fondly called his "ancestral chair." Across the back, in large, Gothic letters, was inscribed, *Ego Hugo.* No one, including the master himself, ever sat in this chair.

"It is contrary to the traditions of my family," Victor said, and Auguste reported to his relatives that this comment was repeated so frequently that Victor soon believed it himself, blithely ignoring the fact that he had invented the tradition.

The ceiling and walls of the main salon, located on the second floor, were covered with a gold lamé cloth that had been made for Queen Christina of Sweden. Around the main fireplace, seemingly supporting it, stand four gilded statues holding a canopy of beaten gold, a Renaissance masterpiece imported by Victor from Florence. The room also still contains a superb table of inlaid ivory that was presented to King Charles II by the Duke of Buckingham, and a tapestry screen that was embroidered by Mme. de Pompadour.

According to tradition, some of the carving in the Oak

Gallery was done by Victor himself, but this story is probably apocryphal. There is no evidence that he ever carved in wood. One of the sights on the third floor is a handsome guest room, which Victor called the "Chamber of Garibaldi," after the great Italian patriot, whom he asked to visit him. Garibaldi was unable to acept the invitation, unfortunately, being occupied elsewhere, and therefore never slept in the huge, Gothic canopied bed that Victor ordered made for the room.

Contrasting strangely with all of this splendor is Victor's solarium workroom, which resembled a monastic cell. Plain curtains of unbleached linen were pushed back from the windows, and a small, plain rug covered the center of the floor. A hinged slab of wood could be let down from one wall to make the desk at which Victor stood while writing. Adjacent to it, on a sturdy stand of unpainted wood was an inkwell, which, on close examination, proved to be an old, chipped water tumbler. Neat racks, placed within reach, held unused copy paper and, beyond them, sheets on which Victor had written.

On the inner wall stood a cot, and within a short time after moving into Hauteville House, Victor began to sleep there every night. In that way he could return to work instantly if he awakened during the night. There were two small chairs, lacking arms, with cane-bottomed seats, and a worn stool that, the author like to claim, had been made by his great-grandfather. Adjacent to the main room was a tiny dressing closet containing two battered wardrobes, in which Victor kept his clothes. There were no ornaments, no bric-a-brac, nothing to disturb the contemplations of a man who wrote for his living.

"I always rise before the cannon on the fort awakens the rest of the island," Victor boasted, and his claim was true. He awakened at 5:00 A.M., and lighting one of the two oil lamps in the room, rang for the cold water he used for washing. A quarter of an hour later he was at work, eating no breakfast and sipping only a large mug of cold coffee. At Hauteville House his work regimen was even more strict than it had been elsewhere. Under no circumstances did he permit himself to end his day's labor until he had written either one hundred lines of poetry or twenty pages of prose. On days when the words refused to flow—rare days, by his candid admission—he kept himself figuratively chained to his desk until late at night.

It was this room, more than any other part of Hauteville House that was Victor's real home for the better part of two decades. He built a small sundeck beyond it, and there maintained the habit of taking cold baths at noon that he had formed in Jersey. It could not have been accidental that Juliette could again watch his ablutions, this time from her private sitting room in La Fallue.

At noon, on alternate days, he either ate at Juliette's villa or with his family. Regardless of where he ate, however, the afternoons always belonged to Juliette, and Victor permitted nothing to interfere. Even the presence of distinguished guests could not prevent him from seeing his mistress.

It was the life of an exile, first in Jersey and then in Guernsey, that made Victor a monogamist again. He had few opportunities, and no desire to stray; his wild years were behind him, and he was as faithful to Juliette as she was to him.

It was in this atmosphere of unaccustomed serenity that Victor edited the poems that soon would appear in *Les Contemplations*. Juliette had become his complete confidante, and on the days he did not eat his noon meal with her, he dined with her in the evening. They had become virtually inseparable, and *Les Contemplations* reflects his new-found calm.

The book was divided into two volumes, the first containing poems written between 1834 and 1843, the year of Léopoldine's death, the second his later work. Victor adapted, reworked, and changed most of the poems that were published in *Les Contemplations*.

Published in Brussels in 1856, the book sold widely in France, the Low Countries, England, the Italian states, Switzerland, and Germany. Everywhere it was hailed as a masterpiece, and Victor was rightly acclaimed as the greatest lyric poet of the century, and one of the greatest who had ever lived. Rarely had any poet achieved such purity of conception, execution, and style.

Each of the poems in *Les Contemplations* appears to be personal, one man's individual reactions to his environment. When viewed in the aggregate, however, a larger and far more grand pattern emerges. Victor's concern was not merely himself; he explored the nature of humankind, and searched for an understanding, in depth, of man's relationship with God.

What, he inquired, was the nature of God? The destiny of man was determined by his ability to comprehend, assimilate, and bow before the altar of the Almighty. Man's acceptance of God's will was paramount, and one succeeded or failed in the search for happiness in accordance with his willingness to subject himself to the disciplines of that will. Similarly, he explored the source of evil, that, he declared, could be conquered by man, under God.

Les Contemplations contained a number of Victor's finest love poems, most of them written to Juliette, but even in these he moved beyond the realm of the purely personal. Even while saluting the beauty of an individual woman and celebrating because of the joy she gave him, he studied the relationship of that woman and that man to God.

He also explored the forces of external nature. Most were kind to man, and could be utilized for his good. Only the sea was excepted, and its fury could inspire terror. The sea, he declared, could be cruel beyond measure. He still suffered intense grief over the drowning of Léopoldine. At the same time he made heroic efforts to understand why Léopoldine had been deprived of her life. Had her death been accidental, which made it stupid and meaningless, or had it been in accord with God's design, beyond the comprehension of mortals?

Perhaps the most celebrated of the poems in *Les Contemplations* was "A Villequier," which was written after Victor had visited his daughter's grave in the village of Villequier. It is a lyric elegy of unsurpassed beauty, and was recognized, immediately upon publication, as one of the greatest poems ever written in the French language. Deceptively simple, it explores the mysteries of death and of nature, of man's religious faith, as well as the grief of a loving father whose sorrow knows no respite. Intellect and emotion combine, intertwine, and separate in "A Villequier." Even Victor's harshest critics freely admitted that he had composed a masterpiece. One of them called it "a symphony of grief."

A few of Victor's enemies criticized *Les Contemplations* because the poet developed no new, central philosophical theme. But when Victor read their comments in the Paris newspapers that were delivered to him regularly, he merely smiled and made no public reply. In a letter to Gautier, however, he expressed himself succinctly:

I believe it is the place of the poet to inquire about God, nature and man, in that order, and to probe, where he can, into the recesses where the bonds that tie the three together are hidden. It is not the function of the poet to expound, to warm and revitalize the philosophical concepts of others in such a way as to re-cast them in a mold that others will call new. Because God is good to me, I am a poet, and do not pretend to be a philosopher.

He could afford to look down his nose at his foes. It had been his intention to overwhelm the literary world with his two-volume work, and he had succeeded admirably, even beyond his own high expectations. After the publication of *Les Châtiments* he had been called a political pamphleteer who had chosen to write jingles, but the authors of such cruel assessments were effectively silenced now.

Perhaps the most remarkable result of the publication of *Les Contemplations* in Brussels was the failure of the French government to ban the work. A decree signed by Napoleon III or one of his subservient ministers would have made the sale of the book illegal in France, and would have deprived Victor of important revenues. But no such action was taken. Victor was delighted when he received a letter from Dumas, who had long since returned to Paris, telling him that the Emperor kept a copy of the two-volume set in his bedroom and was reading it. According to Dumas's story, which may or may not have been the product of his own lively imagination, he had seized an opportunity to sneak into the Emperor's bedroom when invited to a reception at the Tuileries, and had himself examined the dog-eared copy on Napoleon III's bedside table.

Whatever the reason, the royalties that *Les Contemplations* earned in France, forwarded by his Brussels publisher, enabled Victor to live as expensively as ever. It also made possible his unyielding opposition to the man he considered a petty tyrant and the foe of all human liberty.

Chapter
X

VICTOR HUGO, alert and robust, reached the peak of his literary powers during his long sojourn in Guernsey. His reputation is based, in the main, on the books he wrote there. Certainly his vitality was amazing, and, except for an attack of boils in late 1858 and early 1859, his health was excellent.

He himself attributed his physical condition to the life he was leading, and to some extent he was right. The efficacy of his cold water baths in the open air might be questioned, but not his swimming or his daily walks. No matter what the weather, he spent two hours every afternoon hiking briskly along the seacoast of Guernsey, often climbing some of the steep rocks that studded the shore. More often than not he was accompanied by Juliette, although she remained at home when the weather was bad. Victor allowed nothing to deter him, however, and the people of Guernsey thought he was mad when he blithely went into the open during ferocious Channel gales.

He must have been healthy; his prodigious appetites for food and drink would have killed a lesser man. Despite his breakfast of cold coffee, he more than compensated later in the day. He thought of his noon repast as a "light meal," usually beginning with a paté, then omelet or fish, followed by the main course, which was a roast of beef, lamb, pork, or veal. With it were served potatoes and several vegetables, and a salad invariably followed. He became fond of English puddings, and frequently ate one at noon, then ended the meal with slices of three or four kinds of cheese. A different wine was served with each course, and Victor rarely drank less than two glasses of each.

At night he consumed the big meal of the day, regardless of whether he dined with Juliette or shared it with his wife and family. Seafood was plentiful in Guernsey, and Victor developed a prodigious appetite for oysters and mussels, usually eating a dozen or two of one or the other as a first course. Then he enjoyed a hearty soup, one of his favorites being a peasant dish of yellow peas and sausages that Juliette made for him herself. A fish course of which he never tired was boiled or broiled lobster, and he usually managed to down two of them, chewing the shells as well as the lobster meat. Roasted stuffed chicken, served with tiny Guernsey new potatoes and peas, was on the menu several nights each week, and Victor ate a young chicken unaided. The main course was meat, and he developed a craving for a rich English dish, Beef Wellington, which he ate frequently. There was always a large salad, followed by a rich dessert, Victor's favorite being a chocolate mousse with brandy sauce. He ended his meal by eating four to six oranges, which he did not bother to peel. And at night, as at noon, a different wine was served with each course.

It was small wonder that visitors took back to Paris or London a variety of tales about this incredible man, who was both a gourmet and a gourmand. What surprised everyone was that, though he had unquestionably put on weight, he was not fat. His rigorous daily exercise kept him trim, although he was now in his late fifties.

Visitors were also fascinated by the literary and artistic atmosphere of Hauteville House. Everyone was busy. François-Victor, who had mastered English, translated the plays of Shakespeare into French. A number of his efforts became accepted, in time, as the standard translations. Charles composed novels, poetry, and critical essays that were published in Brussels and Geneva. Young Adèle was a musician, and spent hours at her piano each day, composing études and symphonies. Auguste wrote plays, two or three of which subsequently enjoyed modest success.

Even Adèle was busy. Victor required so many copies of his work that Juliette could take on no additional duties, and he would allow no one else to perform this important task. Adèle could handle his correspondence, which was heavy and now spreading throughout the world, so he dictated his letters to her.

The reaction of George Sand was typical. After paying a visit to Victor at Hauteville House, she declared, "There are no idle hands begging for the intervention of the devil at the Maison Hugo. Victor is the grand master of a literary factory!"

In this atmosphere, Victor followed the success of *Les Contemplations* with another literary triumph, *La Légende des siècles*. A huge work of epic poetry in the great medieval tradition, it was published in 1859 in Brussels, a scant three years after the appearance of the earlier masterpiece. Victor's critics were stunned. His versatility was unbelievable, and no one able to read French could deny his genius.

It was Victor's intention, as he stated in his preface, to deal with "successive imprints of the human profile, from date to date, from Eve, mother of men, to the Revolution, mother of peoples." Not satisfied with this lofty ambition, he added still another; to present "the drama of creation lighted up by the visage of the creator," and planned to combine history, philosophy, and theology in a single poetic whole.

He did not, however, intend his theme to be accepted literally, and he left many blanks in history, omitting almost all of Greece and much of Rome, skipping lightly over the Middle Ages, and dwelling only briefly on the long reign of Louis XIV, whom he regarded as a tyrant. Even so, *La Légende* was so complex that he could not say all that he wished in the one work, and added to it in two additional books over the ensuing twenty years.

Victor began with the Bible, opening with the stories of Adam and Eve and Cain and Abel. In them he created sublime poetic moods, and utilized his gifts to create sharp, dramatic impact. His instinct was unfailing and he unerringly selected incidents such as the defeat of the Spanish Armada by a fleet of tiny British ships, to heighten his drama.

The lyricism that made *Les Contemplations* a great work of art was muted in *La Légende*. It is so different in mood, tenor, and approach that someone unfamiliar with the authorship might well think it had been penned by another man. Rarely has any artist given a performance of such virtuosity.

La Légende won for Victor a more widespread fame. Newspapers of many countries pointedly emphasized that Hugo was a refugee, and the thin-skinned Napoleon III was more chagrined than ever. The would-be dictator was at the height of his power and could not tolerate the idea that the world considered him a crude politician. Something had to be done.

Believing his foes impotent, he made a grand gesture. A royal proclamation was published, and under its terms a general amnesty was declared. All political acts against the regime were forgiven, all political exiles were free to come home, and the Emperor gave his solemn promise that no reprisals would be taken against them.

The refugees soon filled the trains and boats. They came from every direction. Tearful, joyous family reunions took place every day in every Paris railroad station, and these touching scenes were duly recorded by the newspapers the regime supported. Statesmen and artists, politicians and writers returned to France by the hundreds.

There was one notable exception. The most prominent of the fish Napoleon III had hoped to land not only eluded the royal net, but trumpeted his defiance to the world. Victor Hugo remained adamant, and issued a statement:

I have been informed that, if I wish, I may return to the land of my birth and that no reprisals will be taken against me. I am assured, also, that it will be my privilege to say and to write what I wish.

I entertain no fears for my own safety, or that of those who are dear to me. Even a bumbling tyrant would not revoke his word and thereby incur the scornful wrath of the world. I take my stand for higher reasons, for sacred reasons.

I grappled with this issue in the pages of Les Châtiments, *and in that book I gave my pledge. I swore that I would remain in exile until the end, either my own or that of Napoléon le Petit. My position remains unchanged.*

I shall share to the end the exile of Liberty. When Liberty returns, I shall return.

This courageous position, taken for the sake of principle, won Victor the respect of millions throughout the world. "His voice," the New York *Tribune* said, "is that of free men everywhere."

"We are proud," the *Times* of London declared, "that Victor Hugo elects to live on British soil, which is enriched and nourished by his presence."

The people of France responded in their own way, and copies of his work vanished from the bookstalls faster than the publishers in Brussels could replenish them. Napoleon III had lost another round in the long-range battle, and was furious but powerless. He tried to persuade Queen Victoria and her government to send the exile packing, but was rebuffed. Even if Victoria herself still sympathized with Napoleon, which was doubtful, no British monarch could snub the world's most diligent champion of freedom.

It had not been easy for Victor to take his intransigent stand, and even his admirers did not know he had been subjected to almost intolerable pressures. Adèle was heartily sick of living in exile, and bombarded her husband with demands that the family return to France. François-Victor, Charles, and Auguste were eager to build their own reputations, which was impossible while living under the roof of the great man in remote Guernsey.

Young Adèle's problem was more delicate. The girl showed symptoms of the melancholy that had destroyed her uncle and afflicted her sister. There were few distractions in rural Guernsey, and two physicians, one of them a specialist summoned from London, indicated that her health might improve in Paris.

Even Juliette hinted that she found life in Guernsey somewhat less than idyllic, and that she would rejoice if Victor chose to go home.

Unmoved and unyielding, Victor stood firm. But the strain, combined with the weariness induced by the pace of his work in recent years, took an unexpected toll. One morning, while standing at his desk in October 1859, he suddenly collapsed.

Adèle could not rouse him, and was so panic-stricken that she sent for Juliette Drouet. For the first time the wife and mistress of Victor Hugo were not only under the same roof, but bent together over his prostrate body.

Guernsey boasted the presence of three physicians on the island; all three hurried to Hauteville House. A thorough examination of the distinguished patient revealed that nothing organic was wrong with him. They agreed that he was suffering from exhaustion, and prescribed a holiday free of all cares.

Victor sat up, drank a water tumbler filled with

brandy, and announced that he would take Juliette to the tiny, nearby island of Sark for a protracted vacation. They left the next day, engaged the so-called royal suite in Sark's only hotel, and spent ten uninterrupted weeks there. The sojourn could not have been much of a vacation for Juliette, who had her hands full. It was her duty to make certain that Victor neither wrote nor thought about his work.

Very little is known about this ten-week period, principally because Juliette took away all pens and paper, and confiscated fresh supplies whenever Victor managed to acquire them. She saw to it that he ate sensibly and slept long hours. Sark being too small for the protracted walks he enjoyed, she introduced him to the joys of fishing and boating, though fishing bored her and she was fearful whenever they set out into the autumn seas of the English Channel in a tiny boat. Her unlimited patience and devotion saw her through the interminable two and one-half months. There must have been times when she wished she didn't have her mercurial lover all to herself.

Victor recovered his habitual vigor and zest for life on Sark. He had forgotten during the years of his exile that not even a genius could spend all his days working. He promised Juliette they would renew the practice of their bygone youth and would take annual holiday vacations. Thereafter he and Juliette made journeys to Belgium, Holland, and Germany. One year, when he was pressed for time, she reminded him of his pledge, and managed to take him off on a return journey to the Isle of Jersey, where they spent several weeks.

Victor continued to maintain a façade of marriage with Adèle because of their children, but also because it was virtually impossible for Catholics to obtain a divorce. Victor no longer paid lip service to the Church, but Adèle still claimed membership. She was horrified whenever she learned that some wealthy, influential couple had obtained a divorce in Sweden or Prussia. But Adèle, like Victor, was chafing under the restrictions of a marriage that no longer existed in anything but name. So many copies of Victor's books were being sold in France that it became necessary for someone to look after his interests there, and this situation gave her the excuse she sought. She would return home for a few weeks—or a few months, if it proved helpful—to hold meetings with various booksellers on his behalf. Perhaps she could also confer with various French publishers who were bombarding him with requests to do his next works.

Victor immediately agreed, and Adèle departed, escorted by Charles.

The day after her departure, Juliette Drouet moved into Hauteville House and took charge. This action was unique in the long history of the affair. Until now Victor and Juliette had observed the proprieties of their era, but they had grown tired of sham. The whole world knew they lived together, and the restrictions in the lives of ordinary people were no longer applicable to him. He and Juliette no longer cared what anyone thought.

Victor's sons and daughters had been close to Juliette since early childhood. They had paid frequent visits to her apartment in Paris, and they saw her regularly in Guernsey, as they had in Jersey. They had good reason to like and respect her, and made no objection when she took command of the household. Life was smoother, their father was more content, and the quality of the meals improved, too.

Victor and Juliette still made a handsome couple. At the age of fifty-seven, his deep-set eyes still flashed, his furrowed brow gave him distinction, and was emphasized by a receding hairline, behind which he still had a full mane of hair. His beard gave still more luster to his appearance. He wrote to George Sand that shaving was a nuisance and interfered with the time he devoted to his writing, but that wasn't his real reason. Beards were now in favor in England and France, and Juliette had convinced him he would look more distinguished with one.

Juliette was in her fifties, too, but looked much younger. Her figure had matured somewhat, but she was still as slender and supple as someone half her age. Her hair was black, and she had no need to dye it, but she wore rouge on her cheeks and lips because Victor enjoyed her use of attractive cosmetics. She wore no perfume, as she and Victor were convinced that the only good scents were made in France, and he refused to send even small funds into the nation ruled by Napoleon III. Victor was so wealthy now that they could afford to indulge her passion for expensive clothes and even more expensive jewelry. On several occasions they entertained diamond merchants from London, and made purchases of consequence. All of Juliette's gowns were made by a woman in Brussels who kept a chart of her exact measurements, and Victor urged his mistress to go to Belgium for fittings, but she refused to leave his side, and insisted that the clothes be sent to her by mail.

The Guernsey natives no longer paid any attention to the famous couple, and were so accustomed to them that no one was shocked by their irregular relationship. Tourists and other visitors to the island found Victor and Juliette the major attraction, however, and sometimes followed them in large numbers when they went on their daily walks. When this occurred, the constabulary of Guernsey quietly intervened and sent the celebrity hunters off to mind their own business.

Victor in his own person had become a symbol of liberty to men everywhere. It was not surprising that humanitarian and social causes in all parts of the world attracted his attention. One incident that startled him occurred in the United States during his absence in Sark, and he did not learn of it until his return to Guernsey.

The fanatical abolitionist, John Brown, had conducted his raid on the arsenal at Harper's Ferry, Virginia. It was his intention to arm the slaves, help them revolt, and establish what he called a black redoubt. But Colonel Robert E. Lee of the U. S. Army was sent with a detachment of troops and Marines to the scene, and quickly forced Brown to surrender. The fanatic, who was considered insane by many of his neighbors, was tried by a Virginia court and condemned to death.

He was executed on December 2, 1859, after conducting himself with such unexpected dignity that even those who were horrified by his acts were impressed. Many in the United States now gave their whole-hearted support to the abolitionist cause, and feelings ran high in Europe, too.

Victor was indignant, and believed that his position forced him to protest, so he published a long, rambling letter to the people of the United States. In it he declared:

At this precise moment, in Washington's fatherland, in the Southern states—and this monstrous contradiction arouses the indignation of the pure and logical conscience of the North—a white man, a free man, John Brown, has tried to liberate these negroes, these slaves . . . John Brown . . . and four of his men . . . were tried by Southerners who had much to gain, or so they thought, if he were put out of harm's way. Their short-sightedness is their eternal disgrace.

All of us everywhere, whoever we may be, all of us whose common country, common homeland is the United States of America, the world's great symbol of democracy, feel ourselves injured and shamed by this sentence.

Brown's execution may, perhaps, reinforce slavery in Virginia, but it is certain that it will shake the whole structure of American democracy. What a pity it is that the cause of freedom should be made to suffer in the freest land on earth! We can only pray that the chimes of freedom will ring out again, across the breadth of that great land, across the ocean that separates us from the land that has been our inspiration and that now has become the degradation of us all.

The efforts of the Italian patriot, Garibaldi, also inspired Victor, and he sent the leader of the Red Shirts a contribution for his cause, as well as another invitation to visit Hauteville House. The supporters of Italian liberty arranged that a meeting be held on the Isle of Jersey in June 1860, and prominent persons from many nations were to attend.

Victor was asked to be the principal speaker, and immediately inquired of the Guernsey authorities whether they would object. As they did not, he went to St. Helier, the capital of Jersey, and was delighted to find that his audience consisted of more than a thousand people. It undoubtedly gave him pleasure to make an address on the subject of freedom in a place he had been asked to leave less than a decade earlier.

"Liberty," he cried in what was later described as his most glorious speech, "is the most precious possession of all mankind. Food and water are nothing; clothing and shelter are luxuries. He who is free stands with his head held high, even if hungry, naked and homeless.

"I dedicate my own life, whatever may be left of it, to the cause of liberty—liberty for all men, everywhere!"

Exile had given Victor Hugo his ultimate cause, and he was not indulging in mere rhetoric for the sake of exciting and pleasing a crowd. No one but Juliette knew it, but Victor was now hard at work on a project that had occupied him, on and off, for many years. He was aware that, if he brought it off, it would be regarded as his masterpiece. His basic theme was that of human liberty and dignity.

It is well to see the project in the context of its times. As always, Victor sensed a change in the mood and reading tastes of the public. But this time some of his colleagues had been the trail-blazers.

Realism had replaced romanticism, social justice had become more important than fine expression, and the sufferings of the common people had become paramount. In England, Charles Dickens was carrying the banner, and in France there were many. Eugène Sue, author of *The Wandering Jew*, wrote scathing attacks on the institutions and mores that shackled the common man. Balzac, regarded as the ultimate realist, was doing the same, as well as Flaubert, whose *Madame Bovary* opened the eyes of thousands to social inequities. Even Alexandre Dumas, king of the romantic sentimentalists, had jumped on the bandwagon.

Victor was in no hurry. He had begun his masterwork immediately prior to the Revolution of 1848, had been interrupted, and had returned to his manuscript sporadically. Showing even greater self-confidence than before, he felt certain that the books of his contemporaries would fade into the background when he published his great novel.

His faith in *Les Misérables*, as he called the book in its final version, was not misplaced. It created a sensation unknown in the history of French literature. And it not only earned its author more money than any other book had ever before achieved, but made its publisher enormous profits, too. Within ten years of its initial appearance it was published in more than forty other countries, and became an unprecedented bestseller everywhere. Since that time it has been reprinted in uncounted versions, many of them condensations, and has been the subject of at least five dramas and motion pictures.

One of the most curious aspects of *Les Misérables* is that critics have been unable to designate its type. More frequently than not, it has been called a realistic novel, but many authorities insist it goes beyond realism into naturalism. It is larger than life, an extreme form of realism. It is also, ultimately, an intricately complex historical novel.

Perhaps such attempts to categorize *Les Misérables* are irrelevant. Certainly the most distinguished of critics have agreed with millions of readers that it is one of the two or three greatest novels ever penned.

Sometime in 1860 Victor assembled the many hundreds of pages on which he had worked through the years, under the old title of *Les Misères*. Then, in a complete reversal of the habit he had developed over a lifetime, he did no writing whatever. He arose at his usual time, went to his desk and spent long hours staring out at the sea. Gradually he blocked out his future course; portions of the manuscript could be salvaged, other parts had to be reworked, still others needed expansion and new development.

Finally, on January 1, 1861, he scribbled a three-word note which the posterity-conscious Juliette Drouet preserved. It said curtly, "Resumption of work."

He had never before observed such a strict writing schedule. At his desk at dawn, he interrupted his task for a brief, light meal at noon, and another, only a little more substantial, in the evening. The twice-daily banquets were suspended, and he limited himself to a single glass of wine at each meal. His evenings were devoted to work, too, and sometimes the writing moved along so smoothly that he continued forty-eight to seventy-two hours at a time, without sleep.

Late in March, Victor went to Brussels, accompanied by Juliette, and paid a long visit to the battlefield at Waterloo. Then, renting rooms in Mont Saint-Jean, within view of the scene, he wrote the superb account of the great battle, which appeared at the opening of the second portion of the novel.

On June 30 Victor scribbled another note: "I have finished *Les Misérables* on the battlefield of Waterloo and in the month of Waterloo."

He was too optimistic, however. Many months of editing and rewriting lay ahead of him, and it was not until May 19, 1862, that the book was actually completed, although the first volume had appeared a month earlier. Victor had made all arrangements for its publication, and signed an unprecedented contract with Albert Lacroix, a Belgian publisher. The author was to be paid a total of one million francs, one-third of it immediately, another third due in 1868, and the final payment to be made in 1874.

Lacroix knew what he was doing. In 1868 his accounts showed that he had already made a profit of more than five hundred thousands francs, and in 1874, when he made his last payment to the author, he proudly announced, "This book has made me a millionaire."

Some of Victor's characters, Jean Valjean and Cosette, Bishop Myriel and Police Inspector Javert, have joined the elite company of an immortal galaxy. The Bishop is a personification of Victor's most tenacious belief: man is basically good. Valjean is used to illustrate yet another tenet: when man commits evil, he can nevertheless achieve redemption. And Javert is a portrait of the close-minded public servant whom Victor despised, the man who interprets the law literally, who ignores the human elements necessary for a compassionate pursuit of his duties.

The complicated story of *Les Misérables* is melodramatic, and Victor utilizes every situation to heighten already intense dramatic values. Some of his situations are not credible, and he has been criticized for them over the past century, but readers of the novel ignore such criticism, just as Victor himself did. His long digressions, which include vast stretches of descriptive material, have also aroused the wrath of the literary world, but, as some authorities have emphasized, they must be viewed as portions of the whole work. That work was very large, indeed: when published without cuts of any kind, *Les Misérables* filled four large volumes.

The critics were overwhelmed when it first appeared, and many found reason to carp about one aspect or another. But the general reading public accepted the book as a work of true genius, realizing what the literary world at first failed to grasp. It has been generally acclaimed as one of the greatest novels ever written. Innumerable details were based on incidents and people of Victor Hugo's own life. The story was more than a condemnation of a social system unjust to the poor; it was also a great story of the Industrial Revolution and man's relationship with God. It was a portrait of the entire century in which Victor Hugo lived.

It is difficult to assess the impact of the book on the world in which Victor Hugo lived. In France and in Belgium, then in other countries, long lines formed outside bookstores when it was learned that copies were available. Republicans rejoiced, and the advocates of monarchy tried to summon valid arguments in favor of what Victor Hugo demonstrated to be an outdated form of government. Socialists and other radicals were eminently pleased, too, although it is going too far to claim, as some of Victor's enemies did, that he had himself become a socialist.

Most men of good faith accepted the basic tenets of

the book, and, in September 1862, the publisher gave a banquet for more than two thousand persons, in Brussels, honoring Victor. Authors, scientists, and statesmen from many lands attended the unique dinner, and many of them made brief speeches.

The principal address was given by Victor, who had never been in better form. He elected to discuss the freedom of the press, which he called essential to the achievement of an improved world, and ended on a passionate plea for liberty, everywhere, for all men.

The evening was memorable in many ways, not the least of them domestic and personal. Adèle had been in London for several weeks, and was planning to go on to Paris when Victor learned that the banquet would be held. He wrote to her, asking her to join him in Brussels for the event.

She replied that her entire itinerary would be disrupted if she changed her plans.

He accepted her refusal, and Juliette Drouet not only accompanied her lover, but sat in a prominent place in the banquet hall. It was her first important public appearance with Victor and, as it was made in the presence of so many prominent persons, signaled that the liaison was no longer even nominally clandestine. Victor and Juliette had decided to ignore the unwritten laws that governed the conduct of gentlemen, and for several days following the dinner, as they visited with some of the distinguished guests, they were inseparable.

Soon after their return to Guernsey, Charles Hugo left Hauteville House to take up his permanent residence in Brussels. There is no evidence that he became angry when

Juliette took his mother's place in the mansion. Nor is it necessarily true that the young man, who was an ardent socialist, could not tolerate his father's somewhat more conservative views. They had argued at the dinner table about politics and the ideal state, but Victor believed in stimulating discussions, and everyone debated vehemently on many subjects at the Hauteville House table.

It seems far more likely that Charles, a competent adult, felt smothered by the fame, as well as the overbearing personality, of his father. He corresponded regularly with both Victor and Juliette after he moved to Brussels, and both were delighted when, two years later, he married Alice La Haene, the daughter of a prosperous Belgian. Victor attended the wedding, but Juliette remained discreetly in Guernsey, probably because she didn't want to embarrass the bride and groom when Adèle was in attendance.

Thereafter Charles and his wife paid frequent visits to Guernsey, and both Victor and Juliette established a close, cordial relationship with Alice.

Meanwhile François-Victor was still at work on his translation of Shakespeare's plays, a task in which he was encouraged by his father. He had, with Victor's help, obtained a publisher for this enormous work, and asked his father to write a preface. Victor was happy to oblige, and rejoiced with his son when the work, in fifteen volumes, made its appearance in 1864 and 1865.

Meanwhile the son's interest in Shakespeare piqued the attention of his father, and Victor returned to his own desk. The unprecedented success of *Les Misérables* relieved him of all financial worries, and he was now in the enviable position of writing whatever he pleased. For the moment, at least, there were no more worlds to conquer in either the field of the novel or that of poetry, so Victor turned to literary criticism, in which he was regarded as a minor figure.

His new book, *William Shakespeare*, was published in Brussels in 1864. The title is somewhat misleading, as the book is a study of literary genius in general rather than that of Shakespeare alone. Victor devoted as much attention to Aeschylus and Sophocles as he did to Shakespeare, and analyzed the plays of Racine and Molière, among others.

He also plunged headlong into a literary controversy that had been raging in French intellectual circles for more than fifty years. It was generally accepted, by this time, that the great literary works of one century should be an improvement on those that preceded it, and Victor's own highly competitive career would indicate that, in all probability, he subscribed to this point of view. He did not.

It would be absurd, he argued, if any playwright-poet should try to surpass Shakespeare. "Art is not perfectible," he declared, and took his stand with those who believed that every artist must be judged exclusively on his own merits. "Comparisons," he wrote, "are absurd. How stupid it would be if one measured the worth of an author's work by weighing his wife's diamonds."

The financial success of *William Shakespeare* surprised no one. Victor Hugo appeared to be incapable of making mistakes, and the book earned far more money than works of literary criticism usually did. But the book also established Victor as a critic of the first rank. "His talents are so formidable that he puts all the rest of us to shame," Gautier said. "We labor to achieve, but Victor is a natural torrent of words."

In spite of his dazzling successes, Victor became a sorrowing man in the mid-1860s. Tragedy struck his family again, and he could not dam the tide of misfortune.

François-Victor was aided in his research and translation by a young lady, a native of Guernsey, who was also a Bard of Avon enthusiast. Émilie de Putron was exceptionally attractive as well as intellectual, and it was the wise Juliette who first detected signs of a developing romance. Immediately after the publication of François-Victor's translations, the young couple announced their engagement, and Victor was delighted. He liked the girl, he enjoyed the company of her parents, and he planned to buy a house nearby for the young pair.

But Émilie suddenly became ill one morning, and by the end of the day she was dead, in spite of the frantic attempts of the island's physicians to save her. All that is known is that she succumbed to what was officially described as a "pernicious fever."

Life lost its savor for François-Victor, and he found life in Guernsey intolerable. No matter where he went, he was reminded of Émilie. He was now completely self-supporting, and his father acquiesced when he decided to take advantage of Napoleon III's amnesty and return to Paris.

Before he departed, he performed one last, important task that involved the honor of the Hugo family. In 1862 young Adèle, whom everyone had thought would marry Auguste Vacquerie, had responded unexpectedly to the advances of a former British army officer, named

Pinson, who was making a prolonged visit to Guernsey, although he had supposedly come for a short stay.

Pinson was responsible for a remarkable transformation in the girl. Young Adèle had grown increasingly morose in recent years, and neither Auguste nor her parents had been able to change her moods. Sometimes, when she had paid brief visits to Juliette, she appeared more vivacious, but even these occasions had become less frequent. Now, however, she was talkative and gay, her eyes were bright, and she played the piano with zest. Victor was grateful to Captain Pinson for the transformation.

Juliette was less impressed with the young man, and Adèle who had returned to Guernsey from one of her journeys, was of like mind. Neither could change Victor's opinion until, one day, they broke precedent.

Neither had ever openly acknowledged the existence of the other. Although they lived within a stone's throw, they could pass on the narrow walks of Guernsey without exchanging as much as a smile or a nod. But on this memorable occasion the threat imposed by Pinson drastically changed the situation.

No one knows whether Juliette first went to Adèle, or whether Adèle first solicited the help of Juliette. Perhaps this detail is unimportant, except for curiosity's sake: they descended on Victor together, or, more correctly, ascended together to his lair.

The one inviolable rule at Hauteville House was, of course, that no one was allowed to disturb Victor at work. No emergency, no crisis had ever been sufficiently grave to permit breaking the rule. For years François-Victor and Charles had joked that, if a fire broke out, their father would be unaware of it until the flames consumed him and his manuscript. No one would interrupt him, no matter what had happened.

Perhaps Adèle and Juliette, singly, would have lacked the courage to open the study door and enter without permission. Together, they were lion-hearted.

It is not difficult to imagine Victor's astonishment when his wife and his mistress burst into his workroom, speaking in shrill, excited voices.

The gist of their joint diatribe was the same. Pinson, they declared, was a blackguard, a cad, and a scoundrel. Above all, he was a fortune-hunter, and he wanted young Adèle's money.

Victor was bewildered by the double-barrelled assault, and protested that young Adèle possessed no money of her own except the five thousand francs, in cash, that he had given to each of his children after the publication of *Les Misérables*.

The good ladies hooted him into silence. The success of his great novel meant that young Adèle would inherit a considerable fortune, and they were convinced that Pinson hoped to marry her so he could get his hands on her future treasure.

Their joint assault was effective. Victor listened, having no choice, and then his own imagination went to work. Soon he was livid, and the ladies departed, their immediate work done. After they parted company, they did not meet again or acknowledge each other's existence for years. They had formed an alliance for a purpose, and having accomplished it, went their separate but parallel ways.

Victor went at once to his daughter, and a thoroughly

unpleasant scene took place. He insisted that she stop seeing Pinson, and the girl refused. The pale, introverted young Adèle defied her father for the first time in her life. His pleas left her unmoved, as well as his threats.

Unable to reach her, Victor found Pinson at the young man's lodging house, and ordered him to leave the island by the night boat to the mainland. If he were found on Guernsey the following day, the irate father declared, he would return to the lodging house with a whip in hand.

Pinson appeared frightened, and gave his solemn pledge that he would depart the same evening.

So he did, but young Adèle went with him.

When Victor came down from his study for dinner, his daughter failed to appear. Her room was empty, and the five-thousand-franc gift her father had given her was gone, as were two steamer trunks of her clothing and other belongings.

It was necessary to wait three agonizing days before another ship sailed to England. Then François-Victor, who agreed to postpone his own departure, went off in pursuit of the romantic fugitives. The chase that followed was an unhappy caricature of an incident in a melodramatic Victor Hugo novel.

François-Victor discovered that Pinson and young Adèle had spent forty-eight hours at a first-rate London hotel, then departed without leaving a forwarding address. A hunt through the establishments of the city's retail merchants eventually led to a gentlemen's tailoring shop, where Pinson had purchased several expensive suits, a cloak, and a half-dozen pairs of shoes. The merchandise had been delivered to a rooming house in Bloomsbury.

The girl's irate brother went there, only to learn that, once again, he was too late. The trail led him to Amsterdam, Rotterdam, and Leyden, and finally to Brussels. There, in a cheap lodging house, he found his bewildered, crushed sister.

Pinson was gone, and so was the last of the girl's money.

In fact, young Adèle was destitute, and her brother had to pay her lodging house bill. She was in no condition to travel, so he took her to a hotel, and immediately sent a letter to his father, which read:

Dear Papa:

I have found my sister, who is penniless and in a desperate physical and mental condition. She swears that Pinson is still in this city, and, until she is strong enough to be returned home, I shall devote all of my efforts to finding him.

Your affectionate son,
F.-V.

Victor's reply was equally crisp:

My Dear Son:

I grieve for our poor Adèle.

If you should be fortunate enough to find Captain Pinson, you may beat him, but I beg you not to kill him, as I reserve that privilege for myself.

Your devoted father,
V.H.

There was no sign of Pinson in Brussels, however, and it was likely that he had sneaked away under an assumed name. So, after young Adèle had been treated by a physician for a week, her brother brought her back to Guernsey.

Her parents were heartbroken, and her father thundered at her, but in vain. She insisted that she and Pinson had been married, and that the ceremony had been legal, but she furnished no details. It was never known whether the alleged wedding occurred in the girl's imagination or whether it had actually taken place. The next morning, young Adèle was no longer capable of taking part in a lucid discussion. The "Hugo curse" had struck yet another member of the family, and she had lost her senses, never to recover them.

She could not be kept at home, and there was no place in Guernsey to house her. Adèle was deeply disturbed by the prospect of putting her daughter in a "foreign" sanitarium in Brussels, so there was only one alternative. François-Victor and his mother escorted young Adèle to a rest home outside Paris and there she remained for another half-century, until her death in 1915, never knowing her own identity, never recognizing any visitors, either her parents or her brothers.

Victor was stricken by this latest blow, but recovered from it in a manner that confounded even his most persistent enemies.

Chapter
XI

*L*ATE in 1865, close on the heels of the tragedies
that marred his children's lives and his own, Victor brought
out a new book, *Les Chansons des rues et des bois*. It was
a volume of light, romantic verse, gay in spirit, delicate in
execution, and was devoted to his remembrance of his own
youth. He recalled his own romances, remembered his own
reactions to the joys of nature when he had been young,
and sang their praises with a clear, pure voice that he alone
could achieve.

It is obvious now, as it was to the perspicacious in
Victor's own day, that *Les Chansons* was an escape from
the stark events that had darkened his own life, and he
took what comfort he could find in the woods and fields, on
a cliff overlooking the sea and beneath the stars. The critics
of Paris, many of whom were jealous of his unvarying
success, attacked him unmercifully. It was beneath the

dignity of a great man, they said, to write poetry that could have been penned by a man one-third his age. *Les Chansons* was slight and ineffectual, they declared, but they were forced to admit that his poems were charming, graceful, and possessed a quality that few others in history had been able to achieve.

As usual, the public paid no attention to the critics, and a new book by Victor Hugo received all the attention that his readers believed he deserved. *Les Chansons* sold out in less than a month, and two more editions were printed before the demand was satisfied.

Meanwhile, in Guernsey, Victor tried to re-order his life. Adèle did not return after taking her mad daughter to France, and was destined to make only one more visit to the island. François-Victor joined Auguste Vacquerie in Paris, but could not tolerate life under Napoleon III, and soon went off to Brussels, where he took an apartment near that of his brother. The Belgian capital, rather than Guernsey, became the family's focal point, and the birth of Victor's first grandchild, Georges Hugo, made Brussels the official gathering place.

When Adèle tired of Paris she went to see her sons, and Victor, finding his grandchild an irresistible magnet, paid several visits each year to Charles and his family. Juliette always accompanied him, and the baby responded to her so enthusiastically that she and Alice became intimate friends. At the end of one visit, Juliette accompanied the Charles Hugo family on a month's holiday, while Victor returned alone to Guernsey. It was the only time he and Juliette were separated for more than a few days, but

Victor was willing to endure any inconvenience for the sake of his infant grandson.

Nothing could stop Victor Hugo from turning out more books, and early in 1866 he gave the elated Lacroix another manuscript. *Les Travailleurs de la mer* (*Toilers of the Sea*), a long, melodramatic novel about the sea, was published soon thereafter. Almost forgotten today, and regarded as one of Victor's minor works, this work created a sensation in its own day that was second only to that achieved by *Les Misérables*.

As Victor would demonstrate in later years, he had not lost any of his formidable talents, nor had they diminished, but *Les Travailleurs* seems to emphasize some of his less attractive traits. There are so many coincidences in his complicated plot that it is almost impossible for an intelligent reader to accept more than a small fraction of them. His melodrama, although breathtaking, sometimes verges on the ludicrous. And he crowds his pages with so many characters that it is sometimes difficult to tell them apart.

Despite this, *Les Travailleurs* is a powerful novel, and some of the sea scenes are memorable. Reading them, it becomes difficult to remember that Victor Hugo gleaned all he knew about men of the sea from observations, not first-hand experience. He watched the sea daily from his solarium as he worked. He often paused at the wharves, during his daily walks, to chat at length with fishermen and sailors, and over the years he accumulated a huge store of sea tales, as well as a vast fund of facts.

He took no notes, but never forgot anything he was

told. Then, after he had stored away a story or a fact in his mind, his ever-fertile imagination went to work. Certainly *Les Travailleurs* reads like a book written by someone who had spent his entire life on the deck of a small vessel, and it was incredible that Victor had never traveled farther on board a ship than across the Channel.

The frontispiece was an impressionistic pen and ink drawing of his own creation that depicted the sea pounding against cliffs, and was made from the heights above the rocks. The drawing received such great praise that, without waiting for his publisher's request, Victor made a number of other sketches that were included in subsequent editions. The critics of his own day were not mistaken when they wrote that, had he not elected to earn his living writing words, he might have become a great artist.

Les Travailleurs in its first days sold at an even faster clip than *Les Misérables* had. Lacroix was delighted to report to the author that in its first week the book was selling more than fifteen hundred copies per day in Paris alone, and that another five hundred were selling each day in Brussels.

François-Victor, who was visiting Paris on business, wrote to his father:

Your success here is enormous, universal. I have never seen such unanimity. Even the triumph of Les Misérables *has been exceeded. This time the master has found a public worthy of him. You have been understood, and that means everything. Because to understand a work like that is to admire it. Your name is in all the newspapers, on every wall, in every shop window, on everyone's lips. You are the great hero of Paris, and it pleases me to think that Napoléon le Petit must be disconcerted.*

The Emperor was not displeased, however, and for a good reason. *Les Travailleurs* was Victor's first book of consequence in years that did not touch on politics, the first that omitted scathing assaults on the ruler of France. Consequently the censors made no attempt to ban it, the police did not harass the booksellers, and the newspapers were allowed to mention it as often as they pleased.

The barrages of publicity and praise did the book no harm, and authors who had heretofore remained silent, fearful that the censors would clamp down on them if they said too much, cheered loudly for the exile. Even Sainte-Beuve, who was supporting the regime and for years had taken no official notice of Victor's work, wrote a review in which he called the novel a "masterpiece of its kind beyond compare."

At the end of the first month following the book's publication, Lacroix wrote to the author that it had sold more than seventy-five thousand copies, and he was not only printing another huge edition, but was embarking on the publication of a translation into English. He did not reveal that he had hired François-Victor Hugo to make the translation. This was kept from Victor as a surprise, and it delighted him beyond measure, when he learned it.

In its first year, *Les Travailleurs* earned Victor more than two hundred thousand francs, at a rate far greater than *Les Misérables*. A Paris newspaper, *Le Soleil*, acquired the right to reprint the book in serial form, and promptly increased its circulation from thirty to ninety thousand.

Lines formed before the kiosks of vendors as people waited to buy newspapers containing the newest installment. Victor felt a deep satisfaction when this was reported to him. He had been told that Charles Dickens enjoyed a similar devoted following in London, and the possibility that another author might enjoy a popularity greater than his own annoyed him.

The year 1867 was important in Paris, and equally important in the life of Victor Hugo. Private industry and the government were joining hands to present a world's fair, the first of its kind, called the Exposition Universel. New, clandestine efforts were made by Napoleon III to induce Victor to come home.

Adèle visited Paris early in the year, accompanied by Charles and Alice, and Sainte-Beuve called on his old mistress in the hope that he could induce her to persuade Victor that it would be in his own best interests to return home. Whether Sainte-Beuve was responsible for the gesture, as he claimed, or whether the shrewd Emperor was behind the scenes, is not known.

Although agreeing to write to her husband, Adèle was never in doubt regarding the outcome of the suggestion, and she was right. Victor not only rejected the idea of returning, but added the spice of insult to outright injury. The enterprising Lacroix was bringing out a guidebook for the tens of thousands of visitors who were expected to flock to Paris, calling it *Paris-Guide*, and Victor came to the publisher with an insidious notion. He would write a preface to the book, and would charge only a nominal sum.

Lacroix was delighted, accepting at once, and Victor wrote the preface, recounting the glorious history of Paris.

He described in glowing detail the contributions of the city's sons and daughters to the intellectual, artistic, and industrial development of the world, and called Paris the cradle of modern liberty. Yet, with all his praise, he made no mention whatever of the present ruler of France or his government.

His silence was even more eloquent than an attack would have been, and was noted by uncounted tourists. Napoleon III was furious, but his censors had no grounds to ban the guidebook, and were forced to allow it to be sold freely. Victor's name on the cover guaranteed large sales.

Sainte-Beuve, having renewed his friendship with Adèle, saw her frequently. On at least two occasions he dined with her in restaurants, and on another he was her guest, along with her son and daughter-in-law. The relationship was certainly platonic, and neither entertained thought of rekindling fires that had burned to ashes so many years earlier. The aging Sainte-Beuve enjoyed his standing as the first literary critic of France, and it is unlikely that he would have taken the risk of ruining his reputation by associating too closely with the wife of Victor Hugo. Adèle must have known it would be impossible to turn back the clock without appearing ludicrous. She was failing in health, finding it increasingly difficult to walk without dizzy spells. It seems far-fetched that she might have been interested in her old romance.

One thought was predominant in her mind; she wanted to undo harm for which she considered herself responsible. It was her great desire to effect a reconciliation between her husband and her former lover. Sainte-Beuve was willing enough, though the precise nature of his willingness is a matter of conjecture.

Adèle made it clear in repeated letters to Victor that Sainte-Beuve hoped he would forget the past. In fact, Adèle bombarded her husband with correspondence on the matter, and one letter in particular, written about three weeks after she arrived in Paris, is memorable:

As we grow older we think more frequently about the close friendships of our earlier years. There were so few of them, and they were so important to us. None was more significant that your brotherhood with Sainte-Beuve. How wonderful it would be if you were willing to forgive the folly of his youth and clasp the hand that is stretched out to touch yours!

Victor's reply was succinct, and perhaps unintentionally cruel:

"I have forgiven—and forgotten."

He had erased Sainte-Beuve's very existence. This could not have been the literal truth, of course, since no one as sensitive as Victor Hugo could have forgotten the man who had changed the basic nature of his relationship with his wife. But Victor no longer cared to bother with a reconciliation. He had made his own life, he had progressed far beyond the point where Sainte-Beuve's opinions, personal or professional, meant anything to him, and he was indifferent to the idea of reforming a friendship that had soured.

Adèle persisted, and throughout the entire period of her five-month stay in Paris she nagged at her husband, hoping to persuade him to change his mind.

Victor simply couldn't be bothered, and, aside from his one comment, did not mention the subject again. Sainte-Beuve belonged to his past, not his present, and had no place in his future.

Napoleon III, if he failed in this approach, tried another. A suggestion was made quietly, through official channels, that the regime would not object if several of Victor Hugo's plays were revived by the Comédie-Française. The officials of the organization immediately wrote to Victor, asking his permission to do *Hernani*.

The great author faced a cruel dilemma. Could he, in good conscience, allow something he had written to be presented on the foremost stage in Paris while he himself remained in exile as a protest against a repressive government? He hesitated, pondering the problem.

A number of friends, among them Gautier, George Sand, and even Dumas, wrote to him at length, urging him to allow the play to be presented. "If you do not," George Sand wrote, "they may find a way around you, and revive the play without your approval."

Gautier's argument was not only more subtle, but far stronger:

It is not an easy matter for anyone who lives in France today to express his longing for liberty. A play by Victor Hugo, presented at the Comédie-Français, would become a symbol of the freedom that so many millions crave. The censors and their masters lack to wit to see than an approval of Hernani *by the audiences who will hurry to see it will be, in effect, a rousing vote in favor of the liberty that is lacking in France today.*

Accepting this argument, Victor wrote to the management of the Comédie that he would grant the right to present *Hernani* and one other play, *Ruy Blas*. He added, "Circumstances well known to everyone concerned make it impossible for me to be present for the performances of my works, so I am designating Mme. Hugo to represent me."

Adèle attended the opening of *Hernani*, accompanied by Charles and Alice, and the audience gave her a standing ovation when she walked down the aisle to her seat. That applause was an indication of what would come. The play was interrupted repeatedly by cheers, and the first-night audience roared its approval. At the end of the performance there was a spontaneous demand for a speech by Adèle.

She had never made a public appearance in her life, so Charles finally mounted the stage. "I thank you on behalf of my mother," he said. "She came here this evening as my father's surrogate, and I know he will be pleased, as he will interpret correctly the nature of your enthusiastic approval."

The cheers welled up again, and did not subside until the management dimmed the house lights.

The secret police gave the Emperor a full report on the reception given the play and members of the Hugo family, and Napoleon III realized he had erred, but it was too late. *Hernani* was hailed more enthusiastically than when it had been first presented. Visitors from many lands who came to the World's Fair vied with Parisians in obtaining seats. The Emperor and his ministers closed their eyes to the triumph, and Napoleon III literally refused to drive past the Comédie-Française in his carriage. He wanted no reminders of the enemy who, once again, had made him look foolish.

When the Comédie announced plans to present *Ruy Blas*, however, a different situation arose. The censors moved in soon after rehearsals began, and insisted on removing lines they found offensive. All references to liberty, in any form, were taken out.

Rumors of these activities spread quickly, and a number of friends wrote to Victor, telling him what was happening. He refused to accept hearsay, and wrote to Charles, asking for a precise indication of what had been removed.

Charles went to the authorities, who stalled. He persisted, making a nuisance of himself, and finally, only a scant four days before *Ruy Blas* was scheduled to open, they gave him a copy of their cut version of the play. He sent it off to his father at once.

Meanwhile Victor's friends passed the word, and the intellectuals of Paris, who had filled the Théâtre-Français on the night that *Hernani* had opened, found it convenient to remain at home, even though they had purchased seats for the new opening. The auditorium was more than half-empty. The actors, aware of what had happened, gave performances that were less than inspired, and the evening was dismal.

Two days later the management of the Comédie received a letter from Victor, who demanded that *Ruy Blas* be withdrawn at once. There were many Parisians and visitors unfamiliar with the intricacies of the situation, and a brisk sale had developed at the box office, but the management had no choice, and the play was withdrawn.

Newspapers subservient to the regime immediately

printed stories to the effect that the revival of *Ruy Blas* had been a miserable failure. Napoleon III felt that this time he had saved face.

But the truth spread, thanks to the efforts of Victor's friends, and soon the students at the Sorbonne were greeting each other with quotations from the play. *Ruy Blas*, Gautier wrote to Victor, became the most quoted play in Paris, and it soon became impossible to purchase a copy anywhere. Victor had good reason to believe he had won his latest duel with the Emperor, even though the last round had ended somewhat inconclusively.

Life in Guernsey remained serene, although it had been complicated by the arrival of Adèle's sister, Julie Chenay. She had come, supposedly to act as Victor's housekeeper during his wife's prolonged absence. The hospitable Victor—and the equally cordial Juliette Drouet—made the newcomer welcome as a guest, but Juliette continued to act as the mistress of Hauteville House.

Then, unexpectedly, Adèle returned to the island, giving no advance warning that she was coming. Juliette promptly moved out of the mansion and returned to her own villa.

It quickly developed that Adèle had no intention of driving her away. In fact, something had happened to Adèle Hugo—a reversal of attitude so complete that it was bewildering. Several explanation have been offered.

Perhaps the revival of her friendship with Sainte-Beuve awakened old guilts, and caused her to reassess her husband's situation. She may have known that her illness, which was chronic, was rapidly worsening, and so wanted to set her husband's house in order before she died. It has also been suggested that Charles and Alice exerted a considerable influence on her, persuading her that Juliette Drouet was a woman of stature.

Whatever the reasons, Adèle astonished her husband and sister by making her way alone down the lane that separated Hauteville House from Juliette Drouet's villa.

Victor's wife and mistress were closeted for a long time. In a letter to François-Victor, Victor, in all probability the principal subject of the ladies' discussion, wrote that they talked for two hours. In another letter, this one to Charles, he said they met for more than four hours.

Juliette made no mention of time in a letter she sent to friends in Brussels, and commented, "Mme. Hugo did me the honor of paying me a visit."

The extent to which Adèle unburdened herself has never been clear, but there can be no doubt that she voluntarily humbled herself before her rival of a lifetime. No one has ever learned what Juliette replied, and if Victor heard what was said at the meeting, he maintained a discretion that was rare in him, keeping his mouth shut and displaying none of his usual verbosity.

The meeting spoke for itself. Juliette returned to Hauteville House that same day, and went to the suite she had occupied for months. Thereafter, for the next ten weeks that Adèle remained in Guernsey, both women continued to live under the same roof.

The long feud had come to an end. Adèle had made her peace with her principal rival, and accepted her as a necessary and inevitable part of Victor's life. The two and a half months that the trio dwelled together appears to have been amicable in every way, and Victor's letters to his children reveal a serenity of mind. He had good reason to feel tranquil, of course, having won the longest battle of his life. It was during this period that he started work on a new novel, *Par ordre du roi*. No matter what happened in his private life, he allowed nothing to interfere with his output.

Adèle finally departed, going to live with François-Victor in Brussels. Charles stayed on in Paris with his little family, explaining in letters to his father and brother that life there was so salubrious he found it difficult to tear himself away. He wanted to establish a new newspaper, and asked his brother to join him, but François-Victor demurred. The short time he had spent in France had made him feel uncomfortable, and he believed it was wrong for a son of Victor Hugo to live in France while the head of the clan remained in voluntary exile.

Charles did not give up easily, however, and asked his father's advice. Victor had not become wealthy by accident, and in a demonstration of his usual shrewdness, replied that he could think of no worse time to found a newspaper. Napoleon III was floundering in his foreign relations; as a result, the strict censorship of recent years would become even tighter. "I'm relieved you haven't asked me to invest in your enterprise," he wrote, "because my good sense and my conscience would not permit me to put one penny into a new Paris journal at the present time. I urge you to wait for a more propitious moment, when one who bears the name of Hugo stands less risk of having his door padlocked by the agents of tyranny."

Charles gave up his immediate plans and returned to Brussels. From that vantage point, in further correspondence with his father, he developed the theme of what he had in mind. The people of the French provinces, he readily admitted, were lethargic. Liberty was only a word, and they tolerated the repressive monarchy of Napoléon le Petit with only an occasional, vague murmur. But a far different spirit prevailed in Paris, where the members of his own generation, much less his father's, were stricken by the freedom-hating, inefficient government. He had talked with friends in many walks of life, and everyone knew he was ready for a new revolution.

Victor's reply was a little masterpiece:

Beware of what your friends tell you! Were it true that life under the yoke of the little Caesar were intolerable, they would follow our example and leave France. He who spends his life in exile hears what he wishes to hear and sees what he longs to see in his homeland.

He makes his life bearable by his reflections that others share his views, his sympathies, his principles. Your old friends sang one song to you, because you would soon leave them, but they sing another tune to the secret police.

Tyranny will continue to exist, in whatever guise it chooses to manifest itself, for as long as the citizens who live under its burdens elect to carry their chains without complaint. Those who truly hate tyranny fight it, either from within or without, depending on their personal circumstances.

If Almighty God is just and loves mankind, as I believe, then He will point the way for the people of France to help themselves. When that moment approaches, and you will recognize it as a time of more than passing dissatis-

faction, then will come your opportunity to help form and solidify the convictions of France. When that time comes, I will give you whatever funds you will need for your new enterprise. But, until that day arrives: wait!

Having delivered himself of sound advice, Victor returned to work, and after putting aside the novel on which he was working, because it would not jell, he turned to another, far larger one. *L'Homme qui rit*, he informed Lacroix, was a story about England and the influence of the English aristocracy at the beginning of the eighteenth century. It would be more than history told in the form of fiction. It would relate to present-day France, and would contain a number of other elements. Like *Les Misérables*, he said, it would be a very large book, and would have to be published in four volumes.

Lacroix knew he would make another fortune, so he replied that he didn't care how many volumes were required.

As the summer of 1868 approached, Victor and Juliette made plans for what had become the annual Hugo family reunion in Brussels. But this year there was a difference: Juliette would not remain with friends, but would live with the Hugos, as a member of the family. Her acceptance was complete, and as Adèle would be staying with Charles and Alice, it was arranged that Victor and Juliette would live in the house of François-Victor, which adjoined the other dwelling. No family could have done more to give "official" recognition to Victor's permanent liaison.

As the time for the reunion drew near, Victor received an extraordinary letter from Adèle. On the surface, she was flirtatious and gay, obviously excited, but the result was rather pathetic. She apparently knew what other members of the family only suspected, that her time on earth was drawing to a close. She said:

As for me, once I have you, I shall fasten onto you without asking your permission. I shall be so sweet and so kind that you will not want to leave me, not then or ever. It is my greatest and final wish on this earth to die in your arms. Only when one reaches my stage in this life does one appreciate all that one previously took for granted through the long years.

The letter made Victor uneasy, and Juliette shared his fear that Adèle's days were numbered. The members of the younger generation paid less attention to Maman's mood. As she had grown older, they said, she had often spoken of her impending death.

Auguste Vacquerie, who came from France to join the family in Brussels, agreed with Charles and François-Victor. Mme. Adèle, he said, was even more a creature of moods than most women, and would soon recover her buoyancy.

The younger men spent their evenings—and some of their days—making plans for their new journalistic enterprise. They drew up dummies, plotted editorial policies and went to great length devising ways to outwit the French censors. Victor sometimes listened and occasionally offered his advice, but he found it more pleasant to play with his grandson and accompany Alice when she went marketing. The variety of foods in Brussels delighted him, and by common consent it was he who planned the family's daily menus. This, he announced, was a far more realistic activity than making plans to publish a newspaper that might never be printed.

Juliette attended most of the Hugo family functions, and sometimes went off alone to spend a day with old friends, many of whom had been prominent in the French theater, had followed the example of Victor and remained in exile.

She received an invitation for a twenty-four-hour visit on August 29, and François-Victor took her to her friends' home. The day was warm and humid, and during the five-course noon meal, Adèle complained repeatedly about the heat. So Charles went off to rent an open carriage, and that afternoon Victor took his wife for a drive into the cooler countryside. During this time they managed to regain something of the spirit that had enlivened their youth.

At dinner, that evening, the Hugo sons looked in astonishment at their parents. Victor was attentive and witty, Adèle was almost adoring. As François-Victor later wrote, "Until that night I could never understand what had drawn my parents together, and had found it difficult to imagine them living as a real husband and wife. Now I not only knew what had drawn them together, but could perceive the life they had lived with each other so long ago."

That night Adèle could not sleep, and at midnight, when she finally dozed off for a few moments, she suffered a nightmare. Her screams brought the rest of the family to her bedside. Victor said he would sit up with her until she became calmer, and sent the younger people off to bed.

At 3:00 A.M. Adèle suffered a severe stroke of apoplexy. Victor immediately summoned his sons, and Charles hurried off for a physician. He returned with the doctor in a short time, but Adèle, no longer conscious, was beyond the help of medicine.

Soon after daybreak she opened her eyes, and although she could not speak, she managed to communicate her thoughts to Victor. He went to her and held her in his arms. They exchanged long glances, and Charles later said that in those moments they silently forgave each other the innumerable transgressions of a lifetime.

Victor's *Diary*, which he kept intermittently, tells the rest:

Died this morning, at half past six, Adèle Foucher Hugo. I closed her eyes. Alas! God will take this sweet and noble soul to Himself. I give her up to Him.

Bless her! We shall carry out her wish to be taken to Villequier and buried close to our dear, dead daughter. I shall go with the coffin as far the frontier. The continuing presence in France of the petty tyrant makes it impossible for me to mourn the passing of my departed wife at her graveside, as is proper.

Charles and Alice, along with the always faithful Auguste, accompanied the coffin to Villequier and saw Adèle to her final resting place. Victor went as far as the French border on the train. Juliette, at her own insistence, declined to become a member of the funeral party, saying it would not be seemly, and she did not want to stimulate additional gossip about Victor. His unaccustomed silence worried the other members of the family, and, although he insisted he neither wanted nor needed company, François-Victor turned back at the frontier with him, and escorted him back to Brussels.

"I don't know what the young fools think I might do," he told Juliette. "All I know is that I love this life too much to perform any foolish deed."

He and his mistress stayed on in Brussels for another month, and during this time Victor was listless. For the first time in his life he could not work, and one day Alice dared to ask him why he grieved so hard for his departed wife.

"I grieve not for her," he replied, "but only for all that might have been."

He had no appetite, lost weight, and found it difficult to sleep. The others held a council of war, and Juliette suggested that she take him back to Guernsey. There, in his familiar surroundings, he might find it easier to recover his equilibrium.

Victor protested that he didn't want to go, but his mistress became adamant, and he succumbed to her demands. The sight of the sea from his solarium had a soothing effect on him, and within two days he returned to work on his new novel. Working for long hours without rest, he once again relished the daily walks along the shore, his gargantuan meals, and, above all, the company of Juliette.

He also found time to continue and expand what had been Adèle's favorite charity. Every Monday evening a group of about forty very poor children, most of them orphans, had been entertained at dinner by Adèle. Victor not only took his wife's place at the table, but gave a large sum of money in her name to the institution where the impoverished children were housed. That fund still exists over a hundred years later, and the proceeds are still used to help the orphans of Guernsey.

Working as intensely and rapidly as ever, Victor finished the manuscript of *L'Homme qui rit* in the spring of 1869, and it was published in early June. He called it a book of "drama and history," and his own analysis of the subject was accurate, but did not go far enough. *L'Homme* was, above all, another in Victor Hugo's long series of character studies about a misshapen human being. His central figure, on Fernain, is mutilated in early childhood, and thereafter for the rest of his life wears a perpetual smile on his face.

Fernain, renamed Gwynplaine, and a little girl he rescues, Dea, are reared by a strange man who keeps a tame wolf as a pet. Eventually the real identity of Gwynplaine is revealed: he is a nobleman, and he tries to take his seat in the House of Lords so he can fight some of the injustices that exist in the world. But his disability hampers him, and no one will take him seriously. Dea, whom he loves, dies in his arms, and he is in such despair over his inability to right the world's wrongs that he throws himself into the sea and drowns.

No such brief plot summary is fair to any book, but, although the story is absurd, the characters unreal, and the setting a warped picture of eighteenth-century English life, Victor had not lost his power as a writer. Some of his descriptive passages were among the best he had ever penned.

The critics, unimpressed by the author's stature, attacked *L'Homme* without mercy, and a number of them called it ludicrous. Victor had not been subjected to such an assault in more years than he could remember, and he was furious.

He replied by sending an open letter to his publisher, and told Lacroix that the critics short-sightedly missed the entire point. He had not written history, he declared, but an allegory. Fernain was the symbol of the world's weak and downtrodden, the man who tries to rise through his own efforts, but finds that the pressures exerted by established society are too strong and push him back down into the mire from which he sprang. His one aim, Victor insisted, had been to arouse the compassion of the reader for those who were unable to help themselves or better their own lot.

Lacroix published the letter, knowing it would help the already booming sales of the book. *L'Homme* was destined to earn its author more than a third of a million francs, so it must be judged a commercial success, although not one of Hugo's more important works.

Victor expected *L'Homme* to create far more of a furor than it did, but he had little time to feel disappointed. Events in the world were distracting him, and he knew the time had come to take action again. With his personal and financial encouragement his sons returned to Paris, and there, with Auguste Vacquerie, Paul Meurice, and two others—Édouard Tockroy and Henri Rodiefort founded a newspaper, *Le Rappel*. This newspaper, *The Recall*, was a revival of their old one, and became, in effect, the voice of Victor Hugo. The time had finally come, Victor decided, for the final fight against the tyranny of Napoleon III.

Chapter XII

*T*HE most extraordinary phase of Victor Hugo's remarkable life began in 1869–70, with the defeat of France by Bismarck and the remarkable revolution of the Communards of Paris. In these events Victor acted a major role and was acted upon. In the beginning his return from the long self-imposed exile in Guernsey was at hand. World-famous as he was, he became a leading player on a very active stage. To relate his life now, it is necessary to visualize first the complex drama that he entered, much as, say, Benjamin Franklin entered on his return from Paris to play his role in the American Revolution as the venerable father-statesman.

By 1869 the people of France were tired of the Emperor's bumbling disasters, and Victor Hugo's description of his as Napoléon le Petit became all too accurate. The beginning of Napoleon III's trouble was his Mexican adventure. In the early 1860s, while the United States was preoccupied with its Civil War, the Emperor believed the time was ripe for re-establishing the French empire in the New World, in defiance of the American Monroe Doctrine prohibiting European powers from seizing territory in the Western Hemisphere. A French expeditionary force was sent to Mexico to conquer that disorganized country. Napoleon III offered the throne to the Archduke Maximilian of Austria, brother of the remarkable Emperor Franz Josef. Maximilian, who was exceptional in many ways, had two handicaps: He was an incurable romantic, and his wife, Carlotta (the Princess Charlotte of Belgium), was as obdurate as she was pretty. Maximilian and Carlotta accepted the offer, and set off for Mexico City.

There they were placed on the throne by French troops, who managed to keep them perched on their pinnacle for a time. The venture lacked any aspect of common sense from the outset. Mexicans of every political persuasion under President Juarez were opposed to the usurper and invader. Maximilian had virtually no support within the country, and it was difficult to keep open the supply lines to the French regiments operating so far from home.

The Mexicans weren't the only people who resented the invasion. Soon after the American Civil War ended in 1865, the United States Government demanded the withdrawal of Maximilian and his French supporters. The threat of direct intervention was implied if the request was not heeded.

The adventure was expensive; French soldiers were dying under the assault of Mexican guerillas. When a general revolt broke out in 1866, the demand for the recall of France's sons became greater. The ambitious Carlotta returned to Europe from Mexico, pleading for additional help from both Napoleon III and the Pope, whom she had previously offended. Without hope, she went mad and was confined in a sanitarium, unable to accept the loathing of the French people for the entire enterprise.

Maximilian stood up well against great odds. In 1867 he was captured by the Mexicans, placed on trial, and executed. French regiments remaining in Mexico were decimated, and few members of the expedition escaped. Not only were the people of France incensed by the collapse, but the morale of the French army was badly hurt.

Then, in 1867, the republican armies of Garibaldi also went down to defeat before a French force near Rome, ruining all chance of forming a democratic government in Italy. Some French battalions mutinied after Garibaldi had been beaten. Now, as a direct consequence of Napoleon III's misdirected policies, all of Italy except Rome and the adjoining Papal states became united as a single country, and that country was strongly antagonistic to France.

The real threat to the security of France came from another, far more formidable, foe. For centuries the keystone of French foreign policy had been to keep the German states weak and separate. Now, however, a master politician was at work. Otto von Bismarck of Prussia, displaying patience, cunning, and a genius not seen in Europe since the time of Napoleon I, was succeeding in unifying almost all of Germany.

Napoleon III made it plain that he disliked what Bismarck's northern Germans were doing, but he was all

I

bluster; the direct result of his activities was disastrous for France. He alienated Germans of various independent states, but took no action when it was still possible to prevent them from banding together under the Prussian banner.

Bismarck had two powerful weapons. One was democratic: he granted the vote to every German male who was twenty-one years of age. The other was his superbly disciplined army that had been equipped with the most modern weapons. It was the best fighting force to appear in Europe since the legions of Napoleon I had vanished, and Bismarck used it with the skill of a virtuoso.

His infantry was supplied with a "needle gun," a rifle that fired five rounds per minute, and overwhelmed its opposition. His artillery included deadly howitzers and the largest cannon ever made. And still another innovation left his foes bewildered: he transported his troops by rail. In 1866 he had his first chance to prove the efficiency of his forces.

Austria, the ally of France, disputed Bismarck's claim to the duchies of Schleswig-Holstein, and Bismarck responded by sending regiments to occupy Holstein. He declared war on Imperial Austria, stunned his foe in a campaign that lasted less than two months, and won a decisive victory at Koniggrätz. Austria was forced to sue for peace, and what came to be known as the Seven Weeks' War came to an end.

Bismarck promptly annexed both Schleswig and Holstein, and simultaneously took possession of the kingdom of Hanover, the free city of Frankfort and the duchies of Hesse-Cassel and Nassau. Napoleon accepted the treaty in his attempt to annex territories along the Rhine, or the French border, but Bismarck merely refused. Prussia, the dominant power, added more than twenty additional German principalities to her growing realm. Again Napoleon III postured but took no action.

Consolidating his hold, Bismarck established a parliament, and representatives were elected to it by all the newly enfranchised citizens. The North German Confederation could now appear before the rest of the world as a free, democratic nation, even though the king of Prussia had become the hereditary head of the new state.

As statesmen everywhere realized, a serious power vacuum existed in the southern German states, among them Bavaria, Würtemberg, and Baden. These principalities had not yet been absorbed by Bismarck, who spread the rumor that France coveted their territory. His agents were active there, and a considerable body of public opinion expressed itself in favor of union with the new German nation that was emerging.

It was just as logical that these southern states join German-speaking Austria. Austria had already been defeated by Bismarck, and the Austro-Hungarian Empire was having other problems of its own. The Hungarians, who controlled the military apparatus, were not in favor of another showdown with Bismarck. In any event, the government was encountering serious troubles in trying to absorb and assimilate its peoples of many languages and ethnic backgrounds.

A logical step to prevent the further amalgamation of the German states would have been a firm alliance between Austria and France, which was the wealthiest of the

Continental powers. There were strong hints from London that, if this bond were formed, Great Britain would also join in the alliance, and would raise her voice, along with that of her partners, in demanding that present borders be respected.

Napoleon III, had he taken an appropriate series of initiatives, could have formed such an alliance, but he vacillated again, and again made pompous speeches. He further alienated the states of southern Germany by ridiculing the temperament and characteristics of the German peoples. In a series of inept speeches and letters he heaped scorn on everything German, and thereby lost the support of the south German principalities, which had been France's traditional allies for more than two hundred years. In their new, nationalistic fervor, they began to look with favor on casting their lot with Prussia, which they had long feared.

As the 1860s drew to a close, people everywhere began to speak of the inevitability of a war between France and the new Germany. Rulers of both nations believed that a war would be to their advantage. Bismarck realized that, in the event of hostilities, the southern German states could be partly bludgoned, partly frightened into joining his new nation. He was aware, too, of the deep divisions that were forming in France; he knew that the opposition to Napoleon III was intense, particularly in Paris. And he reasoned that a defeat might force the petty tyrant from the French throne. A weak, divided France would make the new Germany the most powerful nation in Europe, strong enough to cope with Imperial Russia and almost as powerful as Great Britain.

Napoleon III was unable to admit that the legions

carrying the eagle banners of the first Napoleon were now second-rate, badly motivated troops. A smashing victory over the Germans, he told his advisers, would make people forget the Mexican fiasco, his weak campaigns in Italy where now he held only Rome, and would restore the mystic legend of Napoleonic invincibility.

So he engaged in saber-rattling, and while he talked, Bismarck quietly built up his own forces. Each month a new German regiment was formed, and received the finest equipment that the new munitions plants of Germany could manufacture.

The situation came to a head in 1870, when a revolution drove the queen of Spain from the throne of that country, and a provisional government offered the crown to Prince Leopold of Hohenzollern, a cousin of King Wilhelm of Prussia. The presence of a Prussian on the throne of Spain would mean that France would be surrounded by her enemies, so it was obvious that Napoleon III could tolerate no such development.

To the intense dismay of Bismarck, Prince Leopold, who had no desire to become king of Spain, turned down the offer. It was repeated twice more, and was twice more rejected. But Bismarck, acting in devious ways, persuaded the Spaniards to make the offer a fourth time, then instructed his agents in Paris to release the rumor that Leopold had accepted.

The French ambassador, Benedetti, immediately received instructions to make a formal protest. He went to the German watering spa of Ems, where King Wilhelm was taking the cure, and demanded that Prince Leopold reject the offer. Wilhelm replied mildly—and truthfully—that his cousin would not become king of Spain, and had no intention of sitting on the Spanish throne.

Napoleon III, who was ill, immediately claimed a diplomatic victory. Germany, he declared, had been compelled to back down when confronted by a determined France. Hoping to win an even greater triumph, he sent Benedetti back to Ems with a demand that Wilhelm issue a solemn pledge that no Hohenzollern ever would sit on the throne of Spain. Wilhelm politely but firmly declined, and sent Bismarck a telegram telling him what had transpired.

This was the opportunity that Bismarck had awaited. He released a heavily edited version of the "Ems dispatch," as the telegram was called. The Germans thought their monarch had been insulted, while the French believed their ambassador had been subjected to a severe royal snub. Tempers rose in both countries.

Although the issue of the Spanish crown no longer had a bearing on the situation, Napoleon III, pressed by Empress Eugénie, announced that the issue had become intolerable, and on July 5, 1870, declared war against Germany.

Bismarck had done his work well, and France had no allies. England agreed to remain neutral by extracting treaties from both Bismarck and Napoleon that neither would attack the vulnerable state of Belgium.

The Italians, waiting for the chance to add Rome and the adjacent Papal states to their newly unified country, promptly did just that. Imperial Russia, barred from the Black Sea for the decade and a half, since the Crimean War had ended, moved a fleet into those waters.

The Austrians, natural allies of France in this situation, wanted nothing to do with Napoleon III, who had forsaken them in the Seven Weeks' War. And they held him responsible for the unification of Italy, a new nation on their southern flank. They even favored the cause of Germany, inasmuch as Bismarck had granted them such generous terms after defeating them four years earlier.

The states of southern Germany now reacted precisely as Bismarck had hoped, and committed themselves as his allies. After the short war ended, he painlessly annexed them.

The war itself was almost as brief as Bismarck's Austrian campaign had been. The first skirmishes took place on July 15. On September 2, after the badly trained, inadequately armed French received a crushing defeat at the Battle of Sedan, the main French forces surrendered.

Napoleon III, who had gone into the field with his regiments, was captured, taken off to Germany, and imprisoned in a castle. For him, at least, the war was ended, although hostilities dragged on for months. He took no part in the negotiations that led to peace, the Germans contemptuously bypassing him, and in March 1871 the so-called Assembly of Bordeaux, which constituted the legal government of France, formally deposed him, calling him "responsible for the ruin, dismemberment and invasion of France."

Ailing but unrepentant, Napoléon le Petit went off to exile in England, where he reverted to his former habits and schemed with Eugénie to place his son on the throne. His machinations were cut short in 1873, when he succumbed to a surgical operation.

The Battle of Sedan brought out the sharp differences between the conservatism of the French provinces, which had tolerated the repressive regime of Napoleon III with relative equanimity, and the republicanism of disgruntled Paris. On September 4 (the day Victor Hugo returned home), the city rebelled against the ministers of the Empire and proclaimed a new Republic of France. The German armies marched through France to the city, but Paris refused to surrender, and the enemy placed the great capital under siege. This plight, one of the worst that Paris had ever been forced to endure in her long history, lasted for four months.

Meanwhile the Germans occupied the great palace of Versailles outside the city, and there Bismarck, in an act of calculated effrontery, proclaimed the formation of the German Empire.

Finally, on January 28, 1871, the starving people of Paris opened their gates. There was no government to surrender to the Germans. Bismarck insisted that a constituent assembly be elected by universal male suffrage; and to it he dictated exceptionally harsh terms, which were formalized in May in the treaty of Frankfort. France was forced to pay a staggering indemnity of five billion gold francs, and ceded her eastern provinces, Alsace and part of Lorraine, to Germany. Although many Alsatians spoke German, they thought of themselves as French, and the hostility of France to the cession laid the seeds of World War I.

The election of the new Assembly took place in February 1871, and the country as a whole still thought of republicans as such radicals that more than two-thirds of the delegates were men of monarchist leaning. The National

Assembly, as it came to be called, moved to Versailles from Bordeaux, but the Parisians, who had endured the siege, refused to accept the harsh German peace terms. They set up their own municipal government, which they called the "Commune," and defied all other authority. The city of two million people, which had endured the German siege, was now under attack by fellow Frenchmen, and all that had happened earlier seemed mild.

Karl Marx, then living in England, saw the formation of the Commune as the beginning of the end of the middle classes, but he failed to understand the true nature of the insurrection, as did many others. The spirit of the French Revolution lived again, and the Communards, although opposed to the concentration of wealth in the hands of a few aristocrats, wealthy manufacturers, and clergymen, were ardent, freedom-loving patriots who sought the establishment of a republic.

The fighting between the troops of the National Assembly and the street mobs of the Commune was the worst that Paris had ever known. Battles raged block by block, and the eight weeks that the Communards were supposedly in power saw the city drowning in a bloodbath. In the last, desperate days of their struggle, the Communards burned a number of priceless public buildings to the ground, and inexcusably executed the Archbishop of Paris, whom they had been holding as a hostage.

When the forces of the National Assembly finally gained control of the city, they were determined to stamp out the recurring radicalism of Paris for all time. It was estimated by some that approximately one-third of a million persons were denounced before the Assembly's tribunals.

Other, more accurate, figures tell the true story of the terror. More than twenty thousand persons were put to death for alleged Communard crimes, and another eight thousand were deported to a French penal colony in New Caledonia.

The gestation period that preceded the actual birth of the Third Republic was indecently prolonged. In fact, as the months turned into years without a responsible government, France became something of a laughingstock, a symbol of instability, and generations passed before she could change her image.

A monarchy would have been established overnight had the overwhelming majority in the National Assembly been able to agree on a single candidate. But two monarchist groups, almost evenly divided, fought each other with a vigor greater than they showed in their battles against the republicans. There were Bourbon adherents against those who favored the Orléans branch of the house of Bourbon; neither would yield. The royalist candidates themselves impressed no one with their talents, and the snickers of the world became louder.

Over a long, weary period, the monarchists managed to handcuff each other, thereby delivering a balance of power into the hands of the republicans. Squabbles were so intense that it proved impossible to draft a constitution, and the best that the Assembly could manage was a series of laws that served as a substitute for a constitution.

By 1875 the Assembly finally hammered out a constitution that provided for a president, a council of ministers who would serve under a premier, and a parliament of two houses. The lower house, the Chamber of Deputies, would be elected by universal male suffrage, while the Senate would be elected indirectly through an intricate, cumbersome system. No real change was made, however, in the basic apparatus of government, which controlled the law courts, the government ministries, the police, and the army, all of which continued to function precisely as they had since the time of Napoleon I.

Within two years of its formation, the new government had its initial trial by fire. The President was Marshal Marie Edmé Patrice Maurice de MacMahon, who had won his marshal's baton almost a decade before the outbreak of the Franco-Prussian War, and who was one of the few military men to escape disgrace in the debacle. Severely wounded at Sedan, he recovered in captivity, and in 1873 he became the provisional President. In 1875, when the new laws came into effect, he formally took office, supported by the monarchists, not republicans.

MacMahon had the rigid mentality of the military man who had never looked beyond the visor of his splendid, gold-braided cap. He would have been glad to accept office for a period of ten years, and it may well be, as his foes charged, that he wanted to create conditions that would enable him to seize the government for life.

In any event, a constitutional crisis of the first magnitude arose in 1877, a scant two years after the Third Republic was voted in. Premier Jules Simon, who had the overwhelming support of the Chamber of Deputies, became engaged in a dispute with the President, who ordered him to resign. MacMahon then ordered the dissolution of the Chamber itself.

A new Chamber was elected in the autumn of 1877, and for the first time, to MacMahon's chagrin, was strongly republican in nature. The President refused to take the results of the election as final, and still believing that the provinces outside Paris supported him, appointed a new premier the Chamber would not approve. The republican majority refused the premier funds, and the activities of the government came to a halt. Late in 1877 MacMahon capitulated, and appointed a premier of whom the Chamber approved. That ended the constitutional crisis until January, 1879, when Senate elections gave the republicans a majority in the upper chamber as well as the lower. President MacMahon knew when he was completely beaten, and resigned, retiring to private life. He was succeeded by Jules Grévy, a steadfast republican of no particular stature.

Perhaps the greatest miracle of the era was the industrial and cultural recovery of France in the years following the defeat of the nation by Germany and the domestic upheavals that came in the wake of that catastrophe. If the nation did not regain her equilibrium overnight, as some claimed, it did not take long for her to prosper again. The rural areas, always wealthy, became even richer. Factories proliferated, the Industrial Revolution made greater gains than in any other country, and France soon assumed a place as the world's third largest exporter of consumer goods, especially luxuries. Paris became the women's fashion capital of the world, thanks to the efforts exerted by Worth, the former Empress Eugénie's dressmaker. Life in Paris became more pleasant than in any other capital.

The gutted buildings of Paris were soon rebuilt, and the city became the world's foremost publishing center. In the year 1879, for example, more new books were published there than in London, New York, and Brussels combined. Paris boasted more theaters than any other cultural capital. It was said, only partly in jest, that there were too many artists there for a census taker to count.

The country's political maturation failed to match her advance in other spheres. Paris—and the provinces— were sadly lacking in political sophistication. A hard-core group of aristocrats, the Roman Catholic clergy, and the army officer caste continued to favor the restoration of a monarchy. In addition to the Bourbon and Orléans enthusiasts, a third group reappeared, the Bonapartists. Some wanted to give the throne to the son of Napoleon III (who would live for a few more years before dying in the British Army in Africa). Others preferred another distant relative of Napoleon I. In the main the monarchists were ultra-conservative, anti-Semitic, and opposed all extensions of individual liberty.

The cause of the republicans gradually became stronger. Perhaps the tide turned in their favor after the savage reprisals that had decimated the ranks of the Communards. The great middle class of Paris and the shopkeepers, merchants, and small businessmen of provincial cities had felt a deep mistrust for the more democratic form of government prior to that vicious punishment. Such acts created a great tide of sympathy for the common working man, and the bourgeois elements began to drift toward the republican ranks.

It was not accidental, in 1881, that the republicans finally won control of both houses of parliament. Nor is it surprising that the radicalism of the earlier days gradually gave way to a more modified, liberal outlook. In the 1880s the new majority established democratic, compulsory schooling for all children, at the expense of the taxpayer and free of all clerical controls. The army was forced to grant commissions on the basis of merit rather than proof of one's aristocratic background. Formal censorship was abolished, and France established a degree of personal freedom for her citizens unmatched by another nation on earth, with the exception of the United States.

The advances made in the sciences during the period following the Franco-Prussian War were remarkable. In this atmosphere France produced Pasteur and the Curies. She took first place in invention, and resumed her former place as the banking capital of the world, a place she continued to hold almost to the outbreak of World War I.

Admiration for Gallic charm was unbounded, and the education of young English and American ladies and gentlemen wasn't complete until they had visited the City of Light. The visitors fell in love with Paris, and being outsiders failed to see the deep, ugly cracks below the surface of the social structure.

Meanwhile the French farmer ruled supreme on his own land, and no one starved. If France gradually fell behind Great Britain and Germany in industrial production, leaving the lessons of the Franco-Prussian War unlearned, there were few who knew it, and fewer who cared.

It is significant to note the statistics in the migration of the dissatisfied from the various nations of Europe to the New World. Millions came to America from the British Isles and from Germany, but, between 1846 and 1914, only three hundred thousand French citizens made the journey across the Atlantic.

The French ship of state had almost sunk in 1870, and for the better part of a decade thereafter it sailed through the most turbulent of waters. It was to the France of defeat that Victor Hugo returned home after his long, self-imposed exile, and it was he who had a major voice thereafter in shaping her destiny.

Chapter
XIII

*N*O other newspaper in France had the courage
of the new Hugo publication, *Le Rappel,* that published
its first issues in 1869. Victor once again sensed the temper
of the changing times, and thought that Napoleon III, no
matter how bold and irrational his ventures abroad, had
already alienated so many of his subjects that he would
hesitate to close down a newspaper that printed the names
of the Hugo sons on its masthead. As usual, his instincts
were right.

In 1870, when the government announced that it
would not tolerate the presence of a Hohenzollern on the
throne of Spain, Victor himself wrote an editorial in reply:

*The unarmed lion tamer speaks bravely when he
stands outside the pen, but he would be wise to load his
pistol with real bullets before he steps through the gate into*

the cage of a genuine lion. He who brays the loudest does not necessarily have the most ferocious bite.

In May 1870, just before his declaration of war, Napoleon III ordered a national plebiscite, the results of which, he declared, would prove that his country stood firmly behind him. *Le Rappel* laughed aloud at the Emperor and called the so-called plebiscite a mockery of the democratic process, as it granted the vote to so few.

It is surprising that the censors did not shut the doors of the newspaper by nightfall. The only explanation for this failure to act is that Napoleon III was far too busy to notice the angry hornet buzzing near his head.

When he finally declared war on Germany in July, *Le Rappel* stated flatly that it was madness, and Victor wrote a brief editorial under his own name, in which he said the Emperor was waging a "war of caprice."

Concern over the war made it impossible for Victor to work, and in mid-August 1870, he closed Hauteville House and journeyed to Brussels with Juliette. Few people knew his long-range plans, but he predicted that Napoleon III, who had joined his troops near the Low Countries, would never return to Paris as the monarch of France. The German war machine would smash the French regiments, and Victor wanted to be ready to end his own exile at the first possible moment.

The inevitable defeat at the Battle of Sedan on September 2, reached Brussels the following morning, and Victor Hugo wept. The news of the Emperor's capture by Prussian troops was not confirmed until the following day, and Victor immediately made train reservations for the next night, September 4.

On that memorable occasion he set out for France with Juliette and Jules Claretie, a young author who had become one of Victor's disciples. They were accompanied by others, including Charles, who had come to Brussels to meet him. There were no guards on the French side of the border, which indicated how chaotic the situation had become. Soon thereafter the train halted at the little town of Landrecies where they saw about fifty soldiers, survivors of Sedan, who had escaped the Prussian prisoner-of-war net. They were exhausted men, half-starved, their uniforms covered with grime, and Victor's patriotism overwhelmed him.

Opening his window, he shouted down to them, "Vive la France ! Vive l'armée ! Vive la Patrie !" as they began to board his train.

Learning that the men were hungry, he insisted that the train make an unscheduled halt at Tergnier, and there he bought bread, cheese, and wine for the defeated troops. Leaving his own comfortable coach, he joined them, and with them ate his first meal on French soil in nineteen years.

There had been no opportunity to send a telegram to anyone in Paris that Victor was coming home, as he believed that in the confusion no one would be on hand to receive it. So Victor expected no homecoming celebration of any kind. A rumor reached the train that the monarchy had been abolished and the Third Republic established— at least in Paris—so Victor could imagine the wild scenes taking place there. No one would know or care that a novelist-poet was returning from exile, he told his companions.

It appears that he was not posing for effect, but truly

failed to realize the great stature he had attained in the hearts of his countrymen. But the others knew, and were determined that he not be cheated of his triumph. Jules Claretie told the conductor the identity of the white-haired passenger in the slouch hat, and the conductor sent the news ahead to Paris in a series of telegrams.

The train reached its destination at 9:35 A.M., and from the windows Victor could see that the Gare du Nord was crowded with thousands of people, while thousands more filled the treets beyond it. He assumed that a riot of some sort was in progress, but would let nothing deter him from going home.

He stepped from the train, and a roar rattled the glass panes in the ceiling of the station. Volunteer "police" who were identified by their armbands held back the throngs, and a beautiful young woman walked alone down the platform, bearing two huge bouquets of flowers. Judith Gautier, the daughter of Victor's old friend, had been selected to do the honors, and presented one bouquet to Victor, the other to Juliette.

Then volunteer police formed a flying wedge, and Victor was escorted to the balcony of a small café opposite the station. There he was cheered so loudly and continuously that the brief speech he made could not be heard.

The chant, "Vive Victor Hugo!" rose from thousands of throats.

Victor wept when the crowd spontaneously began to recite entire verses from *Les Châtiments*, his poetic paean of freedom.

Many in the throng wanted to escort the returning

hero to the Hôtel de Ville, but they were dissuaded by another of Victor's old friends, Paul Meurice, who planned to take the party to his own house on the Avenue Frochot, where he had made a suite ready for the travelers.

Someone produced an open carriage, and Victor rode in it to Meurice's house, with Charles and Juliette beside him, his friends following in a line of carriages. Ordinarily the ride would have taken about twenty minutes, but this morning the crowds in the streets were so dense that the short journey required the better part of three hours. When the carriage, together with those containing various friends and admirers, reached certain major squares, the cavalcade was forced to make a complete halt.

Victor was pelted with flowers, and repeatedly heard large throngs break into spontaneous renditions from *Les Châtiments*. Again and again he was compelled to respond with a brief speech, but the precise number of these addresses is unknown. Charles said he made three, in addition to the first one given at the Gare du Nord, while Claretie insisted he spoke six times. Claretie also wrote:

What an ovation was offered him by this tumultuous and revolutionary people of Paris, a people ready for great things, more joyful over its reconquered liberty than frightened by the cannon rumbling at its ramparts. We shall always see the carriage making its way down the Rue Lafayette, the great poet standing erect, with tears in his eyes, uplifted by the throng.

Thousands remained outside the house of Meurice to cheer, and Victor had to make repeated appearances at a window before the throng dispersed. Even then he had no opportunity to rest. Hundreds of old friends and acquaintances came to call on him, and hundreds of strangers came, too, eager to pay their respects.

That night a thunderstorm broke over Paris, clearing the streets. The exhausted Victor was awakened by the rumble and crash of the thunderclaps, and remarked to Juliette, "This, I fear, is a sign of what is to come."

He was right, and two days later the first of the Prussian cannon that would form a ring outside the city appeared near the gates.

On September 9, with his entire family gathered around him, including Jeanne, the infant daughter of Charles and Alice, Victor sat down and wrote an open letter to the Germans who had launched their siege of the city. It was one of the most moving documents he had ever penned, and he informed the Prussian generals they would win the friendship of Parisians for all time if they spared the city. He also presented the argument that it had been the now defunct government of Napoleon III that had declared war on Prussia, and that the new Republic was innocent of all blame.

The Prussian commanders were not literary enthusiasts, and continued the siege.

As the days passed and the "ring of steel" around Paris grew tighter, Victor's peaceful instincts gave way to a surge of violent patriotism. He wrote a new appeal, this one to the people of Paris, and a friend printed thousands of posters, which were pasted on walls throughout the city. Paris could triumph and would triumph, Victor declared, summoning all her sons and daughters to take part in military duty against the invader.

Accepting his own advice, he went to the walls in Montmarte that same afternoon, and after being shown how to fire an artillery piece, he sent a symbolic shell in the direction of the German lines.

His patriotic fervor quickly took a more practical turn. At his direction, the first French edition of *Les Châtiments* was published, at his own expense, and every penny of income was devoted to the purchase of new cannon. He also authorized readings from the book at various theaters, and donated all the receipts to the same cause.

Since it was virtually impossible to find quarters of his own when conditions were so chaotic, Victor and Juliette continued to live under the roof of Paul Meurice, but the novelist-poet felt a need for a headquarters of his own. So he rented or was assigned a large room on the ground floor of the Pavillon de Rohan on the rue de Rivoli, and there he repaired daily for consultations with the leaders of France, his friends, and anyone else who wanted to see him. There in the salon, where he was described by the Goncourt brothers, he was visited by foreign diplomats, including the American ambassador, the ministers of the French government, generals, his circle of great authors and artists, including Daumier.

His sons, both over forty, had joined the defense army manning the walls of Paris.

Most of the prominent men in Paris were already playing their favorite game of politics, but Victor refused. "Stand together," he told everyone who came to his salon. "Remain united!"

His impatience with the impotence of the officials of the abortive Third Republic became greater, and he sympathized with the ultimate goals of the Communards. But he refused to condone their immediate aims. "If you revolt now," he told them, "you will be playing directly into the hands of the Prussians. Wait, and take office by legitimate, legal means."

No voice was more sane, no temperament cooler than that of the famous old man who had returned from exile in time to share the trials of his beloved Paris. To the extent that the people of the city maintained their equilibrium, he was as responsible as any leader. After an absence of almost two decades he had thrust himself into a situation that was beyond the control of any Parisian, but his counsel was sound and his own dignity prevailed.

It became increasingly difficult for the citizens of the beleaguered city to maintain their balance. Prussian cannon were shelling the city methodically, with first one district, then another, receiving heavy bombardments. Familiar landmarks vanished. Churches and shops, private dwellings and schools and public office structures disintegrated into heaps of shapeless rubble.

The voices of the Commune became louder, more insistent, but Victor continued to advise the exercise of patience. His own was remarkable, and he seemed to thrive on adversity. When others began to give in to despair, he wrote the text for another wall poster, declaring, "The soul of Paris is indestructible. Neither cannon nor famine can destroy her!"

The food shortage became increasingly desperate. Volunteers from the Army of Paris went out through the city gates at night and braved the sniper fire of the enemy to pick vegetables, but the supplies they brought back were pitifully meager. The basic staples of Parisian diet were horsemeat and rats. Stray dogs and cats were rounded up and slaughtered, and then household pets began to disappear. A few privileged citizens, among them Victor Hugo, received gifts from the zoo, which could not feed its animals, and on three occasions he dined, respectively, on bear steaks, venison, and antelope chops.

But these were rare treats. The noted gourmet and gourmand not only endured the same privations that afflicted other citizens, but actually seemed to enjoy the sacrifices he was forced to make. In mid-November he wrote a small cookbook that was published as a pamphlet, and in it he gave sound, cheerful advice. Some excerpts:

Horsemeat has never been regarded as a delicacy. When twice boiled, however, it can be delicious, particularly when served with horseradish sauce. This is important, since the supplies of horseradish are virtually unlimited, while those of horsemeat are not. It is significant that the garnish is so pungent it helps kill one's appetite.

Civilized men and women find it difficult to eat ratmeat when it is served broiled or baked. We are the victims of our prejudices. It has been discovered, however, that this meat, when chopped into small pieces to resemble minced beef, makes a palatable filling for meat pies. The use of condiments in liberal quantities is advised.

Garden weeds, lightly boiled, make an excellent substitute for vegetable soup. When the leaves of trees are added, however, care should be taken to cook these leaves for a considerably longer time before adding the more tender weeds. The nourishment that is obtained from this dish may be questioned, but the taste is superb.

On December 1, a brief truce of several hours was observed so that elderly persons and small children who were seriously ill could be sent out for medical treatment. One Colonel von Grabow, the inspector-general of the Prussian forces, sent into Paris a list of prominent persons who, if they wished, also could be evacuated. Bismarck was anxious to preserve at least the façade that his troops were behaving in a civilized fashion, and wanted to avoid the charge than any internationally renowned persons had died during the siege. The name heading the list was that of Victor Hugo.

Immediately aware of the propaganda values of the move, Victor retaliated in kind, and sent a letter to Bismarck, via Colonel von Grabow. In order to make certain that the communication saw the light of print, he also smuggled out copies on the persons of several of the elderly sick who were evacuated. Although he didn't know it until the siege ended, the letter was printed in the newspapers of many countries, including England and the United States. A scathing, contemptuous document, it may have been more responsible than any other influence in winning Paris the admiration and sympathy of the world. Victor wrote, in part:

If I survive your barbarian assault, I will soon be seventy years of age, so it matters little whether I live or die. It is of far greater importance that my infant grand-children be spared, and with them the thousands of other children who, if they do not starve, remain at the mercy of your pitiless, exploding steel devices that each day commit random murder.

Do you suppose that any honorable man would desert his two million fellows and let them lie in their own spilled blood? It is far better that my blood mingle with that of the innocent who are being killed everywhere, in their beds, in the streets, in our churches as they pray, by your mercenaries, the direct descendants of the barbarians who destroyed the civilization of ancient Rome and sent mankind plunging into the miseries of the centuries called the Dark Ages.

I am a Parisian! So here I shall remain until the last spark of civilization flickers and dies!

Copies of the letter appeared on the pock-marked walls of the city, and "I am a Parisian!" became the rallying cry of the day. But courage alone could not defeat the enemy, who increased the pace of his bombardment. By late January it had become obvious that the end was drawing near, and by the 28th the meager food supplies of the city were exhausted, the last of the medicines hoarded in the hospitals had vanished, and it became apparent that a plague might break out at any time. In mid-afternoon white flags were raised over the city gates, and within minutes the Prussian infantry marched through them and occupied the city.

Colonel von Grabow, wanting to assure himself—and Bismarck—that the distinguished citizens of Paris were alive and well, immediately paid personal calls on them, and the first house he visited was that of Paul Meurice.

Victor had to be persuaded to receive him, but finally

came into the drawing room, his hair and beard now a pure white, but his bearing erect. He refused to shake hands, and also refused the offer of food, which orderlies were bringing with them. He preferred to stand in line with his fellow citizens, he said. He and they had shared hardships for four months, and he had no intention of accepting a special status now.

Food poured into the city again, and Parisians began to repair the damage. Then, overnight, political considerations became all-important. Bismarck insisted that elections be held within ten days, and delegates to the Constituent Assembly were directed to report to Bordeaux as soon thereafter as possible.

Victor became a candidate, and his election was taken for granted, so he did not wait until the results became known, but left for the southwest on the evening of February 8, 1871, soon after the polls had closed. Garibaldi, Louis Blanc, Jules Simon, and Léon Gambetta (the opportunistic politician who had escaped the siege by balloon) were also delegates. The facilities of Bordeaux were extended to the limit, and accommodations were exceptionally difficult to find, but Victor was not deterred by such practical considerations. He traveled in his usual style, accompanied by Juliette, both his sons, his daughter-in-law, his two small grandchildren, and three friends. Suitable rooms would be found, he declared, and was delighted when a large house was made available for his convenience.

A number of his old friends grouped themselves around Victor, and so did several younger men of liberal persuasion, among them Georges Clemenceau, who was destined to become the most prominent French statesman of his age. All of them agreed with Victor's stand that the Assembly should refuse to ratify the treaty of Frankfort. Such a rejection would mean a resumption of the war, to be sure, and France already had been beaten to her knees. But Victor was convinced, as were his friends, that the nation would rally and could send another army into the field.

In his major address on the subject, delivered on February 27, Victor was as eloquent as he was emphatic. All hope for the establishment of a permanent peace in Europe would be ended, he declared, if France accepted the treaty: "There will be, henceforth in Europe, two nations to be feared—one because it will be victorious, the other because it will be vanquished."

Even those who wanted the treaty ratified at once recognized the validity of this argument, and applauded.

Two elements in Victor made it impossible for him to refrain from picturing the Europe he himself envisioned. He was a poet, first and foremost, and he was also a patriot. The day would come, he declared, when France would recover her lost provinces of Alsace and Lorraine. They were an integral part of both the soul and the body of France herself, and never could be separated from her.

Then he took an extra step. The day would also come, he said, when France would also conquer the entire left bank of the Rhine River. Then, having returned the insult in full, she would extend the hand of brotherhood to Germany.

He concluded his address on a note worthy of a great poet:

No more frontiers! The Rhine for all! Let us be the same, great republic, the United States of Europe!

Let there be universal, abiding peace! We will shake hands, for we will have rendered service to each other. We will say, "You have delivered us from our emperor." And they will reply, "Now you deliver us from ours."

So we will sit down together, in eternal friendship, and our one, great brotherhood, the brotherhood of all mankind, will be forged for all time.

Even the most fervently patriotic and bellicose of Assembly members shrank from the idea of waging an aggressive war against France's conqueror, or, at the very least, of mentioning such an idea now. Bismarck's observers sat in the visitors' gallery, taking down every word that was spoken on the floor.

Victor was deeply disturbed when, at the beginning of March, the Constituent Assembly ratified the treaty. The parliament, he complained, was dominated by conservative royalists, men who wanted only to turn back the clock. That had happened after the defeat of the first Napoleon, but must not be allowed to happen again.

The events of March 8 were too much for him. Garibaldi, who had fought for France with a small army of Italian volunteers, had been elected a member by the citizens of a grateful Paris, as well as by the people of Algiers. The great Italian liberator had immediately struck up a friendship with Victor, who had admired him so long.

Exercising tact as well as judgment when the monarchists opposed him, Garibaldi resigned his seat from Paris, saying that he was a foreigner, and consequently felt it would be wrong for him to exercise his vote. He made it clear, however, that he would like to deliver an address.

The conservative majority proceeded to insult him, gratuitously, by voting that no outsider had the right to speak before a parliament of elected Frenchmen.

Victor was furious, and was one of a small group who persuaded Garibaldi not to leave Bordeaux. An opportunity would be created for him in the near future to make his address.

But the committee on credentials tried to forestall this event, and on March 8 it took up the question of his election to the Assembly by the citizens of Algiers. It would have been a simple matter to rule that his resignation as a delegate from Paris also applied to his other seat. But, in its anxiety to prevent his speech, the conservative-dominated committee added another insult, and ruled that his election from Algiers was "null, void and without validity of any nature."

Victor could stomach no more. When the vote of the committee was reported to the Assembly, he jumped to his feet and made one of the most violent addresses of his life. "Three weeks ago you refused to hear one of the greatest men of our age. You committed an insufferable deed. Why? Because you are afraid to hear the truth, that France must move forward, not creep back into the stinking rot of a bygone time!"

The conservatives booed and jeered lustily.

Completely losing his temper, Victor called Garibaldi "the only unbeaten general of the war!"

Several of the defeated French army's generals were

sitting in the Assembly as civilians. All were ultraconservative, all were highly sensitive to events of recent months, and all felt their personal honor had been impugned. One leaped to his feet and demanded satisfaction. Another forgot he was taking part in the deliberations of an august assembly, and cursed colorfully and at length. A third tried to rush at Victor and strike him down, but was held back by some of the younger liberals and radicals.

The entire Right believed it had been attacked, and members stood on their chairs, screaming and shouting. The pandemonium was exquisite. Claretie, an observer, said he had never seen such maddening chaos.

Victor, his face a deep red, stood silently, waiting for the hubbub to subside enough to make himself heard. He had felt misgivings ever since the Assembly had started its deliberations, and on several occasions had tried to persuade fellow members to resign together, in a body, as a protest against the timid conservatism of the majority. What other, less courageous men were unwilling to do together, he was anxious to do alone.

No one will ever know the extent to which his anger was feigned. He was upset, certainly, but he committed no impulsive, unpremeditated act. Waiting until the chamber became relatively quiet, he shouted, "You would not hear Garibaldi, and now you refuse to hear me! Very well! I tender my resignation from this farcical Assembly!"

Seizing a sheet of paper, he scribbled his resignation and signature, then stalked up to the Speaker's desk with the document, and walked out. The high drama of his act startled the gathering into temporary silence, and Victor became even more a symbol of the cause of republicanism.

Although Victor no longer had any official reason to remain in Bordeaux, the liberals and radicals still regarded him as a leader, and he was reluctant to leave while the Assembly remained in session. So he assigned himself the task of acting as chief correspondent for *Le Rappel*, which François-Victor was editing in Paris, and in the next few days he sent the newspaper several scathing dispatches, all of which attacked the monarchist-oriented parliament.

On the evening of March 13 a small dinner party was scheduled to be given in Victor's honor at a restaurant. Charles and Alice planned to attend with Victor and Juliette, and a taxi came to pick them up. The two ladies entered it and sat, and were followed by Victor, while Charles, still standing in the street, gave directions to the driver. He never finished his instructions, but suddenly dropped to the cobblestones, and a moment later he was dead, killed by a heart attack.

The unexpected tragedy stunned Victor, but he would not permit his son's death to interfere with the activities that, he was convinced, he was conducting for the welfare of France. He and Alice agreed that Charles should be buried in Paris, in the same plot where Victor's father rested, and the Hugo party sadly returned to the capital.

They arrived on March 18, the day the insurrection of the Communards broke out, and vicious street fighting was taking place as the funeral cortège passed by on its way to the cemetery.

The people of Paris could have arranged no greater tribute to Victor Hugo than they paid him on that occasion. Men who were hurling bricks and firing pistols and rifles at each other halted when they saw the gaunt figure of Victor

Hugo, who sat beside his daughter-in-law in the first carriage. Silently, their civil war momentarily forgotten, they fell in at the rear of the procession. According to several newspaper accounts, a crowd of ten to fifteen thousand persons followed Victor to the cemetery.

There, after Charles had been buried, hundreds surrounded Victor. Unmindful of his exhaustion, they wanted to shake his and, or kiss his cheek, and express their sympathies.

Auguste Vacquerie, who had delivered the funeral oration, tried to extricate him from the crowd. But Victor, tears streaming down his face, refused to leave. "These are my people," he said. "How I love them, and how they love me!"

Two days later, on March 20, as the street fighting mounted in violence, Victor departed for Brussels. Charles's estate had to be settled there, and for the protection of Alice and their children his complicated affairs needed untangling. The widow and her babies accompanied Victor, as did Juliette.

So it was from remote Brussels that Victor observed the excesses of the civil war that erupted in full force on April 2, when the forces of the French parliament marched on the Communards in Paris. He deplored the vicious fighting, and made several attempts, in letters, to persuade members of both factions to desist, to compromise, but the slaughter continued. The situation progressed beyond reason and embattled Frenchmen were no longer listening to anyone, not even to a revered author-statesman.

Victor's feeling of alarm grew intense. In his private opinion, the Communards were going mad in their defiance of authority. But the bloodbath committed against them by the monarchist sympathizers of the provisional government was even more horrifying. Untold numbers were executed and it was reported that hundreds of thousands of republicans were arrested.

He was determined to return to Paris. Juliette, who seldom interfered, would not permit it. He would be in physical danger again, she insisted. Hadn't he already suffered more than any one had right to expect of a sixty-nine-year-old man? The authorities of the provisional regime unwittingly helped her cause when Victor disregarded her advice. He applied for a new passport, but the French Government temporarily denied him the right to return, maintaining that the situation was too inflammatory and that his presence in Paris might rouse further hostilities among the Parisians. They meant the Communards.

By the latter part of May the Communards had been smashed, and the new terror gripped Paris. Both François-Victor and Auguste Vacqueries were denounced, and compelled to stand trial before the tribunals of the provisional government; eventually both were cleared. Scores of Victor's friends and acquaintances, being republicans, were also in danger.

Unable to remain quiet any longer, Victor felt it necessary to speak his mind. The Communards were the lesser of two evils, he believed, and he publicly offered refuge, under his own roof, to any who escaped from the jails, the detention camps, and the execution squads of the reactionary regime.

The Belgian people were divided on the issue, and Victor's statement infuriated those who supported the provisional French government. At night toward the end of May 1871, a mob of several hundred persons attacked Victor's house. Cobblestones torn from the streets were thrown through the windows, the crowd roared threats to drag out Victor Hugo and hang him. And there was a danger that torches carried in the streets would be thrown into the house.

The Brussels police, unable to cope with the crowd, sent for military assistance, half a battalion of troops arrived on the scene before any serious damage was done, and the mob was dispersed.

The Belgian Government had been placed in an untenable position by the great author. Though many officials sympathized with Victor and believed his statement had been inspired by his humanitarian views, they could not permit French passions to spill across their border. So Victor Hugo was ordered to leave Belgium, and was not granted the right to return.

"At sixty-nine," he said dramatically, "I am a man who has no country."

He exaggerated, of course, deliberately drawing attention to his plight in order to gain sympathy. He still owned Hauteville House and its adjoining villa, both of which he could have occupied without any difficulty. But he had no desire to retire again to such a remote spot. It was important, he felt, to watch closely the events in France, and he wanted to return to Paris as soon as the city was safe for the grandchildren he adored and protected, and from whom he would not be parted.

So he took them with Alice to adjoining Luxembourg, and in that quiet grand duchy he rented two small houses in the town of Vianden, overlooking the peaceful Our River. One of these dwellings he turned over to Alice and her children, while he and Juliette lived in the one that stood adjacent to it. There, close to France yet removed from it, he could not only listen and watch, but could turn to his writing, which the turbulent events of the past nine months had forced him to abandon.

It was in Luxembourg that he wrote his new book of poetry, *L'Année terrible*, in which he described the awesome events of the past year. Disillusioned and somber, he nevertheless could not write poetry that lacked beauty, and although the book cannot be regarded as one of his major works, it still had distinction. It was only a mild success when published, principally because France was in no mood to read or appreciate poems, even those written by a master.

By early autumn France had become quiet again, the worst of the terror had ended, and the illness of François-Victor, who was suffering from tuberculosis, recalled Victor to Paris. There he tried, without success, to avoid politics, and to devote himself to his own vocational activities. During the months that followed he managed to revive his reputation as the most lascivious rake in Europe.

Chapter
XIV

$\mathcal{V}$ICTOR HUGO was horrified by what he saw of Paris in early October 1871. The Tuileries had been ruined, the Hôtel de Ville was gutted by fire, and scores of other magnificent buildings were wrecked. The damage was even worse than that done by the Prussians. Friends begged him to intervene, to use what influence he could to save the lives of prominent citizens who were condemned to death by the provisional government, and he tried, without success, to make appointments with several leading officials.

Reduced to using a public forum, he wrote an editorial, under his signature, for *Le Rappel*. The appearance of his by-line sold out the issue, and all Paris read what he had written, but his appeal saved no lives. Members of the government made no secret of their hatred for him.

In July, his name was entered in the elections for the

new national Chamber of Deputies while he was still in Luxembourg, and he was defeated, much to his humiliation. After his return to Paris, he was again roundly defeated in the run-off elections in January 1872, to his own astonishment. The people of Paris, unutterably weary after the German siege, the excesses of the Commune, and the violent reprisals taken by the provisional government, wanted only peace. And Victor, the voters reasoned, was too sympathetic toward the men who had been prominent in the Commune.

Rebuffed in politics, Victor began a new novel, closeted in the large house he rented for himself, Juliette, and his family. He was interrupted in his labors by the management of the Odéon Theater, which wanted to present a full revival of his play, *Ruy Blas*. He gave his consent, and immediately was plunged into the hectic life of the theater.

In the months that followed, Victor shocked the world and amused Paris by becoming involved, simultaneously, in several intense, hectic romances. Théophile Gautier's daughter, Judith, one of the loveliest young women of the period, was married to Catulle Mendès, a noted poet. Herself a poet, the black-haired Judith, who boasted a breathtaking figure, had attracted Victor ever since she had met him at the Gare du Nord on his return from exile.

She returned his ardor, and he spoke of taking her to Guernsey with him. Whether this was his serious intention is not known, but Mendès became so jealous that he left his wife, thereby creating a scandal of some proportions. Victor was now seventy years of age.

His second affair of consequence, conducted at the same time, was even more spectacular. A young girl with a magnetic personality, burning eyes, and a willowy figure had been given the role of the queen in the play, a part in which Juliette Drouet had been cast so long ago. The young actress was not beautiful, but she had an electric quality that captivated everyone who came in contact with her, and no one who heard her speak ever forgot her voice. Not yet twenty-seven years of age, her real name was Rosine Bernard, but she had taken the stage name of Sarah Bernhardt.

The woman who would become "the divine Sarah" took one look at the great poet-novelist and fell under his spell. Victor was similarly enchanted, and their affair began while *Ruy Blas* was still in rehearsals.

Not satisfied with these dalliances, both with girls almost young enough to be his granddaughters, Victor had twenty to thirty other affairs. Some were great ladies, some were actresses, some were pretty nobodies whom he found attractive. All were young. He thought nothing of bedding a passing conquest in the afternoon, then climbing into the bed of either Judith or Sarah in the evening. He had resumed the passionate stance of younger days, and was indefatigable in his pursuit of the ladies.

But this was different from his former philandering. He no longer wrote love letters or poems to his mistresses. He was growing older, he said, and had to hoard his words. Then, too, he no longer concealed his activities from the incredibly patient, loving, and understanding Juliette Drouet.

Alice Hugo was aghast, and could not understand how Juliette remained so placid, so undisturbed.

A smiling Juliette merely shrugged and shook her head. "His vanity," she said repeatedly, "demands these little pleasures, and he would grow old before his time if he were denied them. But I have no fear that he will desert me. Victor needs me, and knows it as well as I do, if not better."

So, while the world whispered, Juliette waited, and every night Victor came home to her.

Ruy Blas was the greatest success in the theater that Victor had ever known, and he was inundated with offers from other theatrical managers who wanted to present new productions of all his plays.

To their surprise, he demurred. In a letter to the management of the Comédie-Française, he said, "The time I must spend in the rehearsals for one play makes it impossible for me to write another. Time has become my enemy. There is much that I carry in my mind and wish to write, so I must husband my dwindling store of energies."

Apparently it did not occur to him that his affairs occupied his time and depleted his energies, and he continued to sleep with many women through the winter and early spring of 1872. He and Sarah Bernhardt soon lost interest in each other, which opened her to the charge, never proved or disproved, that she had entertained the affair only because of the widespread publicity it had given her. But he continued to see Judith until the day, in mid-spring, when he suddenly departed for Guernsey, taking Juliette, Alice, and his grandchildren with him.

The time had come for him to engage in serious writing, and he could do his best work in his quiet solarium overlooking the sea on his remote Channel island.

He made something of a sentimental journey, stopping for a few days in Jersey before going on to Hauteville House. Although he made no known comment to anyone, the irony of his situation could not have been lost on him. For nineteen years he had remained in voluntary exile, awaiting the day when he could pick up the threads of his life again in his beloved Paris. But now, when he could live there if he chose, he found conditions so uninviting that the could no longer engage in serious work projects there.

François-Victor, too ill to maintain his duties as editor and publisher of *Le Rappel*, followed his father to Hauteville House, where Juliette and Alice nursed him. Juliette was becoming increasingly arthritic, so little Georges and Jeanne took her place in the afternoons and accompanied their grandfather on his long, rambling walks.

The children loved Guernsey, and had to be restrained from bathing in the sea when they were alone. But their grandfather taught them to swim, and they went with him into the surf daily. They explored paths, climbed high onto the rocks, and soon felt completely at home on the island.

Their mother did not share their contentment. The young widow of Charles Hugo was bored. Although she was devoted to her sick brother-in-law, she longed for a more active life. François-Victor was restless, too. He felt that he had come to Hauteville House to die, and the thought depressed him. If he were in Paris, he felt, he could become active again to the extent that his physical condition permitted. He would write editorials for Auguste Vacquerie, and on his "good days" he could stay at the offices of *Le Rappel* until he grew tired.

Victor could not counter the arguments of the

younger people, and was forced to let them return to Paris. He wept at the thought that his grandchildren would be leaving, but agreed that they would receive better schooling in the city than on the little island. So, on October 1, 1872, François-Victor and Alice departed for Paris, taking the children with them. Victor described their departure as a terrible wrench, and wept copiously.

Now, except for the servants, he and Juliette were alone at Hauteville House.

Constant pressures were applied by Paul Meurice and other friends, who urged Victor to return to Paris, too. Meurice wrote, "I cannot sleep for fear another little tyrant will seize the throne of our poor shrunken country, and will deprive our people of the liberties for which they have shed so much blood. There is one voice of reason to which the people of France listen, the voice of Victor Hugo. I beg you, come home and prevent a new, horrible catastrophe."

There had been a time when Victor would heed such a call for help. But experience had finally taught him that the voice of one man could not stem a tide. He remembered that the voters of Paris had rejected him in January, when he had been a candidate for the new National Assembly. So he took Meurice's words with a large pinch of salt.

His reply was succinct. After thanking his friend for his flattering words, he added, "I have so little time left that I must concentrate on my own writing. And I find I accomplish more in a week, here, than I could in Paris in a month."

The tables had completely turned. Juliette no doubt enjoyed life at Hauteville House far more than she did in Paris, too. Here she had no young rivals; Victor completely abandoned the chase, and gave her the undivided attention that she had come to expect as her due, at least when they were in Guernsey.

A letter she wrote to Alice in November indicates that both were happy in Guernsey. Papa, she said, was sleeping better than he had in many months, and his appetite had improved a little too much. For the first time in Victor's life, his meals were being restricted. He would listen to no one but Juliette, but he did not grumble when she gave him meals that any ordinary person would have considered ample and that he thought too meager. Juliette's arthritis had responded to the sun, she declared, and she could accompany Papa on his walks at least two or three days each week.

She was also busy copying his work as fast as he turned it out, and became excited about his current projects: "Not since *Les Misérables* has he done such magnificent writing!"

Two major books occupied Victor. One, which he considered relatively minor, was a new, expanded version of *La Légende des siècles*. The other was a novel of the French Revolution of 1793 that, he felt would be the natural successor to *Les Misérables*. He called it *Quatrevingt-treize* (*Ninety-three*), and worked out a careful schedule. "I begin this book today, December 16, 1872," he wrote in his journal. "I am at Hauteville House." He also noted that he intended to complete it on June 10, 1873.

So precise were his work habits of a lifetime that he finished the novel exactly one half-day ahead of schedule. He knew what he was doing, and worked methodically, but the result was no pot-boiler. Completed when he was seventy-one years of age, he considered it by far his best historical novel, and in France it compared favorably with all of his other work.

Victor had for a long time seen a parallel between the political turmoil that had been tearing France apart in recent years and the events of the French Revolution of 1793. France, he believed, was the one nation in Europe where men were willing to die for their political and philosophical convictions. So *Quatrevingt-treize* is, above all, a novel of ideas. Since it was written by Victor Hugo, it also had characters portrayed in depth, and high drama. It suffered, to be sure, from the usual Hugo faults: the melodrama was unbelievable in part, the dialogue was somewhat stilted in passages that required little action, and the arm of coincidence sometimes proved to be astonishingly long.

Nevertheless, *Quatrevingt-treize* must be regarded as a great book. In France, where all the nuances of the revolution in 1793 were clear to all citizens, it has long been regarded as a work more or less on a par with *Les Misérables*, but it has suffered from inferior translations, and could not be fully understood in the United States, Great Britain, and other English-speaking countries.

Victor's research in preparation for this novel was far more intense than for any similar work. In his library at Hauteville House were forty-three books on the French Revolution that he read with great care, and an examination of them reveals that many were heavily marked. He used minor incidents as well as major political events, and no detail was too small to escape his attention. His imagination did the rest.

His memory was still remarkable, and he relied on it

repeatedly. He recalled a medieval tower that he and Juliette had seen thirty-seven years earlier, when, in the late spring of 1836, they had paid a visit to Brittany. The tower was located in Juliette's birthplace, the village of Fougeres, and at the time it had fascinated Victor. He re-created it in his book, moving it to a deep forest and using it as the scene of a siege, where a republican force is trapped. Juliette, who remembered the tower well from her own childhood, was astonished at Victor's ability to re-create it in infinite detail.

Juliette spent her mornings copying what Victor had done the previous day, and finally she felt moved to write him a letter. Although they were now living together permanently, she could not rid herself of the habits she had formed through the years. And it was possible she found it easier to express some thoughts on paper. "I am speech-less with admiration before the catalogue of your master-pieces," she wrote. "Your genius is unmatched in our cen-tury." Her assessment may have been heavily prejudiced, but it was accurate.

By now Victor could not write ordinary prose, and the soul of a poet shines through his descriptive passages, even seeping into his action. A few paragraphs in this novel that were devoted to a description of a large cannon break-ing away from its lines on board a warship have been used in countless literature courses as the perfect example of the purest of style.

Victor's story is centered on the long fight between the forces of the new Republic and those of the opposing royalists to take control of France. Such historical figures as Marat, Danton, and the genius of the Revolution, Robespierre, appear in his pages, and are memorable, but he does not dwell on them. His principal characters are drawn from his own distinctive imagination.

Lantenac is the compleat royalist. He is a man of honor, a man who believes in tradition and is loyal without question to his Bourbon king and the Church. Highly civilized, he nevertheless becomes a ruthless killer in a civil war. Perhaps no greater tribute could be paid to the artistry of Victor Hugo than the recognition of the extraordinary feat he accomplished in creating Lantenac.

The hero of Victor Hugo's novel of the Revolution is a character named Gauvain, and much has been written on the subject since Victor Hugo's day because of this. Juliette's real name had been Gauvain; generations of graduate students writing theses for higher degrees have attempted to trace the political sympathies of Juliette's ancestors. Such efforts proved to be irrelevant. By giving his protagonist Juliette's name, Victor was doing no more nor less than paying his mistress a graceful compliment.

"You are always in my thoughts when I am working," he told her on many occasions, and his protagonist in this novel is proof that he meant what he said. Juliette's pleasure was great, and she told Victor she was overwhelmed.

Gauvain, the "coincidence" of his name aside, is probably the most complicated of the book's characters. He is, by birth, a royalist, but has become an ardent advocate of the Republic. He is an idealist, and therefore the views he expresses and the convictions on which he acts make him something of a mouthpiece for the author.

Victor Hugo had come far from the starry-eyed idealism of his own youth by the time he wrote *Quatrevingt-*

treize. If Gauvain speaks for him, it may not be accidental that there is a strong, cynical touch at the end of the book: Gauvain betrays the Republic for which he has fought with such determination and unflagging courage. The betrayal is not intellectual, but grows out of his own humanity. He is incapable of ordering the execution of enemies who must be removed. Gauvain is a true patriot, a son of France who does credit to his cause and his country, but he is, above all, a man of compassion, a man who must put his love for his fellow human beings above every other consideration.

The last member of the trio was Cimourdain, the complete and dedicated revolutionary. Cruel without recognizing his inhumanity, dedicated to the core, Cimourdain was not only a three-dimensional fanatic of the French Revolution, but he might have taken his place in the councils of the Commune that had been abolished some months before he appeared on paper. He is the prototype of the extremist who has lived in every age, and such is the genius of Victor Hugo that Cimourdain well could be the prototype for any period that has come after. The revolution that Cimourdain advocates is all-important, the individual means nothing. There is no room in his makeup for pity, compassion, or any other regard for humankind; the revolution will cure all ills, and if individuals are killed or maimed, hurt or broken, their sacrifice is necessary so the aims of the revolution be achieved.

Viewing the book exclusively as a historical novel, the reader marvels at the ability of Victor Hugo to recreate the atmosphere, the sights and smells and sounds of the year 1793. This year, he insisted was the turning point in human history, and he may be forgiven if he ignores the upheaval of 1775–76 in North America that preceded the social earth-quakes that shook France. He concentrated on the achievements of his own nation, of the people he knew. His fundamental argument is valid: all men are entitled to liberty and equality, but the nature of man is such that neither right can be taken for granted. Both must be earned. If they are neglected or contravened, they will be lost.

It can be argued that in no other work did Victor more thoroughly portray his own dedication to the principles in which he had come to believe. He was a man who not only typified the noblest of his own age, but of the century that followed. In the best sense, he was a twentieth-century man.

It is ironical that Victor, the sensualist who had bedded more women that he could remember, saw no need to mention, much less dwell, on the erotic. At this period such subjects simply weren't portrayed by gentlemen, and there was no need, in a major Hugo novel, to portray scenes of the bedchamber.

Quatrevingt-treize contained all the elements of a classic, and the news that it was in preparation aroused the interest of the entire publishing world. When word seeped out that a major Hugo novel would be ready in the spring, every publisher in Paris became excited, and every day's mail at Hauteville House contained new, unsolicited offers.

Lacroix, sitting in his plush Brussels office, became concerned. It was true that he had published Victor's greatest successes, but he had done them at a time when no French publisher was permitted to print them. The Belgian's worry grew, and he finally sent Victor a telegram:

"How much must I bid for the rights to your new novel?"

Victor's reply settled the problem:

"You already have the rights. Pay whatever you think will earn both of us a profit worth our efforts."

The Belgian expulsion order had not been rescinded, and Victor could not visit Brussels, so Lacroix came to Guernsey, bringing with him a bank check for two hundred fifty thousand gold francs.

The publisher's faith in his author was justified. The first printing appeared in mid-summer of 1873, and was sold out within two weeks. Subsequent editions sold just as rapidly. The people of France saw the parallels between the French Revolution that linked their distant to the recent pasts of the Commune. Foreign reaction to *Quatrevingt-treize* was somewhat less enthusiastic, however. Readers were inclined to take the story literally, missing its universal qualities, and the citizens of most nations at the time had only limited interest in the France of 1793. The British were heartily sick of the French Revolution and its consequences, the Americans were still rebuilding their own country after their Civil War. The Germans wanted nothing to do with anything French.

The popularity of the novel was spotty in France, too. After enjoying an initial success that was sustained through the 1870s, the book went into a decline in the 1880s. Other Hugo works continued to sell, but this did not. By the 1890s the indifference gave way to active criticism. *Quatre-vingt-treize* came to be regarded as a lesser Hugo work, a novel marred by too much violence.

Most scholars agree that this gradual change came about for specific reasons. By the 1880s a relatively stable France was trying to forget the horrors of 1870–72. Paris had become the most sophisticated and glittering of all the world's capitals. People, particularly those who read and criticized books, were busy earning a good living and spending their money. They had no desire to be reminded of the French Revolution, and of the later insurrection that had disgraced the country. France looked at its recent history passively in the 1880s, and by the 1890s rejected it.

So *Quatrevingt-treize* suffered a severe and unwarranted decline in reputation, for decades obscured by other Hugo works. Only after World War I was interest in it revived, and only in our own time has it received the recognition it deserves.

Victor celebrated the end of his work on the novel by turning to his new version of *La Légende*, but Juliette called a halt. He had no need for money, he had been straining himself at his desk, and he was in need of a long holiday. There were other, equally compelling, reasons for them to return to Paris. François-Victor's health was gradually declining, and Juliette had kept this from her lover while he had been working on the new book. She knew how much he missed his little grandchildren, so it wasn't too difficult to persuade him to return to Paris.

The children delighted him. "Georges reads!" he exclaimed. "And Jeanne now speaks in complete sentences! Childhood is a miracle, and I am blessed beyond my worth!"

But his joy was tempered by the illness of his son, into whose house on the avenue des Sycomores he and Juliette moved. François-Victor could no longer leave the house, and it was an effort for him to walk into the small, enclosed garden off the dining room. He no longer did any work for

Le Rappel, although he tried to pretend, for his father's sake even more than his own, that he was planning to write a new series of articles on the current political situation.

Alice spent most of her waking hours looking after her children and taking care of her brother-in-law. Juliette felt desperately sorry for her, and Victor knew she deserved more in life, so he hired additional servants, and took over some of her nursing duties himself. Alice should remarry, he decided, and to her extreme embarrassment he began to bring eligible bachelors to the house, then praised her appearance, her intellect, and her domestic virtues, not caring whether he spoke in her presence. It was no easy task to be Victor Hugo's daughter-in-law.

A temporary change took place in Victor's personal habits. He no longer indulged in sexual excesses, and remained faithful to Juliette, although he still appreciated the beauty of attractive women, and could be relied upon to flirt with every pretty girl he saw. His temperance was caused by neither a decline in virility nor desire, but by a pall cast over him during the illness of his son. And his delighted absorption in Georges and Jeanne made him less eager to engage in affairs.

For months he did virtually no writing. Every afternoon he held open house in the drawing room, and at his insistence, François-Victor always received with him. The son sat in a huge armchair, his face waxen, his breathing labored, and Victor stood beside him.

It was not easy for the son to converse, though few ever found it necessary to say more than a few words when Victor was present. Guests were shown into the room, where Victor conducted a non-stop monologue for several hours, and then they departed, usually feeling uncomfortable. Friends and acquaintances continued to come because Victor was a figure of such gigantic importance that he could not be ignored. But the afternoons were a far cry from the brilliant salon that Victor and Adèle had conducted so many years earlier.

Nothing was allowed to interfere with Victor's mornings, devoted to his grandchildren. He read to Jeanne, insisted that Georges read to him, and composed fanciful stories for both of them. Sometimes adults came to the door and listened to the doting grandfather weave his tales of adventure and delight, but he permitted no one to enter.

The children also accompanied him on his daily walks, late in the afternoon, and one or two days each week he took them to the zoo. He had not forgotten the kindness of the zoo keepers to him and to Juliette when the Prussian siege had cut off all outside food supplies, so he quietly gave large sums of money for the expansion of the zoo, but insisted that his gifts be received in the names of Juliette and his grandchildren. He wanted no publicity, and although his generosity fooled no one, he was content.

One afternoon his callers included Judith Gautier Mendès, who was now more beautiful than ever. Juliette and Alice left the room and would not receive the younger woman, but they had no cause for fear. Victor discussed Judith's poetry, quoted extensively from his own, and then bent over her hand. That was that, and he did not seek her out in private. One of the facets of Victor's sensitivity was his unerring ability to realize when an affair had ended. He had achieved a new plateau of inner dignity, and apparently knew he would look absurd if he publicly formed a new, serious liaison with someone of Judith's age. So he was content to behave gallantly while keeping his distance.

The emergence of Marshall MacMahon as a prominent political figure worried Victor, and he entered his name as a candidate for a seat in the new Assembly that would be elected early in January. But the illness of François-Victor, which suddenly became much worse, prevented him from campaigning actively.

Christmas Day was dreary. François-Victor was dying; only the presence of the children in the house made the day bearable. Victor spent as much time as he could with the children, but was recalled repeatedly to his son's bedside. In the early hours of the morning of December 26, 1873, the last of Victor Hugo's sons died. Only his daughter Adèle remained, in her living death of insanity.

Victor was more depressed than he was willing to admit.

François-Victor was buried beside his brother and grandfather in the family plot. Victor insisted, as he had at Charles's funeral, that there be no religious ceremony. Convinced that organized religions had failed the people, he refused any association with them. Strangely, however, he did not object when Georges and Jeanne were sent to a school operated by a convent.

"All I have left now," he remarked after the funeral, "are my grandchildren, may God preserve them."

On New Year's Eve Victor was awakened from a sound sleep by a line of prose that came into his mind, and arose to write it down. Juliette and Alice were horrified when he showed it to them the following day:

"I have but one function left to perform upon this earth: to die."

His lethargy frightened them, and when he complained of a severe toothache a few days later, the first time he had ever mentioned a physical ailment, they knew something had to be done. First, it was necessary to move him out of the house in which François-Victor had died, although he insisted it was all he wanted for his declining years.

Alice and her children were François-Victor's heirs, and Alice said she had been advised to sell the house now, when she could obtain a high price for it, so she disposed of it. Juliette found a huge house at 21 rue de Clichy, which she knew would appeal to Victor, and she was right. He purchased it, then busied himself filling it with the decorative bric-a-brac he loved. Juliette also insisted that he buy himself a new wardrobe, and may have shuddered when he ordered frock coats with velvet collars, silk shirts with flowing cravats, and pointed, calf-high boots of patent leather.

She was familiar with all the signs, so she knew, as did Alice, that there soon would be another parade of young women through his life.

The family moved into the new house in April 1874, and Victor no longer spoke of his defeat in the Assembly election, but seemed to take the loss for granted. The house absorbed him. There was a whole succession of parlors, drawing rooms, and receiving rooms. The children had their own bedrooms, and shared a small library, a sitting room and a playroom. Alice had an extensive suite of her own, which was large enough for the entertainment of guests, if she wished. Juliette had a similar suite, directly above that of the younger woman.

Victor reserved a large, plainly furnished bedroom on the fourth floor of the house for himself, and placed his new study next to it. He could work there without disturbing anyone else, and was far enough from the children, so he couldn't hear them when they were playing. His own children had been taught to play quietly when their father was at work, but the doting Victor placed no such restriction on his grandchildren.

One bedroom, with its own entrance, was located on the ground floor. This chamber was furnished with special care. Victor explained his curious choice of its location by saying it might be used by guests who wouldn't want to inconvenience others. Neither Juliette nor Alice needed further explanation, and soon after the family occupied the house, the bedroom became a busy place.

Victor had decided that his dignity made it impossible for him to engage in affairs at the homes of his conquests or in hotel rooms, so it was better if the girls came to him. But he was careful to observe the amenities, and to shield his grandchildren. The youngsters usually ate their evening meal at 6 P.M., in a small, upstairs dining room. It had become customary for Alice and Juliette to sit with them while they ate, and then to dress for their own dinner hour. So this became the time of day Victor selected for his sexual encounters.

The usual procession of girls came and went. There were the wives and daughters of men high in society, there were actresses and nobodies. And there were members of a new breed known as fashion models. All thought Victor

Hugo fascinating, charming, and a delightful lover. Victor's memory was unimpaired, so it must be assumed that he remembered the name of whoever came to him on any given day.

The routine was always the same. Victor opened the outside door, and his mistress of the evening slipped into the secluded bedroom. Thirty minutes to an hour later she departed again, not having set foot in any other part of the house. Then Victor went up to his own room to change for the evening, and appeared at dinner displaying his accustomed hearty appetite. If Juliette and Alice thought his behavior childish, they kept their opinions to themselves. He had recovered from his depression, he was writing again, and he was filled with a new zest for life. They could ask for little more.

Victor's health, for a man seventy-two years of age, was magnificent. He still read omnivorously, and his eyesight was so good he had no need for glasses. He could mount the stairs two at a time to the top floor of the house without losing his breath. After his aching tooth was extracted he had no more pain, no more complaints. He slept soundly every night, and his appetite was still prodigious. Friends always knew, when he and Juliette were invited for dinner, that Victor required double portions of every course. He could crush another man's hand in a grip, and at the end of a hard day, when others were exhausted, he remained fresh, strong, and as cheerful as he had been at breakfast. He still took walks daily, and said he was sad that he couldn't swim.

His work output remained prodigious, although he published nothing for several years. Some people mistakenly assumed that he had given up his career and was content to rest on his long record of notable achievements, but they soon would learn otherwise.

Meanwhile he kept up his interest in politics. At his afternoon salon sessions and his own dinner parties and those of others, he continued to preach the theme of reconciliation. He watched the Republic being forged, and felt great hope for the future, though the monarchists still made him uneasy. He concealed his disappointment with the Communards from no one. Their irresponsible violence still shocked him, and he equated the fanaticism of one extreme with that of the other. "Only moderate men of good will should be allowed to participate in the affairs of government," he told his old friend, Louis Blanc. "I begin to wonder whether democracy shouldn't be tempered to exclude those whose sole political purpose is to destroy democracy and replace it with a fanatical system, either of the left or the right."

Various friends continued to urge him to return to the political arena, but he refrained from becoming a candidate again. The demands of that raucous profession were too great.

By 1876 the new division in parliament had been well established, and some of Victor's close associates saw an opportunity that would enable a distinguished man of seventy-four to participate in the affairs of government without being forced to trade verbal blows in the Chamber of Deputies. The new Senate, they decided, was the right place for someone of Victor Hugo's stature.

The idea is believed to have been Clemenceau's. In any event, it was he who took the initiative and saw the plan through to completion. Victor was formally proposed as a candidate for the Senate, and, under the complicated voting system that had been devised for election to the upper chamber, he won his seat on the second round of balloting. He remained a member for the rest of his life, and was to play a prominent role in the MacMahon crisis, when he defended the cause of the Republic with vigor and skill.

In 1876 he published *Actes et paroles*, a collection of various pieces he had written over his lifetime, and in a series of prefaces he demonstrated the gradual growth and development of his basic political philosophy. The book created a stir only in the large circle of Hugo admirers.

In that year he also did some work on a comedy, *Philémon Perverti*, that he never completed. The protagonist is an elderly man who, still dreaming of the sexual conquests of his youth, continues to have affairs with girls young enough to be his granddaughters. Philémon, the protagonist, has a loving and devoted mistress, but he fails to appreciate her many virtues, and at the climax of the play casts her aside for an amoral young woman who is interested in him only because of his wealth and fame. Philémon is presented as a pompous, bumbling old fool who cannot admit to himself that he had grown too old for the chase, and who, as a consequence, is scorned by everyone who knows him, including those who have long respected him.

The unfinished play reveals, of course, that Victor was aware of the absurdity of his own sexual pursuits. He had the sense and wit to stand apart from himself, envision his own folly, and sympathize with Juliette, whom he was mocking in his fleeting affairs. Rarely has an author castigated himself more severely than Victor did in *Philémon Perverti*.

Yet even with such insight, and in spite of the unhappiness he knew he was causing Juliette, he did not mend his ways. He hinted to various friends that the bait of a lifetime, although meaningless, was a compulsion too strong for him to break.

What he failed to comprehend was that Juliette's patience had worn very thin. Because she had loved, admired, and respected him for the better part of a half-century, she had tolerated his flagrant infidelities. In the early years of their relationship, when her own position had been precarious, she could have walked out had she chosen. Later, after he had become her whole life, she knew his weaknesses and needs, and displayed a gentle tolerance that was extraordinary.

Gradually, however, her feelings changed again. She was afraid that Victor's excesses would cause him physical harm. And now at last, her own sense of dignity, of propriety, was outraged. As 1877 approached, the year in which Victor would be seventy-five years of age, she told Alice that unless he changed, she would be forced to take action.

Victor as yet had no idea that he soon would face the most important crisis of his life.

Chapter XV

THE year 1877 was one of the most important, personally and professionally, in Victor's long life. He himself was the first to recognize its significance, naturally, and he told Louis Blanc, "If I had never accomplished anything until this year, posterity would not find my achievements totally lacking in meaning."

He was, for a change, being modest. A new, longer version of *La Légende des siècles* was published early in the year, thereby expanding his ambitious history of all human kind, or at least those portions that he found worthy of comment. The book was praised as much for its youthful vigor as for its content, and this critical acclaim has remained valid to the present time. Victor, the poet, observer, and philosopher, like Victor the lover, simply refused to grow old.

In mid-May still another book was published, *L'Art d'être grand-père* (*The Art of Being a Grandfather*) became one of his greatest successes. He had become incapable of putting anything on paper that was lacking in broad popular appeal. Written for and about his two grandchildren, he had begun this series of poems in 1870, composing most of them over a period of five years. In it are some of his finest love poems, the love of a grandfather for a little boy and a little girl whom he adored. Although a few of these verses have been criticized as overly sentimental, most achieved a balance of warmth and wit that made them refreshing little works of art.

To an extent, *L'Art d'être grand-père* was a record of Victor's own experiences with his grandchildren. He recalled an occasion when Georges broke a valuable vase, and was afraid his mother would punish him. He was rescued by his doting grandfather, who took full blame for the mishap. He recounted visits to the zoo, and recaptured the thrill of children when they first watched an elephant. And he became mystical as he described the forging of bonds between the children and their grandfather as they took long walks together, sometimes in the city, sometimes in rural Guernsey.

L'Art d'être grand-père also included fairy tales, very special fairy tales that the author fashioned for a readership of two small children, who appeared in them as the protagonists. "L'Épopée du lion" is a typical fairy tale poem. A little boy, who happens to be a prince, is kidnapped by a ferocious lion. A brave knight is sent to rescue the boy, but the lion kills and eats him. A hermit who is also a holy man tries to persuade the lion to release the child, but the lion is vastly amused, mocking and confounding the theological arguments that the hermit presents.

The king, in desperation, sends a company of his best soldiers to rescue his boy, but the cagy lion outwits the troops, and in an exciting climax, sends the men fleeing for their lives. Meanwhile, however, the prince's little sister, who is still at home in the palace, misses her brother so much that she goes out into the wilderness to find him. After experiencing several adventures she discover him with the lion, and sits down to discuss the situation with the beast. The little princess succeeds in so enchanting the lion that he not only releases her brother but escorts the two children back to their parents' palace to make certain they come to no harm.

Perhaps the work of the greatest literary merit in *L'Art* are the poems devoted to the physical beauty and wonders of nature. Victor had always excelled in his descriptive poetry of this sort, but here he achieved a different view, describing nature as seen through the eyes of a small child. Never becoming saccharine or cloying, never writing down to his small readers, he succeeded brilliantly.

The book ends on an inspirational note: Victor wrote five poems for his grandchildren to read when they became adults. Here he preached the principles of liberty and equality, the need for the formation of the United States of Europe, and urged them to show respect for all human dignity.

To the surprise of everyone in the French literary world except the author, *L'Art d'être grand-père* not only became the largest-selling book of the year, but was destined to be regarded through the following decades as a classic. Fifty thousand copies were sold during the first two months after publication, and a year later more than a quarter of a million copies had been purchased.

Georges and Jeanne Hugo became the most famous children in France. When their mother bought them new clothes, thousands of other parents faithfully bought the same. Occasionally, when the youngsters were recognized on the street, crowds formed around them, especially when they accompanied their grandfather.

The year 1877 was significant in the life of Alice Hugo, too. After six years as a widow, she fell in love again and remarried. Her new hasband was Édouard Lockroy, the editor of *Le Rappel* and a leading republican member of the Chamber of Deputies. It could not have been accidental that Lockroy was a great admirer of Victor Hugo, or that Victor heartily approved of him.

To some extent it was Lockroy who persuaded him to become more active in the political arena. Late in the spring of 1877 Victor introduced a bill in the Senate to grant complete political amnesty to the Communards and restore the rights of citizenship that had been taken from them after their insurrection. Victor's address in the chamber was one of the most moving of his career, and he used, as its model, Abraham Lincoln's Second Inaugural Address, from which he quoted at length.

Few men shared Victor's compassion or sense of forgiveness. Only nine Senators voted in favor of his bill, and the measure was killed.

Victor played a for more important role in the great constitutional crisis of 1877. President MacMahon, asking for the concurrence of the Senate, dissolved the government, dismissed the Chamber of Deputies, and ordered a new election. His target was Jules Simon, the head of the Chamber. It appeared that a coup was in the making, with MacMahon becoming the permanent head of the state. As Simon was Jewish, the virulent anti-Semitism of the monarchists had again come into the open.

Victor immediately returned to work on a play that had occupied his attention for short periods over the course of almost twenty years. It was called *Torquemada*, and dealt with the career of the fanatical anti-Semite who had been the chief of the notorious Spanish Inquisition.

As he could not complete the play overnight, and the political situation required prompt action, Victor leaped into the battle with the vigor of a man half his age. He delivered an address in the Senate opposing dissolution of the government and the Chamber on the grounds that these moves were illegal and unconstitutional. The republicans in both the Senate and the Chamber hailed the speech as the most cogent yet delivered, and republican newspapers called it a masterpiece of rhetoric.

Victor was dissatisfied. The monarchists still held a majority in the Senate, and voted in favor of dissolution, the author's splendid words changing no minds or votes. So he was one of the first to take the issue direct to the public, hoping to influence the electorate in the coming vote for a new Chamber of Deputies.

At his writing desk, Victor quickly revised his powerful indictment of tyranny, *Histoire d'un crime*, that he had written more than a quarter of a century earlier. Bringing portions of it up to date, he stressed the ever-present need for vigilance against the efforts of would-be dictators to destroy the liberties that Frenchmen regarded as dear.

The book was rushed to print in a new edition, and Victor made it clear that he would contribute all his royalties to the election war chest of the republicans. The timing of the maneuver was perfect. *Histoire d'un crime* appeared on the bookstalls just two weeks prior to the election, in October, and in that short, fourteen-day span it sold an astonishing total of more than one hundred fifty thousand copies.

This was the election that resulted in an overwhelming victory for the advocates of a republic, and MacMahon might have won his goal only if he had been willing to call out the troops loyal to him, using force to prevent the new Chamber from convening. It was obvious to him, however, as it was to his opponents, that any such move on his part would plunge the country into another civil conflict. And it was equally plain that, in the event of such turmoil, Bismarck would not hesitate to inaugurate another war on flimsy grounds and add portions of the eastern provinces of France to his own, growing realm.

MacMahon remained in the presidential palace, sulking for another year, until the election of a republican Senate demonstrated that his cause was permanently lost, and he resigned.

Victor was hailed as one of the principal architects of the great republican victory that gave France a new political stability and made certain that the Third Republic would endure. Others worked as steadfastly as he did to sway the electorate; it is an exaggeration to claim, as Hugo idolators have done, that he deserved all the credit. Yet, his contribution to the cause was vital, and he was universally regarded as the patriarch of the Republic.

At about this time Édouard Lockroy moved with his family into a house at 132 avenue d'Eylau, and a pleasant surprise awaited Victor and Juliette. Édouard, coordinating arrangements with Paul Meurice, rented the adjoining townhouse, at number 130, from its owner, the Princesse de Lusignan, and presented Victor with the key. So Victor could be near his grandchildren, and he and Juliette could be assured of privacy when they wanted it. Also, it would be easier for Victor to work in a dwelling that was not inhabited by two boisterous children.

Almost overnight the new Victor Hugo house became the principal salon of the Republic. Members of the Senate, newspapermen, and most of the prominent figures of the era—Louis Blanc, Garibaldi, Kossuth—came to call in the afternoons. Members of the Chamber who visited the house of the increasingly powerful Lockroy found it convenient to drop in next door. Victor was at the height of his popularity.

He continued to ignore his own health, and exerted himself far too much. He was working on still another version of *La Légende* and several other projects. He campaigned actively in behalf of Jules Grévy, his republican friend, who had become a candidate for MacMahon's post as President of France. Acting against the advice of Juliette and various friends, he not only accepted the position of president of the International Literary Conference that was held in Paris in the spring of 1878, but insisted that he not be given a mere honorary place. He drove himself harder than anyone else at the task of organizing the meeting. And he gave a stirring oration at the celebration of Voltaire's centenary in May 1878. And, with all this, when Juliette went to the Lockroy house early each evening to sit with the children while they ate their dinner, he continued to engage in his never-ending sexual affairs.

He and Juliette often entertained at dinner, and one such occasion became memorable for unfortunate reasons. On the evening of June 27, 1878, Louis Blanc was one of the guests, and initiated a discussion of the relative merits of Voltaire and Rousseau. Both men had consumed large dinners and copious quantities of wine, and became embroiled in an absurd argument. Blanc, an economist, historian, and politician, not only praised Rousseau, but called him the greatest of eighteenth-century French authors.

Victor, like all partisans of Voltaire, despised Rousseau, and pronounced his friend ignorant of literature. Blanc retaliated by calling Victor stupid. Tempers rose. Victor roared, shook his fist, thundered, and toppled to the floor, gasping for breath and clutching his chest.

Juliette, who had not intervened while the great men engaged in the dispute, immediately took charge, and sent someone for a physician. Until he arrived she sat on the floor, cradling Victor's head in her lap and allowing no one near him. Two physicians came to the house at the same time, and several others arrived soon thereafter. It was no small matter that the most famous living Frenchman was taken ill.

Victor's ailment was diagnosed as a slight heart attack. The physicians agreed that, though the attack had not been serious, it was a sign that he should start taking life easier. Victor protested, insisting that he had no intention of changing his routine, and the doctors were cowed.

One person was unimpressed by his stand. Juliette, following the doctor's verdict, informed Victor they would leave within the week for Guernsey, where he would do no writing or other work, and would spend all his time recuperating.

Victor defied her, and at first refused to go. But on the evening of July 3 they left Paris, and arrived at Hauteville House the next day. Ordinarily the housekeeper was the only person on duty there, but a letter from Juliette had forewarned her, and a full staff of five servants had been assembled by the time the couple arrived.

Juliette established a strict regimen. She supervised the menu, and permitted Victor no rich foods. She not only accompanied him on his daily walks, which taxed her strength, but sat on shore and watched him while he went swimming. She allowed him to read as much as he pleased, but locked his study to prevent him from working on a new manuscript.

One of his little habits puzzled her. Victor insisted on walking to the gate every morning to meet the postman. To the best of her knowledge he was expecting no important mail, so she watched from the house, and saw that on several occasions he stuffed letters into a pocket, but did not mention them. At her first opportunity she investigated, and discovered he was receiving love letters from some of the young women of Paris with whom he had been having affairs.

After living with Victor for the better part of a half-century, Juliette Drouet suddenly lost all patience and created the deepest crisis they had ever faced in their life together. If Victor wanted his cheap little romances, that was his privilege, and he was free to return to Paris. He could do what he pleased and live as he pleased, without interference from her.

But, if that was the life he wanted, she had no desire to share what might be left of his love. She would not accompany him, and preferred to remain at Hauteville House, where she would spend the rest of her days alone.

Victor was startled by her unexpected stand, and devastated to discover that she meant every word. He tried to argue with her and protested that she was treating him the way a schoolteacher dealt with a bad boy.

Juliette remained adamant. If he wanted anything more to do with her, he would give up his little affairs at once, and would never indulge in another. She would make no exceptions, and if he could not give her his pledge, and felt incapable of changing his ways, she was willing to accept his decision, and would bid him a final farewell then and there.

When the horrified Victor could not budge her, he became panic-stricken. Juliette had been his emotional bulwark for a lifetime, and he knew he could not manage without her. Tears streaming from his eyes, he dropped to his knees and swore several oaths—one on a Bible, and another on a copy of *Les Misérables*—that he would give up his affairs for all time, and would be true to her as long as he lived.

Juliette felt certain her confidence was not misplaced, and accepted his word.

Victor did not disappoint her, and never again, even

after her death, sought out any other woman. For the first time since the early years of his marriage to Adèle, he was faithful to one woman, and took no interest in others. He was now seventy-six years of age.

Tranquil at last in his personal life, Victor returned to Paris with Juliette after a four-month sojourn in Guernsey. Neither realized they had seen Hauteville House for the last time.

No matter how serene and ordered Victor's private existence, he could not avoid turbulence in his professional life, and soon after his return to the house on the avenue d'Eylau he published a long, highly controversial poem, *Le Pape*. In it he contrasted two events of that year, the election of Leo XIII as Pope, and the one hundredth anniversary of the death of the great, anti-clerical Voltaire.

The much-heralded liberalism of the new Pope was a delusion, Victor declared, and he attacked Pope Leo's first encyclical in detail. He liked to think of himself as Voltaire's successor, but in spite of the realism he had developed, he was still far friendlier to the Church than Voltaire had ever been.

In *Le Pape* an unidentified Pope falls asleep, and the bulk of the poem deals with his dream. The imaginary Pope dresses in sackcloth, smears himself with ashes, and goes out into the world to preach the Gospel. Living a life of poverty, he practices the essential spirit of Christianity. Doing good deeds wherever he goes, he spreads the doctrines of charity, equality, and humility before God. Finally, when the Pope awakens, he says, "What a frightening dream I have just suffered."

Victor's followers and most of the anti-clerical elements in France hailed the poem as a milestone in the history of developing theology. True enough, *Le Pape* was a modern study of the Church, but no more. By portraying what might be done, Victor proved that despite his thin veneer of cynicism he was still the idealist who thought that a reformed Rome could accomplish wonders on earth.

In the next three years Victor published several other long poems, and the world marveled at his continuing production. He kept to himself the fact that he had done virtually all the work on them in past years.

On February 27, 1881, the Republic of France saluted Victor Hugo in a tribute that no other author has ever received from a government or a people. This was Victor's eighty-first year, and his friends made history on his behalf.

The day was declared a national holiday by law, the avenue d'Eylau was decorated with flags and laurel wreaths, and was renamed, permanently, after him. Trees were planted in his honor, and a great parade was held in the new avenue Victor Hugo. President Jules Grévy of the Republic of France acted in the role of grand marshal, and later joined Victor, Juliette, and the two Hugo children on the balcony of Victor's house to review the parade.

As befitted a man of letters, the entire membership of the Academy marched first, followed by the Senate, the Chamber of Deputies, and the municipal council of Paris. The faculty of the Sorbonne turned out, as did the entire student body, and there were scores of literary societies and other cultural organizations.

The schoolchildren of Paris marched, too, group after group reciting lines in unison from *L'Art d'être grand-père* as they moved past the balcony. Bringing up the rear were the people, who came by the tens of thousands, then the hundreds of thousands. Émile Zola, the young social reformer-author who considered Victor a god, wrote in a newspaper account that one and one-half million took part. Other newspapers estimated that the throngs had exceeded one million, a figure with which the British ambassador agreed in his report to London. The disgruntled monarchists issued their own estimate, and tried to damn the affair by saying that "no more" that half to three-quarters of a million participated.

Victor responded, in the main, with the grace and dignity befitting a man in his extraordinary position. He inclined his head, he waved, and he smiled repeatedly. When President Grévy read a tribute to him, tears came to his eyes. And he replied to the salute of the municipal authorities with words that have since been chiseled into the cornerstones of hundreds of buildings:

I salute Paris, the great city.

I salute her, not in my name, for I am nothing, but in the name of all that live, reason, think, love and hope here below.

It proved too much for Victor to remain staid all day, and he added a touch to the festivities that was uniquely his own. Scores of bands took part in the parade, and occasionally he was so carried away by the music that he hurried down to the street, seized the baton of the leader, and himself led the playing of a military air.

The day was memorable in other ways. Tons of flowers were given to Victor, and he ordered them sent to hospitals and orphanages. The armed services remitted all minor punishments, and so did the universities and even secondary schools of the country.

That night a great banquet was given in honor of the author, and he attended with Juliette at his side, followed by Alice, her children, and her husband. Speech after speech was delivered, but when the time came for Victor to reply, he was so overcome he could not speak. Tears came to his eyes, and he sat down, his hands trembling.

Although the night was still young, Juliette judged that he had been subjected to enough emotional strain for one day, and took him home.

Thereafter Victor loved it when friends addressed mail to him:

> M. *Victor Hugo*
> *in his own street, Paris.*

The February celebrations were the first of many that year. On July 14, Bastille Day, Victor was the guest of honor at the national celebration held by the government. On July 21, St. Victor's Day, another banquet was given in his honor, and on this occasion he made another resounding speech. A whole series of Hugo dinners, receptions, and other affairs occurred between August 21 and September 15, and, in order to husband the strength of Victor and Juliette, they stayed at the house of Paul Meurice during this period. Juliette was now being hailed in her own right, and was publicly acknowledged by everyone as though she were Victor's wife.

Sometimes the question was asked in these later days: why were Victor and Juliette not married after the death of Adèle? Nothing stood in their way. Although friends urged them to marry, they refused, saying that they would appear foolish in the eyes of the public if they changed their status after living together unofficially for so many years.

In the autumn of 1881 Victor published, concurrently with the celebrations, a new book of poetry, *Les Quatre Vents de l'espirit*. It contained the work of a lifetime, some of the poems having been written in the early 1840s, others penned as recently as 1875. Included were two short plays, *Margarita* and *Esca*, both of them comedies that were blends of cynicism and sentiment.

These plays were unlike anything Victor had ever before published, and the reading public was astonished that a man of his age could change his style so completely that even the Hugo addict found it unrecognizable. Victor refrained from telling anyone that the plays had been written almost twenty years earlier.

It was also in that year that he finished *Torquemada*, publishing it early in 1882. This work was Hugo's answer to the anti-Semites of the aristocratic monarchist circles and of the army hierarchy. The play was no more accurate historically than was much of Victor's other work, and his Torquemada barely resembled the Grand Inquisitor. But he wrote with his usual passion, and his warped, fanatical Torquemada made the anti-Semite look absurd, which was his intention. The play enjoyed a good sale, but was not intended for theatrical production, and was not performed in Victor's lifetime.

Another celebration took place on November 22, 1882, this one as much in Juliette's honor as in Victor's. Émile Perrin, the managing director of the Comédie-Française, decided to revive Victor's play, *Le Roi s'amuse*, which had opened precisely fifty years earlier, on November 22, 1832, and subsequently had been closed by the censors. Juliette and Victor occupied the royal box and were accompanied by the Lockroys, Georges and Jeanne Hugo, and Victor's steadfast friend, Auguste Vacquerie.

The President of the Republic, Jules Grévy, occupied the box on the other side of the theater, and an audience of notables attended. Victor and Juliette were cheered on their arrival; at intermissions they held court in their box. Another ovation rang through the theater at the play's end, and the audience paid the couple another extraordinary tribute. Not one person left the auditorium until Victor, with Juliette on his arm, had departed. They made their way out through applauding lines of the most important men and women in France.

Victor didn't know it, but Juliette suffered excruciating pain that night. She continued to feel ill, and a few days later a physician examined her at the Lockroy house, the arrangement for the meeting having been made there to conceal her condition from Victor.

Juliette was not surprised to learn that she had cancer of the stomach, and had not long to live. The news was kept from Victor, and she went to great lengths to prevent him from learning it. No matter how great her pain, she appeared every evening at the dinner table, playing the role of hostess for his guests. Others saw the heavy applications of cosmetics on her increasingly gaunt face, noted that her clothes were hanging loosely on her thin frame, and knew that her gaiety was forced. Some of them guessed her condition, but it was not until she had to take to her bed at the beginning of April 1883 that the truth finally dawned on Victor. Until then he had known only that Juliette was always on hand, as she had been for fifty years.

For the last six weeks of Juliette Drouet's life Victor Hugo literally did not leave her side. When she begged him to take a walk or go to the dining room for a meal, he refused, staying in her bedchamber.

Two physicians took up residence in the house, one to attend Juliette and the other to keep a discreet watch over Victor. Alice Lockroy and her husband confided to friends that they were afraid Victor would not survive Juliette.

On the morning of May 11, 1883, after a romance that had lasted for a half-century, Juliette died in her lover's arms. She was seventy-seven years of age. She did not speak at the end, but was conscious and rational, and she died as she would have wished, while Victor was kissing her.

She was buried near the grave of her daughter, beneath a tombstone that she herself had chosen. Auguste Vacquerie delivered the funeral oration, as he had done for so many members of the Hugo family.

Victor did not attend the funeral. He collapsed after Juliette died, and had to be placed under sedation. His own condition was so precarious that a team of physicians ruled it would be too dangerous to permit him to attend.

Newspapers treated Juliette's death as an event of

national importance. Jules Claretie wrote an extraordinary obituary in *Le Temps*, which had become the nation's first newspaper saying:

The white-haired woman whom we have lost will be inseparably associated in literary annals with the imperishable memory of Victor Hugo. There is a majestic dignity in the figure which she presents to us. France and the world share Victor Hugo's loss, and we mourn with him. She was a lady of virtues far beyond the ordinary.

The loss of Juliette was a blow from which Victor never fully recovered. Overnight he became an old, feeble man, indifferent to the life around him. Until Juliette's death he had been vigorous, witty, interested in politics, the arts, everything in a world that was moving rapidly. Now only his grandchildren could cause him to smile.

What Juliette had meant to him was revealed by one fact: after her passing, Victor never again wrote a single line of either poetry or prose.

The public had no idea that he had abandoned his career, however. The final series of *La Légende des siècles*, which he had actually completed earlier in the year, was published in the autumn of 1883, the last of his works to appear in his own lifetime.

So great was his output, however, that a number of Victor Hugo works were published posthumously. They included several books of poetry: *Le Théâtre en liberté* (1886), *Toute la lyre* (1888), *Les Années funestes* (1898), and *Dernière Gerbe* (1902). Two travel books also appeared in the years between 1887 and 1900, *Alpes et Pyrenées* and *France et Belgique*, as well as a book of essays,

Choses vues. The quantity as well as the quality of Victor's lifetime of work was remarkable.

Even his will, written two years before Juliette's death, had a literary quality. He may well have known that posterity would be interested in the document, but it is also possible that his style, by this time, had become an integral part of his nature, making it impossible for him to think in more mundane terms. The will read:

God. The Soul. Responsibility.

This three-fold idea is sufficient for mankind. It has been sufficient for me. It it the true religion. I have lived in it. I die in it. Truth, light, justice, conscience: It is God. Deus. Dies.

I leave forty thousand francs to the poor.

I wish to be taken to the cemetery in a pauper's coffin.

My executors are MM. Jules Grévy, Léon Say, Léon Gambetta. They may choose associates whom they please.

I leave all my manuscripts and everything which may be found written or drawn by myself to the Bilbliothèque Nationale in Paris, which will one day become the Library of the United States of Europe.

My literary executors are MM. Paul Meurice, Auguste Vacquerie, Ernest Lefèvre. I charge them with responsibility for the publication of such writing of mine which has not yet been published.

I leave behind me an infirm daughter and two grandchildren. My blessings upon them.

Apart from the eight thousand francs annually necessary for my daughter, everything of mine belongs to my two grandchildren. I mention here, as sums which must be set aside, the yearly income for life which I give to their mother, Alice, and hereby increase it to twelve thousand francs. The annual income for life of twenty-four thousand francs which I give to the courageous woman who at the time of the coup d'état saved my life at the risk of her own, and who subsequently preserved the trunk containing my manuscripts.

I shall close my earthly eyes, but my spiritual ones will remain open, wider than ever. I decline the prayers of all Churches. I ask for a prayer from every soul.

Victor Hugo

With death very much on his mind, he added a brief codicil to the will a few weeks after Juliette died:

I give fifty thousand francs to the poor.
I wish to be carried to the cemetery in their coffin.
I refuse the prayers of all Churches.
I ask for a prayer from every soul.
I believe in God.

Victor Hugo

Although Victor gained a measure of his equilibrium after the death of Juliette, and his mind remained lucid and sharp, his physical decline was obvious to everyone. Alice Lockroy took complete charge, and he spent most of his time with her and the two children. Eventually he began to give small dinner parties again; the table talk was stimulating, but the spark of wit that had characterized Victor as a conversationalist was gone.

On his eighty-third birthday the Republic of France and the literary world saluted him in public ceremonies, and again a banquet was given in his honor. But he was too tired to await the after-dinner speeches, and the Lockroys took him home.

On the evening of May 13, 1885, Victor gave his last dinner party. As always, he dominated the conversation, and appeared to be in relatively sound health. But on May 15 he felt ill, and Alice sent him to bed. He was suffering, his physicians said, from "the general disabilities of the aged." Seventy-two hours later the onset of pneumonia complicated his condition, and on May 22 the end was at hand.

Victor spent that afternoon bidding farewell to his old, close friends. Inexplicably addressing Paul Meurice in Spanish, he said, "Death will be very welcome."

The spirit of a poet still burned brightly within him, and he said to Auguste Vacquerie, "Here is the battleground of day and night."

Shortly before sundown his grandchildren were admitted to the sickroom. He urged them to seek happiness by giving love, and after they had kissed him, he was heard to say, "I see black light." He closed his eyes, passed into a coma, and died.

Both the Senate and the Chamber of Deputies, which were in session, adjourned immediately when they received word that Victor Hugo was gone. President Grévy designated May 24 as a day of national mourning, and the casket containing Victor's remains was taken to the Arc de Triomphe. Horsemen holding lighted torches sat at each of the corners of the Arc; flags bearing the titles of Victor's works were placed at intervals around the coffin. The Arc itself was draped in black crêpe.

The following day six addresses were delivered at the Arc de Triomphe, and the speakers included the President of the Republic, the President of the French Academy, the President of the Senate, the President of the Chamber of Deputies, the dean of the diplomatic corps, and Auguste Vacquerie. Auguste had written the first major biography of Victor a few years before.

Following the addresses the funeral procession, with regiments of cavalry and infantry, moved through the streets to the Panthéon, which would be Victor's final resting Place. The pauper's coffin was carried on a mule cart, in accordance with the author's wishes.

Never in history had any member of Victor Hugo's profession been accorded such honors by any nation. But it was the response of the people themselves that was overwhelming. The population of Paris was two million, and according to every newspaper account, a greater number crowded the streets to watch the funeral procession. The Panthéon was filled. Victor Hugo was laid to rest beside Voltaire and Rousseau.

All government offices were closed that day, as were business firms, factories, schools, and shops. Most restaurants shut their doors, as did retail establishments of every sort. Under a special, imaginative dispensation, however, the shops and stalls of booksellers remained open, and before the day ended, they had sold out all of their remaining stock of books by Victor Hugo.

Victor, had he known, would have been very pleased.

Principal Bibliography

Berret, Paul, *Victor Hugo* (Paris: 1927).

Biré, Édmond, *Victor Hugo*, 4 vols. (Paris: 1883–1894).

Brunet, G., *Victor Hugo* (Paris: 1929).

Charetie, Jules, *Victor Hugo* (Paris: 1882).

Duclaux, Mary R., *Victor Hugo* (Paris: 1929).

Dupuy, Ernest, *Victor Hugo, L'Homme et le poèts* (Paris: 1886).

Escholier, Raymond, *La Vie glorieuse de Victor Hugo* (Paris: 1929).

Grant, Elliott M., *The Career of Victor Hugo* (Cambridge: 1946).

Guimbaud, Louis, *Juliette Drouet et Victor Hugo* (Paris: 1914, 1927).

———, *La Mère de Victor Hugo* (Paris: 1930).

Hugo, Victor, *Correspondance*, 6 vols. (Paris: Imprimerie Nationale, 1896–1898).

———, *Works*, 47 vols., ed. by Paul Meurice, Gustave Simon, *et al.* (Paris: Imprimerie Nationale and Librairie A. Michiel, 1902–1946).

Hugo, Mme. Victor, *Victor Hugo raconté par un trémoin de sa vie* (Paris: 1863).

Josephson, Mathew, *Victor Hugo* (New York: 1944).

Mabilleau, L., *Victor Hugo* (Paris: 1893).

Maurois, André, *Victor Hugo and His World* (New York: 1956).

Sainte-Beuve, Charles-Augustin, *Volupté* (Paris: 1834).

Vacquerie, Auguste. *Mes Premieres Années à Paris* (Paris: 1872).

Numerous other works were consulted, among them the various books on Victor Hugo by Gustave Simon and Louis Barthou.

Victor Hugo's extraordinary range of interests as well as genius have produced an unbelievably extensive library of books concerning him. As with any man who was a legend in his lifetime, many who wrote of him in his own time introduced numerous errors of fact that later scholars have attempted to correct. Yet some conflicting evidence is almost impossible to judge.

Index

Index

INDEX